GOD KNOWS
THERE'S NEED

"You're right, there has to be justice. There has to be a judgment day, too, when God will judge us all. What you gonna tell him you did to this child when that day comes?" "There's no need—" he began, but she interrupted him. "There's need," she said, "God knows there's need." Her voice was awesome, biblical. "God knows."

—Dorothy Allison, *Bastard out of Carolina*

GOD KNOWS THERE'S NEED

CHRISTIAN RESPONSES TO POVERTY

SUSAN R. HOLMAN

OXFORD
UNIVERSITY PRESS
2009

OXFORD
UNIVERSITY PRESS

Oxford University Press, Inc., publishes works that further
Oxford University's objective of excellence
in research, scholarship, and education.

Oxford   New York
Auckland   Cape Town   Dar es Salaam   Hong Kong   Karachi
Kuala Lumpur   Madrid   Melbourne   Mexico City   Nairobi
New Delhi   Shanghai   Taipei   Toronto

With offices in
Argentina   Austria   Brazil   Chile   Czech Republic   France   Greece
Guatemala   Hungary   Italy   Japan   Poland   Portugal   Singapore
South Korea   Switzerland   Thailand   Turkey   Ukraine   Vietnam

Published by Oxford University Press, Inc.
198 Madison Avenue, New York, NY 10016

www.oup.com

Oxford is a registered trademark of Oxford University Press

Library of Congress Cataloging-in-Publication Data
Holman, Susan R.
God knows there's need : Christian responses to poverty / Susan R. Holman.
p. cm.
ISBN 978-0-19-538362-1
1. Poverty—Religious aspects—Christianity—History of doctrines.   I. Title.
BV4647.P6H65 2009
261.8'325—dc22   2008032929

1 3 5 7 9 8 6 4 2

Printed in the United States of America
on acid-free paper

for R.D.H., R.S.H., and R.M.H.

CONTENTS

ACKNOWLEDGMENTS

When Charles Marsh first suggested that I write a book engaging personal narrative to reflect on responses to poverty in early Christianity, in his invitation to join the Virginia Seminar on Lived Theology at the University of Virginia, I was not sure it could be done. But soon I began to discover partial phrases and unfinished ideas for exactly such a book scribbled on random scraps that had been shuffling around in my notes for years, buried and suppressed under more orderly, systematically academic (and, frankly, easier) tasks. Still I was chary. In fact, the Seminar became the ideal academic writing group; without it, this book would still be buried in my subconscious and the piles on my desk. Thanks are due above all to these friends and conversation partners who made the journey possible and even fun: Charles Marsh, Carlos Eire, Mark Gornik, Patricia Hampl, Alan Jacobs, Charles Mathewes, and Rebekah Menning. A Christian Faith and Life Grant from the Louisville Institute funded the final year of writing, convincing me beyond doubt that there was an audience for such a book. I am immensely grateful to Dr. James Lewis and the Institute's Board for this gift. Several chapters and sections of other chapters developed from invited lectures and conference talks. Friends, colleagues, and academic audiences at Harvard Divinity School, Episcopal Divinity School, Holy Cross Greek Orthodox School of Theology, Gordon Conwell Theological Seminary, and Hartford Seminary helped me think through the relevance of these texts to ethical practice and congregational life. Parishioners and clergy in Episcopal, Lutheran, and Eastern Orthodox settings listened to my more "ministry"-related talks with an interest that astonished me, and asked tough questions. At the Catholic University of Leuven, Drs. Johan Leemans and Brian Matz enabled my thinking on the common good in modern Catholic Social Thought. Drs. Yaacov Lev and Miriam Frenkel's invitation to be a Visiting Scholar at the Institute for Advanced Study at Hebrew University in Jerusalem, as part of their research group on piety and charity in the ancient Mediterranean world, made it possible to explore these issues across several religious traditions that shape modern societies. In Israel, Dr. Joseph Patrich, Yisca Harani, and Dr. Galit Noga-Banai opened my life and heart to the intersection of past and present need in the Judaean Desert, Jerusalem, and the Galilee. An alumni award from the Friedman School of Nutrition Science and Policy at Tufts University confirmed that such a project might indeed serve a profession I once feared I had abandoned by choosing to study religious history. Academic colleagues in early Christian and patristic studies have patiently, if sometimes quizzically, tolerated this outside-the-box venture into the applied subjectivity of modern paradigms. Cynthia Read, executive editor at Oxford University Press, saw possibilities from the start, and garnered a group of what must be the world's wisest and best anonymous peer reviewers to midwife the narrative into a shape that worked. Cynthia's assistants, Meechal Hoffman and Justin Tackett, and production editor Joellyn Ausanka showed extraordinary care in guiding every detail into a work of art. No one is more aware than I of the limitations of such a book. Poverty, hunger, and need remain perpetual components of the human condition, endlessly testing our empathy and discernment even as they shape our remembering, our stories, and our hope.

Cambridge, Massachusetts

Feast of All Saints, 2008

GOD KNOWS

Empathic Remembering

In a song inspired by his native county Durham, English folksinger Jez Lowe envisions the seventh-century monk, Bede, revisiting his ancient haunts in modern times and weeping. Viewing the stark poverty of the region today, the old monk "feels the curse of all their debts and damns their debtors. If just one could stand high, and say we'll take no more," the singer laments, "but their will's been broken...the wind blows all day saying more's the fool you...and Bede weeps."[1]

Indeed, the countryside where Bede wrote his *History of the English Church and People*, the same region that gave birth to the magnificent *Lindisfarne Gospels,* is a place that today is scarred by closed mine pits, high unemployment, and a working class focus on survival. The coastal town of Whitby, which I know best, has three heroes: St. Hilda (or Hild), Captain Cook, and Dracula. Despite its summer crowds, chips shops, and lean and haggard hotel-keepers, Whitby is a bleak place, a beautifully spare town, pared by centuries of misfortune, where the wind indeed blows all day. The Vikings decimated St. Hilda's seventh-century monastery (which Bede describes) so cleanly that its remains consist of a few tombstones, bookbinding clasps, writing *styli*, spindle-whorls, loom weights, and combs—and one lead *bulla*, a seal from a lost document authorized by Boniface, archdeacon of Rome from 654 to 685, possibly his papal reply to the abbess's complaints about the obnoxious bishop, Wilfrid. The gaunt abbey shell that is visible for miles, like an etched lithograph of skeletal darkness, is twelfth century, founded by one Reinfrid who, "pricked to the heart" by the sight of the ruin and desolation he saw (and likely caused) at Whitby during the carnage of William's conquest, gave up soldiering to become a monk. The abbot's book, begun around 1160 and preserved today in the town museum, describes among the ruins forty roofless monastic oratories, abandoned monastic cells. Fond to repeat the pattern, Henry VIII deroofed Reinfrid's abbey; the only remaining shelter in the enclosure is a narrow eastern stairwell that is dark with pigeons.

A mile inland on another hill facing the sea, modern nuns in honor of Hilda keep a castle and the ancient traditions and records; their numbers, too, are slowly diminishing. It was from Whitby that Captain James Cook fled a life of poverty to learn seamanship. He was so successful that the Hawaiians ate him in 1779. Like stylites, North Sea gulls honor his statue on Whitby's West Cliff in an endless vigil from their perch on his head. Winds off the sea still claim several lives a year, and the town's August rains call to mind the New England hurricanes of my childhood. Perhaps Dracula is Whitby's third hero because he could keep his balance.

Whenever I visit Whitby—taking the slow bus from York over the moors to walk the coast and worship with the castle nuns—I enter anew these tangible encounters with the process of Christian history, as it knits together its fragile present with the threads, bones, and weaving and binding tools of its past. From the cold stillness of steep and narrow sheltering stone alleys, or from the green and sunny headland, gazing north toward the Viking longboats or south toward the Conquest, I am met by pieces of a past that is paradoxically rich in its very poverty, its need, and its power to impoverish those of whom nothing now remains but stories. Repeatedly I find myself—a scholar of early Christian social history—faced yet again with the realization that the Christian narrative of power and dogma is built on such living relics of human need. This book reflects on some of these interconnected narratives and explores the traces that link issues of need, past with present. Using a narrative of stories, these essays focus on connecting early Christian responses to need, justice, relief, and poverty with modern responses to those issues in Christian tradition today.

In the Anglican church calendar, October 12 is the feast of St. Wilfrid, that troublesome bishop who caused such disturbance at the "synod" Hilda hosted at Whitby in 664. Gathered to present differing views on Easter to the king, whose primary concern was to establish a uniformity of practice rather than doctrine, the local bishop and most of the Northumbrians defended the traditional Celtic date and practices, while Wilfrid championed the Easter date and liturgical practices of the Romans, who had appointed him bishop of York. Bede, a keen admirer of Hilda, diplomatically records the gist of Wilfrid's eloquent appeal for Rome. Wilfrid won the day; Reinfrid's medieval abbey would follow the Roman Benedictine model. But not before Wilfrid was chased out of town by those he had trumped. Wandering through the south of England during a famine, Wilfrid succeeded at converting the Saxon "pagans," using borrowed eel nets (again according to Bede) to teach them how to fish, rescuing them from starvation. When the nets dragged in hundreds of "fish of various kinds," the grateful Saxons distributed a third of the catch to the poor and a third to those who owned the nets; they ate the rest, happily welcoming Wilfrid, who soon baptized them all. When king and bishops again exiled him a few years later, he traveled to Rome to strengthen the support he needed to occupy the episcopal seat at York that he believed was his. By 705 the Northumbrians gave up, and Wilfrid spent his last four years "in peace," dying at Ripon near York in 709.[2]

I often think of Wilfrid around October 12 when, in alternate years, the Anglican daily office directs readers to Jeremiah 38:1–4. In this passage, written centuries earlier and hundreds of miles from the Whitby ruins, an equally troublesome messenger is thrown into a deep cistern to die of hunger and thirst because his enemies view his message as subversive. As Jeremiah was being sucked into the mud, encrusted with the wet earth of time, his voice muted by the echoes of that dank, hollow, space, an imperial servant snuck out in the night with a pile of old rags and worn-out clothes to rescue him. While Wilfrid's voice as a preacher was saved (for a time) by his own eloquence and political strategies, the servant who saved Jeremiah accomplished his task using rags and old clothes, tying them together into a rope that he then passed down into the cistern to rescue the prophet. Perhaps the servant found a spot of firm ground some distance away to gain leverage, stabilizing himself and the rope against some solid object—a tree? a wall?—to ensure a secure, steady pull that would not land them both in the mud. When all was ready, he took position and pulled. Jeremiah soon stood on solid ground, and the voice of the dissident preacher was once again a force for reckoning with the world.

This prophetic image—of using old rags, a firm, steady grip, good leverage, and an attachment to conventional structures to right imbalances and to bring suppressed voices up from the earth to speak into the present—has always seemed to me to be a very powerful metaphor for the modern scholar engaged in early church history. And among the voices from the past that have been left in (or thrown into) the dark storage places of the earth and abandoned, unnoticed and unheard, there have been, until quite recently, a number of early Christian texts about poverty, need, hunger, physical sickness, and other social calamities. Because these texts often existed only in their original or ancient languages, such as Greek, Latin, Syriac, and Coptic, those who study modern medicine, national and international public health, policy issues, and social services—that is, those who might find them most interesting—often knew nothing about them. Because such texts were, like the proverbial prophet, coated with the material of everyday social circumstances, the "scum" of a very earthy past, many theologians and classicists with the necessary language skills to edit and translate tended to overlook them to pursue the study of more "philosophical" or "theological" themes. As a result, in the long and tangled web of discourse over theology, "orthodoxy," "heresy," and even discussions of the body, many early Christian texts on wealth and poverty, written, preached, and applied in the centuries between the New Testament and the medieval era of St. Francis of Assisi, have received short shrift.

Who knows, for example, that the "Great Orphanage" that trained some of ancient Byzantium's best musicians, theological leaders, and administrators probably had its roots in an Arian or "heretical" foundation? Or that some of the most beautiful poetry to equate the poor with Christ and the earth is from a Syriac author once marginalized (in the West, at least) as heterodox? In the Latin-speaking West during the Middle Ages perhaps only a monk here and there copying and translating a rare manuscript in a cold library remembered the classically "orthodox" sermons in Greek from Cappadocia with their vivid depictions of leprosy, obscene wealth, greed, and starvation. One or two sentences from such texts crept into papal decrees but few later sermons tell us how these earlier writings might have been used in historical practice. One exception is that of John Chrysostom, a fourth-century monk-bishop who littered every sentence so densely with comments on the poor that until the computer age his sermons defied the systematic organization that might have filtered out his "social gospel." Indeed, John Calvin built his vision for the diaconate on Chrysostom's writings, but not many Presbyterians know that. Was Stephen Colwell, that eminent if eccentric Presbyterian trustee of Princeton seminary (discussed in Chapter 4), aware of this patristic influence on his own tradition when he tried to confront American Protestants with their "creeds without charity, theology without humanity" in his 1851 *New Themes for the Protestant Clergy*? How many of his contemporaries read either Colwell's book or the translation he financed in 1857 of the French Catholic Etienne Chastel's *Études historique sur l'influence de la charité durant les premiers siècles chrétiens*? Indeed as Colwell discovered, nineteenth-century France was one of his generation's best resources for patristic texts about social issues and poverty relief. Jacques-Paul Migne censored nothing from his massive *Patrologia Latina* (PL) and *Patrologia Graeca* (PG), typeset in Paris as the nineteenth century French republics faced one social crisis after another. French political administrators used

Migne—or at least cited his texts on social welfare—in defining new policy
goals for several republics. Even as modern scholars growl over Migne's
careless typography, they owe this maverick priest an enormous debt for
pushing the envelope of the patristic canon.

The English-speaking world of Colwell's day was more selective, even
as it, too, brought ancient texts to light that had relevance for modern
issues. Colwell was no admirer of John Henry Newman's Oxford Movement, but Newman also sought to influence his peers with a renewed
knowledge of early church writings in English translation. Yet most of
Newman's spiritual heirs, like Newman himself, display little of Colwell's
passion for patristic texts on social welfare. Few such texts were translated into English in the series inspired by Newman's legacy and vision,
the AnteNicene Fathers (ANF) and Nicene and Post-Nicene Fathers
(NPNF) series that were until recently the "standard" Protestant source
for patristic texts from the second to seventh centuries.

Growing up in the Protestant tradition, I found the ANF/NPNF long
before I heard about the abbé Migne or discovered the existence of these
never-before-translated texts on religious responses to poverty, hunger, and
disease in the ancient world. Indeed, such texts, whose stories are traced
in this book, have until recently languished in obscure corners of manuscript repositories and the dusty shelves of reference libraries, at least in
the English-speaking world. Those who might have dragged them from
the past, out of the dust-filled cisterns of these ancient repositories, were
more often busy, like Newman's "high church" colleagues and their suc-
cessors, doing social action itself, applying literal "rags" to more immediate and pressing concerns, eager to wash the wounds of those with present
human need, to act and lobby for justice, human dignity, and rights in the
modern world. Christians who care about poverty and social action tend
to go into the ministry, politics, medical training, or other service vocations that leave little time to study the shells, bones, and original sources
on religious responses to human need in history.

And yet the early Christian writers of such texts on social issues are
in many ways potential allies for those of us who seek ethical voices that
might both inform and challenge our contemporary dialogue about relief
and social justice. Patristic writers—that is, early Christians between the
second and seventh centuries—have left us dozens of narratives, sermons,
letters, hagiographic biographies, and other treatises that give voice to
issues that are relevant for social welfare in any age and religious tradition. And just as we may bring our own issues to modern relief dialogue

(as discussed in Chapter 2), the personal voices of patristic authors often intersect and elide with the stories they tell about the others in their world. Their situations have certain features in common with our own. Like us they too faced risk, insecurity, destructive responses, and violence in a world that seemed to be tottering on its very foundations. Like us they too faced enormous social problems that threatened to (and often did) swallow up every resource at hand. Like us, they had biases and prejudices; they faced similar difficulties in deciding how best to use philanthropic resources. They too made choices that may inspire us and choices that may appall us. As in our own world, early Christian concerns for social issues coexisted within a complex social and environmental network of theological disagreements, inflation, war, floods, fire, hail, drought, and constantly changing politics.

There are many differences, of course, between the social contexts of these authors and our own time and place. These differences are discussed in some detail throughout the following pages, along with suggestions for applying several paradigmatic models to guide a narrative reading of such texts that might enable us to practically apply them to social welfare issues today. The twenty-first century is radically different in many ways from the world of late antiquity between the second century and the seventh century. But are not our friends often very different from ourselves? Do we not value our best companions for their counterpoint, their ability to broaden the depth of our own perceptions, and their power to get us "out of ourselves"? Even when we hold certain beliefs and opinions with kind but firm conviction, do we not also gain wisdom by listening to others, open to their diversity and new perspectives?

Simply reading and being familiar with these ancient texts does not in itself ensure their critically constructive use in modern discourse. Early Christian writers and social activists did not always treat the needy poor as we might wish. Different societies and cultures vary in how they define and apply religious and ethical ideals, even when those ideals are (at least in theory) the same as our own. Consequently there is always a risk of quoting from these authors out of context, with unhelpful, or even harmful results. And yet the challenge to sensibly apply these ancient moral writings to related problems in our own world also offers exciting opportunities. Exploring such texts in depth may enable us to reevaluate and reshape traditional views and practices in ways that offer new perspectives, encouraging fresh approaches to issues of poverty and social justice. This book explores just a few of those opportunities.

AN INVITATION TO EMPATHIC
REMEMBERING

The stories in this book are discussed using an approach that I have called empathic remembering. The word "empathy" is from the Greek *en* (in) and *pathos* (passions), meaning the capacity to participate in the visceral emotions or thinking of another. It differs from sympathy, which is a slightly more distanced feeling alongside the other person. Simply put, to sympathize is to feel *for*, while to empathize is to feel *in,* as if the other is part of one's very self. Individuals influenced by Christian traditions often explain the second half of the "Golden Rule," "love your neighbor as yourself," in terms of such an empathy that expresses itself in action. While empathy involves closely identifying the other person with yourself, it is not about confusing or transgressing interpersonal boundaries. Philosopher Edith Wyschogrod writes that both empathy and sympathy are part of embodying the other and that "in empathy I do not merge with the others but retrace the lines of the others' affect."[3] Those with whom I may empathize—whether they are early Christian writers, the needy poor, or both—remain ever "other," ever "not-me," different from myself in many ways, and worthy of dignity and respect for their differences, whether they live in the distant past or share my present space. Relief narratives and social actions are too often a sharp delineation between "us" and "them." An approach characterized by empathy allows both the self and needy "other" to stand together yet to be distinct within the same encounter.

Pairing empathy with the concept of "remembering" invites that hopeful reconstruction of the past that is always at work as we shape our present. "Remembering" can have several meanings, and two possibilities are most relevant here. First is the ordinary sense of the word, the internal recall of personal experience, things we ourselves have seen, felt, known, or learned from others. But the word can also signify a reconstruction. This is the act of membering again, or "re-membering" the needy voices and bodies of the past, internally refiguring through an imaginative but carefully empathic reconstruction, and in the process giving them new consideration and engagement in the present. Such "re-membering" requires both empathic reconstruction of the other and recall within the self. In such an act, we must remain ever acutely aware that although we take the greatest care with historical sources, reconstruction remains a thing that we have made; others' reconstructions will often differ from our own.

Indeed, the original "reality"—of early Christian responses to the poor, of Wilfrid's role in the distribution of fish from the eel nets, of Reinfrid's inspiration to build a monastery at Whitby—might be something very different again, even perhaps unrecognizable from the stories that shape our own constructions. While "remembering" is used here in both ways, I have chosen to avoid the hyphenation of the second concept precisely because both meanings perpetually intersect in the subtle encounter of present mind and historical construction.

By its appeal to empathic remembering, in an exploration of stories from very different periods in Christian history, this book is in the end a creative narrative. It reads both past and present with an imaginative caution, even as it also offers broad conceptual guidelines to link the past with the present in religious responses to social need.

This book is more personal than I had originally intended. Although most of my work is in the academic study of early Christian texts and issues of social justice, health, and human rights, the early Christian history of social welfare cannot be neatly boxed into academic scholarship, confined to the classroom, lecture hall, and job market. It speaks to us all, oozing and bleeding into contemporary life and into our own personal experiences and memories of encountering needs and poverties both in ourselves and others. Historical studies on religious responses to poverty provide a vital foundation to this topic but are not sufficient for those who struggle to develop practical ideologies that can be applied to modern problems of needs, injustice, hunger, and related issues from an informed historical and religious perspective. Similarly, the packaged solutions and neat, time-defined projects and political consensus documents that usually characterize modern social action are limited in their potential to build an empathic creativity that opens new possibilities for talking, thinking, and acting on these concerns and issues. These essays occupy the space between these two worlds: between historical textual studies and contemporary social action and between the life of the academic library and the life that strains toward effective prayer. As a result it is, I hope, a book that might interest anyone bothered by the problems of poverty and injustice in the world, whether they believe they can do anything about it or not.

The most difficult task has been the challenge to include some of my own experiences and my own stories. While I have never personally suffered from the more catastrophic effects of poverty or many of the other crises of need that we find in these texts from the ancient world, I could not apply an "empathic remembering" to these stories without also considering my own journey to this topic. This required me to lower the screen of academic, objective distance. Consequently, the book borders at times as much on memoir as on religious history. As I wrote, I spent months pushing away first-person narratives only to find them breaking through repeatedly, clinging to my lined yellow writing pads like Styrofoam droplets from a package gone awry. Ultimately I was forced to ask if I had the guts to be vulnerable about myself where it touches on these issues, and not limit the narrative to a voyeuristic adventure into the needs of others. The texts from the past are hardly objective, after all. Early Christian writers ultimately tell their own stories. They are constantly bringing personal agendas to their plans and ideals for private relief, social outreach, and philanthropic institutions. In exploring the practical relevance of their ideas for today, could I speak of what "need" means to me as well, as it relates to this complex issue? Did I dare to mix in my own relevant engagement with liturgy, my explicitly structured designs and models for reading and engaging with these writers from the past? Surely the equal transparency of an author's subjectivity has a place. Most of this personal narrative is in Chapter 2.

BETWEEN THE LINES: INTERPRETIVE CHALLENGES

The issues that this book explores are not just for readers within the Christian tradition, although that is the source of most of the stories and the direction that I personally have chosen to take in writing from within my own tradition. These ancient religious voices on poverty and need may speak to anyone who shares broad humanitarian concerns. Those engaged in international aid in a world after September 11, 2001, are no longer put off by discussions of religious history, as they were when I studied nutrition and public health food policy in the 1980s. In those days, it seemed taboo to discuss "religion" in international food aid or human rights except to identify religious beliefs as problems that might, for example, blockade agricultural initiatives or bias community and household food distribution. But now we find, for example, Catholic liberation theology as a central theme in books such as physician-anthropologist Paul Farmer's *Pathologies of Power: Health, Human Rights, and the New War on the Poor.* The nonprofit corporation Farmer founded, Partners in Health, explicitly appeals to liberation theology in its publicized commitment "to making a preferential option for the poor."[4] And recent "secular" international policy recommendations on reaching needy children in poor countries often promote support for local faith-based initiatives, recognizing that "community organizations, in particular faith-based organizations, have an unparalleled reach in sub-Saharan Africa and enjoy high levels of approval and trust among the people they serve."[5] Christian patristic texts construct a rhetoric of philanthropy that also has much in common with modern Hasidic and Conservative Jewish teachings on *tzedakah*, a word that fundamentally means "restorative righteousness," but is usually translated as "charity."[6] The early Christian narratives themselves, such as the fourth- and fifth-century stories explored throughout this book, as well as the paradigms that can inform how we "read" them, offer resources that are at once ecumenical and cross-disciplinary.

Historical texts that discuss problems such as poverty, hunger, injustice, and the moral use of wealth have a perpetual immediacy in any age. But the adventure into such cross-disciplinary readings is one fraught with certain risks and challenges as we attempt to "read between the lines." It is helpful to be aware of these challenges from the start.

One obvious challenge in reading about the past is understanding its context. What a text says and what it means will depend on where it is coming from, culturally and socially, its literary genre, who the authors are, their explicit as well as unstated agendas, and the background world broadly understood, as it relates to our own. Modern theologians and seminarians are usually trained to interpret the New Testament in light of contextual issues, but may have little formal training in the equally complex issues of reading materials written several centuries later. The quest to understand context is a particular challenge when we are also hoping to find in the text any common ground that might help us to explore ancient and modern worlds comparatively without oversimplifying their many differences from our own world. If we (however innocently) twist the text to say what we want, we do it and ourselves an injustice. Context may be deeply nuanced, so the more we know, the more useful our application can be. Cross-disciplinary readings demand respect for the expertise of companions in the very different disciplines that share these common interests and bring different angles to the reading—disciplines such as history, theology, archaeology, political thought, public health and human rights, anthropology, and economics.

Another challenge is the vocabulary that different cultures use to discuss social problems, need, and poverty. The basic vocabularies of poverty issues in fifth-century Constantinople, for example, do not necessarily—even in translation—have the same meaning as seemingly identical word concepts in the twenty-first century West. Furthermore, vocabulary depends on genre as well as ideals. The language of ancient sermons, poems, letters, chronicles, saints' lives, and church disciplinary manuals may not "transfer" or apply in exactly the same way to modern Catholic, Orthodox, Protestant, and secular government practices or international nongovernmental organizations (NGOs) and programs.

Finally, these texts are also often laden with biases and complex agendas. Their images of the poor are constructed, or even perhaps invented, through the words of those who were often rich and powerful church leaders and skilled wordsmiths; such elite, male, educated narratives do not necessarily represent the common views of their time.

These are not reasons to give up on these texts. Despite certain differences, both the early Christian authors and their subjects were made of human matter and touched one another's nerves in some way. Their vision of things is an opportunity that directs viewers, including ourselves, to another incarnation: to divine engagement with the body of the poor and to the religious call to put concrete substance into divine justice, service, and mercy. Both Christian sermons and human bodies change little in their functions and purposes through the centuries, even though the norms and expectations into which they and we speak and live can change.

As broad, general guidelines, I find it most useful to keep four particular points in mind. These points, outlined in the following sections, may serve as signposts on the journey into any initial effort at a constructively critical reading of the texts whose stories fill the chapters that follow.

Looking for Trouble

First, to avoid accepting the agenda of these texts at face value, I must, as a reader, be open to those places where the story troubles me. For example, the practice of "helping the poor" in the ancient world did not always ensure "social justice" as we may understand it. A story about a failed alms distribution during a fourth-century controversy over theological authority is one example.

In the year 347, the emperor Constans, son of the famous emperor Constantine, sent two imperial officials from Rome to North Africa with a large monetary gift that he ordered to be distributed equally to both Catholic and "Donatist" communities. Optatus, the Catholic bishop of Milevus who describes the event, says that the gift was intended as "alms to relieve the poor, so that they might breathe, be clothed, eat and rejoice."[7] Donatists were followers of Donatus, bishop of Carthage, who had split from the Catholics over what he and others considered to be compromising concessions of some clergy during the early fourth-century persecution, concessions that (the Donatists believed) invalidated ecclesiastical legitimacy. In response, the Catholics condemned the Donatists as "schismatics." An imperial gift equally meant for both was unusual, to say the least. Meeting the imperial emissaries at Carthage, Donatus recognized that this official largesse of "alms" was in fact a Roman stratagem intended to convert his congregations by force. When the officials "told him that they were going through the several provinces and would give to any who wanted to receive," according to Optatus Donatus "said that he had sent letters everywhere to prevent what had been brought from being distributed anywhere to the poor."[8] That is, he not only ordered his churches to refuse to accept donations from these visitors, but ordered that distributions be actively blocked. Scholars have shown that Donatus's hunch was right: the embassy was indeed an imperial commission to investigate him, and the use of alms was to function as patronage-propaganda to assert "Catholic" (and with it imperial) power.[9] Donatist bishops throughout the countryside reacted; the bishop of Bagaia went so far as to incite certain radical activists, called "Circumcellions," to rouse a mob to lynch the imperial messengers. For their part, the imperial messengers were no less severe in punishing those who resisted the forced unification. The ultimate fate of the alms, purportedly intended for generous unbiased distribution to the poor, is lost in bloodshed and theological polemic. Such stories are more than historical tales; religious aid "missions" often remain an explosive topic today, the controversies as often about power, ordination, and politics as they are about human need. To read Optatus's story at face value, we might assume that the emperor was just trying to be nice and that the schismatics overreacted. We need only scrape the surface to see that the account is not so simple.

Seeing the Frame

Second, I must keep in mind that most historical texts about responding to poverty were written by authors who accepted the context of a society that was framed and defined within a patronage model entirely unrelated to modern ideals of democracy and inherent political equality. The world of late Roman antiquity, for example, tolerated slavery, reserved equal rights for male citizens of equal education and privilege, and even often understood Christianity itself differently than we might in many respects. We know, for example, that the church as an organization owned slaves. These slaves were often transferred from the bishop's personal property to become church "property" when he, as a bishop, was expected to divest much of his worldly wealth. In his will, for example, the fourth-century Greek bishop Gregory of Nazianzus mentions a number of (male) slaves he had freed, but he also orders that after his death two of his (female) slaves be assigned to serve one of his aging relatives, a dedicated virgin, for the rest of her life.[10] Perhaps even more troubling, in 599 the Latin-speaking Gregory the Great, bishop of Rome, ordered Vitalius, rector of Sardinia, to help Gregory's agent purchase local pagans as slaves for the church, so that these pagan slaves would then do the mundane and dirty relief tasks for a Roman parish ministry to the destitute poor.[11] Such scenarios reminds us that these are the voices of Christian leaders who functioned within a cultural framework very different from our own. Chapter 3 explores this further through the stories of fourth- and fifth-century bishops responding to social crises of famine, homelessness, and disease.

These patronage frameworks still remain an everyday aspect of life in many cultures today, and some nations still practice slavery. Even in "democratic" nations, patronage is often promoted unapologetically by wealthy philanthropic organizations, whose donors, for example, are listed in descending dollar amounts in fund-raising materials. In North America, patrons continue to be lauded for their "handouts" to good causes and are often rewarded with tax breaks. While we may view patronage patterns as admirable in the foundation grants that fund educational programs, start-up initiatives, research, and academic sabbaticals, patronage remains problematic in local and international relief dynamics, where those in need often continue to find it demeaning, perpetuating status quo inequities rather than empowering human dignity, healing, and social change toward justice and civic autonomy. In 1847, a terrible year across Europe, J. van Leeuwan looked at the many church models for handouts, housing, medical, and relief programs in Holland and noted that "the church does not concern itself with transforming the individual pauper into a constructive member of society."[12] This is often as true today as it was in late antiquity.

Reading Gender

Third, as a constructively critical reader of ancient texts on poverty relief issues, I must be aware that such texts usually say very little about the women's issues that so powerfully touch our own modern understanding of justice, and they say almost nothing about the gendering of poverty. Women are more likely than men to face the challenges of poverty, and their dependent children (girls and boys) suffer as a result in ways that often cripple their own potential for growth, health, and maturity. Family and community support in the ancient world was somewhat different from our world, but widows and children have always been recognized in religious charity texts as a group at special risk. Widows in antiquity had no legal power over their underage children; they frequently fought a losing battle for power over their late husbands' goods and property, and often their own property or inheritance as well. The church often perpetuated such inequities rather than correcting them. Nor were gendered inequities limited to widows. For example, Basil of Caesarea, famous for his radical social models of equity in material redistribution and justice to the poor, advises women in abusive marriages to "endure" and not leave their husbands for any cause because the husband is "the most honored" part of the marriage body (although, to be fair, he does not condone the abuse).[13] We may find ourselves in agreement with early Christian writers' views on some issues, but this does not require us to accept their views on everything. The dominant patristic focus on poor *men* is less than half of the story. Chapter 5 presents a more extensive discussion of the issues involved in gendering poverty.

Recognizing Diversity

Fourth, just as Christian individuals and groups today may differ on how to approach the issue of poverty and relief, as a careful reader I must be aware of points at which the ancient authors also differed among themselves. Although the survival of the external Christian structures of faith and worship followed a certain broad consensus on some particular issues, there are many topics in which early Christian leaders continued to differ, and where their views clearly differed again from those of many faithful believers in their communities. Basil of Caesarea and Gregory of Nyssa, for example, lobbied for a social equality that often sounds quite compatible with modern ideas of equality and even idealized socialism. In contrast, John Chrysostom, their near contemporary who today is often painted standing (literally) side by side with Basil and Gregory of Nazianzus in the iconography of the Orthodox church, adamantly defended the value of maintaining social hierarchy and a static social order.[14] Other areas in which different but equally respected authors vary widely include views about property, the characteristics of a beggar who deserves to receive alms, and effective philanthropic divestment styles. Such patristic diversity on social issues, explored throughout the book but particularly in Chapter 6, opens the door to modern religious dialogue that freely grants and even welcomes a diverse range of options for the discussion of "Christian" views.

BUILDING PARADIGMS

With these issues and their associated risks and opportunities in mind, how might we build on the positive challenges of bringing ancient voices into the conversation about modern issues? How might such early Christian narratives on social issues be used as constructive cross-disciplinary and ecumenical bridges for applying religious ideals on social welfare issues, past and present, to modern dialogue? How might we understand and interpret their nuances in a manner that is fair to both their world and to ours? Throughout these essays, I offer three interpretive paradigms for such a venture: sensing the poor, sharing the world, and embodying sacred kingdom. Each of these three will be defined and described in more detail. These three concepts or paradigmatic ideas encompass particular categories that might be used to apply bits of the complex past to present issues while respecting ancient nuances and cultural differences. These paradigms are not fixed ideological systems but rather function as flexibly constructive tools for discussing and interpreting these texts in light of later or contemporary issues. They permit, and I hope encourage, a shared discussion of common images that trace broad ideals that are present in most religious philanthropy texts. Because they have meaning that is relevant in the present as well as in the past, they offer building blocks that we may use to link this Christian vision across time.

Sensing Need

First, "sensing need" (the focus of Chapters 2 and 5) is the initial process in any rhetoric about physical and social needs that happens at the level of creating or awakening personal perception. By "sensing" I mean the individual's literal experience of the "other" through the physical senses. Because the focus of this book is on religious responses to poverty, the phrase "sensing need" is sometimes used interchangeably with "sensing the poor": the difference between these two concepts (the importance of distinguishing just whose "need" we are sensing) is discussed in Chapter 2. Sensing is that process by which we are aware of persons outside of ourselves who are effectively "touching" our nerves in response to particular concerns. It is that basic encounter that brings these images into direct contact with our own bodies through the senses. We must be "tuned in" before we can take any of those next steps that are more commonly associated with narratives of poverty relief and that are discussed further in the second paradigm, "sharing the world." In the initial sensory piece of the process, responses are limited to our own bodies. Such sensing might consist of emotional experiences, such as anger, compassion, shock, tears, or disgust; as an empathy; or as an overwhelming grief or even repulsion. Or "sensing" may be less emotive, simply a new awareness of something that then influences decisions about how to use time, relationships, and resources.[15] It is precisely because such internal and personal sensory awareness is so important—and has not been adequately considered in other books on poverty relief—that these chapters draw so heavily on narrative examples.

Once tuned into the role of "sensing" in relief rhetoric, it is not difficult to identify sensory engagement in relation to the destitute needy as a recurrent theme in early Christian sermons on the poor. John Chrysostom, for example, often describes the needy in very deliberate language of the theater—appealing to the eyes, ears, and emotions—to tease out dramatic response. The three "Cappadocian" bishops discussed at length in Chapter 3—Basil of Caesarea, Gregory of Nyssa, and Gregory of Nazianzus—often repeat the phrase, "I have seen…" as they appeal to internal responses to persuade their audience to initiate more external activities. For example, Gregory of Nazianzus encourages embodied involvement by appealing to emotive visual experience: "There lies before our eyes a dreadful and pathetic sight: persons alive yet dead, disfigured, a wreckage of what had once been human beings."[16] We may "sense" the poor today through the media, travel, engagement in social ministry, or other personal experience of poverty, and we, too, most often describe these sensory perceptions by relating what we have seen.

Although these texts appeal to a primacy of visual experience as the leading "sense" for most encounters with need, I have chosen to use the word "sensing" rather than "seeing" here in order to deliberately include within this paradigm the full range of human neural responses. Describing such encounters as "sensing," rather than using more common emotional terms such as "feeling," allows the reader more broadly to engage with the spectrum of ways that the ancients discussed their own perceptions.

In ancient Greece and Rome, both the senses and the "passions" were understood in terms of bodily behavior. Yet emotions or "feelings," including pity, were rarely viewed as ideals that could be admired independent of ethical action (such as piety or justice) or ascetic self-control; indeed, one important function of Christian asceticism was its focus on maintaining all "feelings" in an ideologically proper balance. So if we speak of internal bodily "senses" rather than "feelings" as being the first step, the first thing that "happens" in this encounter, we are then in a position to explore how personal issues of need, value, and prejudice might play a role in the next steps that may (or may not) follow: responses and actions that affect the needy other more directly.

This choice, to begin with the personal as we ponder human need, also allows us breathing space to think seriously about what responses may be most constructive. It may help to prevent uncritical reactive and ineffective behaviors, the kind of "kneejerk" leap that often characterizes sensory reactions when others with evident needs enter one's perceptual "space." Facing demands for food, clothing, and justice, social action may too often trump careful thought. Before we *do* anything in this traditional way, we must (even if only for an instant) first perceive the other in relation to ourselves so that our actions might be most sensitive, empathic, and effective, recognizing our own position and our ability and desires to address the real issues, whatever they are. Modern human rights are more likely realized by effectively changing systems (even if only at the personal level) than by guilt-induced reactive volunteerism.

This breathing space often gets lost in modern social and religious action. Friends who are engaged in relief programs have told me that they welcome the reminder that it is okay to take time out and "just" think. One friend, Jodi, wrote, "I have to admit that sometimes the poverty and depravity [are] so overwhelming that I need to sit and pray a while." She wrote this as she was serving remote villagers in Nepal who subsisted in a shocking chronic state of malnutrition, slow starvation, and destitution.

One of Jodi's photos captures a moment that I have found prayerfully helpful in this paradigm of "sensing need." The girl in the photograph, who is holding her baby brother in her arms, was living barefoot in a poorly heated hut high in the Himalayas, in the winter. Her dress is in shreds and her brother is visibly malnourished. Sensing the poor in such a frozen photographic moment offers a viewer the luxury of distance and, with it, only a small piece in the human reality of the situation. For example, what

A young girl and her brother in Humla, Nepal. Photo copyright © Jodi Winger. Used with permission.

the viewer cannot see is that this girl is deaf. Nor does our gaze here tell us that the infant, visited again several months later, was even more malnourished. It is difficult for any sensitive person to encounter such situations without an instant rush to "do" something, often coupled with a sense of hopelessness that anything might make a permanent difference for these particular children. It seems to me that such photographs must be treated with great reverence, as way-signs that direct us to see more clearly the neighbor who, made like us in God's image, awaits whatever our gifts and vocation call us to do in ethical response. Although ancient texts about the needy are not as "objective" as such photographs, they too are often way-signs to captured moments in human history that can guide action now even if it cannot begin to touch those who lived in a time and place beyond our reach, whose stories spur us on. With this deliberate awareness, our reading of ancient texts may take on new meaning as we take time out from action to "sit and pray a while." Intentional "time out" allows us to see in a new perspective the needs that might otherwise threaten to overwhelm. It is sometimes hard to think theologically while we are frantically serving in a soup kitchen, fighting insects in a tent from a famine relief station somewhere in Africa, washing bodies in a hospice, or driving a needy family member to the doctor's office. Harried to speed up our pace of addressing the perpetual anguish of the other, we might instead give ourselves permission, for example, to take vital time to equally respect our own needs, to close the door and re-evaluate our perspective, alone or in community.

The intentional sensing of such visual meditation or reading can be a form of prayer, promoting mindfulness of other human beings and need that goes far beyond ourselves. Simply sensing needs and injustice may not change the world, but for Christians it is often part of an inward "Lenten" journey, a moral obligation such as that mentioned in Hebrews 13:1, to "remember those in prison, since you also are in the body." In such an awareness of our own act of sensing need in others, we may come closer to sharing God's view of these issues and divine concern for the human body.

Sharing the World

The second paradigm, "sharing the world," denotes the full range of actions that might logically follow this initial sensory encounter. Most religious texts on poverty and justice focus on this concept, that most basic common denominator of relief and philanthropy in any culture. To speak of social justice and poverty relief is usually assumed to mean "giving" to "charity" or "alms" or taking part in some kind of "social action." In this process, our inner perception and prayer moves outside, laterally, to physically engage with the other in any of a thousand different ways. Sharing the world is incarnational giving, broadly defined. It may include empowering justice by sharing goods, sharing space, offering hospitality, sharing gifts by volunteering, practicing, or lobbying for global divestment, sharing ideas, or sharing poverty.

Just as the first paradigm emphasizes "sensing" rather than "seeing" in order to construct as broad a concept as possible, so in the second I emphasize the word "sharing," not "giving," because real justice, relief, and cosmic healing are never one-way activities; they are engagements in reciprocity and relating to one another equally at the level of creation. Two chapters focus on this paradigm. Chapter 6, where the story begins in the past, considers the tensions of religious divestment options through the primary lens of a sixth-century narrative about one woman and the choices she faced. Chapter 7, where the story begins in the present, explores this theme with particular attention to three issues: contemporary ideas about the "common good," human rights, and hospitality, focusing on what "doing rights" might actually mean within these specific action-oriented ideals.

Embodying Sacred Kingdom

Most relief programs, whether religious or not, support and are founded on some ideal of global wholeness or cosmic, eschatological unity and resolution as the ultimate goal and realization of their work and mission. Thus the third paradigm, "embodying sacred kingdom" (discussed in Chapter 8) deliberately acknowledges that body matters in the dynamic of engagement with one's philosophical or spiritual ideals, that is in Jewish and Christian traditions, with the divine. In Christianity, to embody sacred "kingdom," ultimate "cosmos," or *eschaton* is to bring body and its brokenness into direct relation with that divine urban finale, usually called either the kingdom of God or the kingdom of heaven. Although the word "kingdom" is problematic, evoking images of gender inequities and colonial domination, I have retained it here because Christian texts that use it as a standard word for the ideals of eternity do not essentially imply a toleration of such associations in eschatological space and time.

Chapter 8 explores issues of modern social welfare and justice as they relate to this third paradigm, using an understanding of liturgy (in Greek, *leitourgia*) that is perhaps best described by Alexander Schmemann when he wrote, "It is only because the Church's *leitourgia* is always cosmic, i.e., assumes into Christ all creation, and is always historical, i.e., assumes into Christ all time, that it can therefore also be eschatological, i.e., make us true participants of the Kingdom to come."[17] In the Roman world a public "service" *was,* by definition, a "liturgy" or *leitourgia.* Liturgies used the body to serve both the divine and the community. Thus liturgy means both "service" *and* "worship"; the two ideas cannot be separated in Christian discussions. Liturgy is thus an ordered service that addresses human need in a manner that is in every sense a sacred act. The most popular Christian image for this relationship is that from the parable of Christ in the poor, in Matthew 25:31–46, where at the last judgment people are assigned to either heaven or hell based on how they treated those in need. Liturgy sanctifies and is defined not only in terms of service but also by association with "sacred" objects: the fourth-century bishop John Chrysostom, who repeatedly alludes to the Matthew passage, calls the poor who were lying in the streets "altars," on which, he says, his congregation should offer sacrifices. And early Christian widows were also called altars because the church brought them material goods and they offered up prayers.

The embodiment of sacred kingdom is more than an external liturgy, however. It is something that engages personal inner wholeness. To think of liturgy in this way is to consider all of life as an engagement in the sacred realm. Each of the world's monotheistic religions contains this concept in some form: the idea that bodily actions in the here and now have or contain the potential power to build (or damage) the realm of reality and divine order in some manifestation that goes beyond what we can understand in the temporal present. Patristic texts on the eschatologically present meaning of the cosmic or the natural world often build on this assumption in their writings about care for the poor and needy. Texts on Christian healing often also include an element of *social* healing, a new life in relationship and community. The ancient idea of social healing also lends itself easily to dialogue about modern relief and philanthropy. Modern Jewish charity contains an ideal of *tikkun olam,* "remaking the world." Such restorative restructuring is, too, the foundation of liberation theology, sometimes described in terms of cosmic ecological concerns. In *Cry of the Earth, Cry of the Poor,* for example, the Brazilian liberation theologian Leonardo Boff suggests that viewing the poor as Christ's body with ultimate rights may also be extended to reflect on the destruction of the rain forests as a violation of this social and sacred body of the earth.[18] While not all Christians would view sacred kingdom in this way, this is one of those many places open for dialogue, where past and present Christian responses share similar concepts. In the fourth century, Basil of Caesarea wrote, "If you give heed to yourself, you will not need to look for signs of the Creator in the structure of the universe; but in yourselves, as in a miniature replica of cosmic order."[19] The needy poor were often seen as embodying this sacred kingdom, guarding the doors of heaven against those who treated them unjustly in this life. Voluntary ascetics are often defined by this image of the poor as embodying sacred order, as they embraced a larger social role that often cast them as ambassadors for social justice. The book concludes by exploring this image and its relationship to all three paradigms using one particular example, an icon of Basil of Caesarea and the holy poor beggar of Edessa, known in some traditions as "The Man of God" and in others as Saint Alexis.

These three paradigms, applied in more detail throughout this book, are intentionally very broad. It is my hope that in this way they might offer a wide, flexible, and useful framework for thinking carefully about potential situations and practical applications in the dialogue of social responses to human need.

CONCLUSIONS

In conclusion, this study of the past functions in constant intentional mindfulness of the present location, not just our own present location but that of those who have read these texts throughout the centuries to use them to help the needy. Christian texts on welfare, relief, and justice have been used in many different ways in history. It is the legacy of such transmission (the focus of Chapter 4), through a chain of filtered readings and choices, that brings each of us to the point at which *we* personally begin our study of these texts. These pages explore only a few of the links in this historical chain.

Most books on early Christian responses to poverty focus on either past or present, on history, policy, or practical ministry, rather than negotiating the complex network of ideas that influences the intersecting space between such very different areas. Yet it is within these intersecting historical spaces that each of us lives and works. By engaging in this broader approach, I intentionally invite dialogue across the disciplinary spectrum. There is no single, neat, definitive answer to how we "solve" poverty and the social problems of mortal need and injustice in our troubled and troubling world. Early Christian texts contain narratives that suggest a range of response possibilities. Through such narratives, this book invites readers to engage with these possibilities in new ways, creatively, imaginatively, and hopefully.

In his memoir *Istanbul: Memories of a City*, Orhan Pamuk writes, "Pay close attention, dear reader; Let me be straight with you, and in return let me ask for your compassion."[20] In this book I, too, must be honest about my own limits. In particular, I am not a social activist. I can empathize with Pope Paul VI when he wrote that "Private property does not constitute for anyone an absolute or unconditioned right. No one is justified in keeping for exclusive use what is not needed, when others lack necessities."[21] But I find this terribly hard to live by. I am more at home with the view of a priest I once heard who said, preaching on charity and divestment during Lent, "God values personal property so highly that He wants everybody to have some!" While the book is broader than my own personal story, it is within the complexity of such personal narrative that the voices of these ancient writers from the past—and many of their modern contemporaries—come together to tell their tales, shape their cries, and rise up from mud and rags.

REMEMBERING AS
PERSONAL STORY

> Christ alone feels hunger with the hungry, and He
> alone feels thirst with the thirsty. And therefore,
> insofar as it pertains to His compassion, He is in need
> more than others.
>
> —Salvian of Lérins[1]

From Marseilles and the island of Lérins in southern France, as he watched
the Goths invade his culture and change Roman civilization forever, a fifth-
century monk named Salvian wrote an impassioned treatise condemning
his fellow Christians for not taking seriously the gospel teaching that God
would judge them by how they used material goods to encounter Jesus
in the bodies of the poor. Roman Christians were by their materialistic
greed causing a social disintegration far worse, Salvian charged, than the
external devastations they were experiencing at the hands of their more
moral and disciplined conquerors. Drawing on the Matthew 25 image to
emphasize Christ's neediness, Salvian noted that "every needy person is in
need only for himself and in himself, but Christ alone begs in the univer-
sality of all who are poor."[2]

Salvian's choice of images, to emphasize the universal *neediness* that in
his view defined Christ's compassion, evokes that encounter with Jesus
that Rowan Williams suggests is essential for Christian transformation
when he writes that "mature Christian identity is at home with the past—
with diverse aspects of it, in diverse ways, but always as posing the question of relation with Jesus. Without this encounter with Jesus in the days
of his flesh and in his life in his corporate Body in history, the believing self
remains untouched by transforming grace."[3] But what does Salvian mean
when he says that Christ in the flesh was "in need more than others"?
What is this need? Indeed, what does the word *need* itself mean in light of
our first paradigm, "sensing need"? Attentive, empathic engagement with

the needs of others must always begin within one's own body, in seeing, hearing, sensing, and perceiving a sensory link with the other that we call *empathy*. But how we then personally respond to others' needs—and perhaps also how we respond to Salvian's idea of Christ's greater neediness in proportion to his compassion—will likely be influenced by how we view our own needs. Given the body's natural tendency to jumble together its needs, wants, preferences, urges, biases, overreactions, and personal tastes into one raucous sensory shout, we can best wisely distinguish and perceive what are truly *needs* if we begin with some idea of what the word *need* actually means.

REMEMBERING NEED

Need is a word that has so many different nuances that I must look it up in the dictionary. There I find that it can be a noun, an adverb, or a verb, all synonymous with some variant of "lack." Its broad meaning is "distress, force, necessity." It may derive from the Old English root word, *nēo*, meaning corpse, and the Old Norse *nār* and Goth *naus*, both meaning "to be exhausted." The noun can mean a necessary duty or obligation, a want of something that is required, desired, or useful; a physiological or psychological requirement for the maintenance of the homeostasis of an organism; a condition requiring supply or relief; or want of the means of subsistence.[4]

Modern economics is built on a theory of need. What would it take for us to live without need, to feel that we were truly free to opt out of constant market distractions that divert us from whatever we hold most dear in life? Is our answer to such a question shaped by a quantity (that is, we could be "need free" if only we had a certain amount of money or material security) or is it a state of being (that is, if only we had certain ideal inner qualities, usually identified in terms of dispassion, freedom, and love)? We use the verb so indiscriminately that it may seem to have no meaning at all. We need coffee in the morning, or a job, a raise, a break, or a vacation. We tell others what (we think) they need, and define others by how we judge their needs. The many different ways that we use this simple word constructs the boundaries that we use to create order in life.

I am surprised by how basic and how varied the dictionary definition is. Using the word so casually in affluent American society, would I guess that the root words relate to death and exhaustion? Need has nothing to do with desire or personal preferences. Its true double edge—obligation and relief—suggests a balancing act: need is an obligation whereas want requires relief. Your needs may (or may not) be my obligations, and vice versa. Need is more than a simple emptiness; it carries with it a driving energy toward its own annihilation. In this way need is more commonly experienced as a demand. As Karmen MacKendrick reminds us, "lack is a potent force in itself" and "power is as needy as vulnerability."[5] We may feel threatened or trapped by the evident needs of others, particularly if they are tied to us by family or other relationships. Faced with his homeless and alcoholic father, for instance, Nick Flynn shut the door and wrote frankly, "If I let him inside I would become him...the drowning man would pull me under."[6] The despair of overwhelming need may lead to a sense of self-annihilation. Eve Ensler captures this desperation well when she writes, "Here on the road, I am nothing, an erased being, down to the zero of myself."[7]

What does it mean to be a Christian faced with such a potent force in a world in which wherever we turn, we encounter those who have a literal "want of something requisite or useful; a physiological or psychological requirement for the maintenance of the homeostasis of an organism"? How do we face their human needs as well as our own? Sensing the poor means entering into the perpetual tension of such questions, recognizing that the dilemma of poverty and relief begins, fundamentally, with the personal. Need is all the more complicated because it is rarely logical or consistent. To face the needs of others as clearly as possible, for example, I must begin by facing and understanding my own needs.

Personal need is complex. Even if we face the truth about our own past, our own narrative, and our own needs, and commit nonetheless to a lifestyle of self-giving, such choices have risks. The very poor, often legendary for their generosity, face social risks that can include victimization, denigration, violence, and preventable illness due to inadequate health care. But there are other risks that may follow the social conscience of a deliberate choice to embrace voluntary poverty, economic simplicity, and divestment in order to work for the global good. We who may choose to take this road—whether for social action, as part of our studies, or as a monastic or ethical lifestyle—risk overlooking our own limits. We may risk letting the ideals of others (or our own) push us to extremes that disregard our personal temperament, gifts, and the equally valid vocations and gifts of interdependent family members who are affected by our choices. Trying to be "good" and trying to win approval by sacrificial generosity, we may fail to respect our own integrity enough to affirm the limits of our personal psychological makeup, the limits of our bodies, and the limits of our available support, time, and space.

It may initially seem counterintuitive, even narcissistic, to cultivate empathic "remembering" of the needy poor in the world by first becoming more consciously aware of personal needs. Considering religious responses to the needs of others in a war-torn and troubled world is often defined as "forgetting self." Yet in that moment of exchange between ourselves and those we seek to help, it may be our "forgotten" self who influences how we define the division between "them" and "us" in choosing the best response. Considering the needs of others is inevitably intertwined—sometimes unconsciously—with how we view and respond to our own history of need, poverty, and economic and social choices.

In her reflections on working with Bosnian women war victims, Eve Ensler emphasizes the importance of remembering her own needs before she could bring herself to these women as a whole human being:

> I realized that if I wasn't "saving" these women—offering solutions—or transforming them into literary substance, I had no idea what to do. My ways of relating were hierarchical, one-sided, based on me perceiving myself as a healer, a problem-solver. All of this was based on a desperate and hidden need to control—to protect myself from too much loss, chaos, pain, cruelty, and insanity. My need to analyze, interpret, even create art out of these war atrocities stemmed from my real inability to be *with* people, to be *with* their suffering, to listen, to feel, to be lost in the mess.[8]

For Ensler, this meant coming to terms with herself and the violence she had personally experienced as a child. By recalling the past, she could open herself up to new responses and face new understandings of herself and others. It was neither easy nor simple. But it was a beginning. Her experience resonates with many early Christian teachings, where it is the needy poor who are the teachers, offering spiritual healing to the rich.

Remembering or recalling our own experiences of personal need can be uncomfortable, awkward, and perhaps even painful. Overwhelming need is never pleasant, and such memories have a way of attaching themselves to our bones, creating body memories that remain whether or not we have a conscious awareness of them or words to describe them. For example, personal memories of need may include some momentary panic, fear of abandonment, a parent suddenly out of sight, or a terror when faced with something new and incomprehensible, perhaps experienced so early in life that we barely remember it. Or perhaps there was a source of distress that we remember very well, such as, for example, an accident that needed immediate medical attention, a learning problem, or a complex disability that could not be addressed without asking for help. Perhaps we felt no conscious needs until we lived on our own for the first time or until a loved one died. If early encounter with need did not include consistent nurture or wise support, our response to such memories may be complex indeed. When caregivers ignore a child's true needs, the child may have difficulty identifying, accepting, and handling personal needs as adults. If those in power gloated over our childhood weakness and took advantage of it for their own personal ends, the child, grown up, may deny having any needs at all, or may prefer to exercise an emphatic or excessive control over adult circumstances lest we be hurt again. If adults blamed our needs on our behaviors, we may do the same to others. If, alternatively, they emphasized their self-sacrifice on our behalf (whether we wanted it or not), we may feel guilty, believing that we too must practice extreme sacrifice simply to justify our existence. Or if, on the other hand, our every desire was treated as a legitimate need or we strongly assert our right to "make up" materially for a "deprived childhood," we may harm others unconsciously by focusing excessively on adult desires or wants, over-reacting when the genuine needs of others appear to threaten and compete with our demands, our sense of entitlement, and our pleasures. Often the past is some mix of these things; it always calls for a healthy balance of adult responses. Whatever cognitive lessons we receive about responding to the problems of the world, for example in moral and religious education, personal response is ultimately shaped by personal stories, priorities, how apt we are to feel empathy for others, and maybe even by birth order and the childhood behaviors of siblings. Even if we think we care, we may sometimes be functionally oblivious to the fact that others have any needs at all.

In the face of needs that can never be addressed adequately or solved definitively in this life, we may find it possible to survive, contribute to society, even to breathe only by constructing with care certain personal boundaries, not as metaphoric walls but as well-hung doors, with good latches and oiled hinges, to open and close with wise discretion. Edith Wyschogrod notes that "both empathy and sympathy lie along the same gradient of feeling-acts that one may occlude or 'run into' the other";[9]

that is, both can either generate action or end in feelings without external action, but the repeated choice to take no action may cause both empathy and sympathy to dry up entirely. As we seek to remain vulnerable to other human beings on some positive level, and not to use our readings of the past to lock us away from all potential of pain or hurt in the present, we may find a constructed space that fosters nurturing support, energizes us to go on caring, and feeds us in solidarity, even on those occasions when we may choose the solitude necessary to listen to these ancient Christian voices. The better we understand our own needs, the more equipped we may be to live out what we truly believe.

As Salvian faced the Gothic invasion in the fifth century, the passion of his appeal to Christ's neediness suggests that he could not detach his generation's injustices to the poor and needy from his own place as a member of that society. His appeal to fellow Christians to see and act on the needs of Christ in the poor was part of his own personal story, as one who had consciously chosen material divestment. Although we know little about Salvian's life, we do know that he was married, with a daughter, and possibly had a sister named Cattura who was a nun.[10] We know that when he and his wife chose to take up the celibate, monastic life, his wife's parents were so angry that they broke off communications with the couple for more than seven years.[11] It is not difficult, therefore, to guess that when Salvian argues, for example, that parents ought to generously divest themselves of wealth to help the poor rather than saving their wealth for their children, he has in mind some piece of his own personal experience. For Salvian as for us today, remembering the poor was inevitably part of a personal story even when the "poor" consist of those others outside ourselves, at the edges of our distant awareness.

CHOICE NEEDS: A JOURNEY INTO PERSONAL SPACE

These issues have particular meaning for me as I experience the world through the lens of my own narrative. While this subjectivity is true for each person, I have chosen to explore here my own personal narrative journey as it has led toward developing a concern for religious responses to social issues. As a teenager who viewed the "needy" as simply those with less material stuff and fewer opportunities than I had, it startled me to meet people who chose to live the life of the poor. In junior high and high school during the late 1960s and early 1970s, I began to meet those for whom living simply, even to the point of real "lack," was a genuine preference: this included social workers, teachers, doctors, and others committed to justice and humanitarian aid, not just the familiar clergy and missionaries who intentionally opted for a minimal or substandard salary to "do God's work." It seemed to me that those most responsive to social responsibilities such as ecological awareness, "simple living," and the move "back to the earth" were the elite of society, people with the most education or the most money. Their choices startled me because they were so different from the working class values of so many people I knew, whose chief aim in life was not divestment but acquisition. They also differed, radically, from my East Coast Maritime-Yankee family's scorn for any material or fiscal risk. The view that prevailed in our family was that a desire to impress the neighbors was foolish, but choosing to live poor was insane. We had been there during the Great Depression, said my grandmother. In the years when she lived with us, it sometimes seemed that we were there still.

I wandered into the early Christian world and its writings on the poor quite by chance. In our Lutheran church the "patristic period"— the four or five centuries of early Christian writers who lived after the New Testament—was rarely mentioned. In fact, when *Time* magazine in 1943 called the eloquent and charismatic Lutheran radio-preacher Walter A. Maier the "Chrysostom of American Lutheranism," Maier's son Paul, writing his father's biography for a Protestant audience, had to explain to his readers that John Chrysostom was a fourth-century patriarch of Constantinople who was called "golden-mouthed" because of his eloquence.[12] Yet Chrysostom's passion for helping the poor and the needy was, like Chrysostom himself, unknown to most of the Lutherans I knew.

Dissatisfied with their Methodist and Congregational roots, my parents had chosen, in the late 1950s, to join the Lutheran Church-Missouri Synod (LCMS) because of its liturgy, doctrine, and music. As we grew up in this tradition, my brother and I were drenched, from infancy, in scriptural readings and ancient liturgies. We recited creeds, chanted canticles, memorized *Luther's Small Catechism,* and feasted on German potluck dinners. Our pastors, good men from middle America, deliberately balanced law and grace in every sermon. Under their direction, church history from the pulpit and in Sunday School led us through Genesis to Jesus to Paul, briefly acknowledging as scripture the dicey books of James, Hebrews, and Revelation, then leapt directly to Martin Luther, with a flying nod at

Augustine. Theology was embedded within creeds, sermons, the Lutheran *Book of Concord*, and rare (usually negative) references to modern theologians.

Ours was an unlikely mission parish for a Boston suburb, established in an urban region better known for its Roman Catholic politics, Jewish intellectuals, Armenian artists and merchants, East Coast atheists, and international graduate students. It was my friends from these other traditions who shaped my world during the week. The persuasive Irish Catholic girl across the street enchanted me with ideals of the nun's vocation, even as my own tradition taught that Martin Luther called monastic life a blasphemous divine service full of idolatry that pious people should leave.[13] In third grade, an Armenian friend shocked me profoundly as we played "church" one day, when she pretended to pull me up to the altar to "kiss the cross." In fourth grade my best friend, a British Anglican girl, delivered a similar shock when she whispered the facts of life to me as we walked together to school. The Jewish boy who had once collaborated with my classroom giggles and hijinks abandoned us all that year for an elite private school across town, and it was nearly a decade before I saw him again. Into high school my best friend and sparring partner was an atheist with a shared love of fantasy and folk guitar, who introduced me to liberal politics and Arlo Guthrie, and happily played devil's advocate in our running theological arguments.

I had no illusion of theology as an idyllic pursuit. As I prepared for college, our parish cracked and bled in a national denominational split over liberal–conservative tensions, a controversy that was to rock the denomination for a decade. The conservatives (and my mother) encouraged me to hold fast to the foundations of Lutheran doctrine. The liberals (and my mother) also encouraged me to pursue seminary and ordained pastoral ministry, something not yet possible for women in the Lutheran church. When I finally got my first Bible, at the late age of sixteen, I scandalized my mother by studying it with Pentecostals, Episcopalians, and Southern Baptists. As a child I was allowed to visit the religious sanctuaries of any friends I wished—except the Catholics. Only once was I bold enough to visit a Catholic church on my own, but the door was locked. While these experiences provided a solid grounding in understanding religious diversities, tolerances, and tensions, the prevailing theological atmosphere did not lend itself to learning about early Christian saints, monks, and martyrs. Later a Lutheran college text on the history of the English Bible would briefly mention Hilda of Whitby, but the professor quickly pressed on to what he considered a far more interesting subject: Luther's influence on Tyndale.

Despite this strong post-Reformation focus of my own tradition, the early Christian world began to intrude into my senses even within the walls of our tiny white New England church. It crept across these silent boundaries through the liturgy, canticles, creeds, and powerfully haunting hymns attributed to mysterious names from antiquity such as "Ambrose," "Clement," "Prudentius," and "the liturgy of St. James." Yet past and present did not cross paths in a conscious way until the summer I was sixteen, when I lived with a Catholic family in Aachen, Germany. There far from home I first greeted real-life nuns, although it would be another decade before I had a conversation with one. And it was there, in Aachen, that I sat in entranced meditation for long hours on warm afternoons in the old city, as the magnificence of Charlemagne's ninth-century palace chapel and its twelfth-century "modern" sanctuary opened my vision to see beyond the cheap pottery statues and effusive Catholic piety that had always put me off. Glimpsing pilgrimage for the first time, I entered into the multiple past tenses that lived and intersected in its history. Breathing the incense of centuries in that rotunda, I peered up in the silent afternoons at its nineteenth-century dome mosaics, one of Christ in glory, another of the holy Jerusalem, four angels, and the river of life. Despite being a late reconstruction, Aachen's rotunda mosaic of Christ in glory is based on a charcoal sketch that was found in the original dome, which, although I did not know it then, may have guided my vision back to fourth-century Jerusalem. For we know that Charlemagne modeled his palace chapel on the *Anastasis*, the rotunda church of the Holy Sepulcher in Jerusalem as it stood in the year 796, after the Persian pillage but before it was damaged by an earthquake in 810 and then razed to the ground by an insane caliph in 1009. Sitting beneath the Aachen dome I was captured, willingly, as if a trap door in my world had sprung open and a windy vortex pulled me down past the invisible sixteenth-century walls that had shaped my universe until that moment. And later in a museum—for this no other place would have done—I faced the first *pietà*—a carved statue of Mary holding her broken and dead son's body—that truly moved me with its sorrow, a sorrow I had until then believed must be expressed aniconically, that is, without any fixed and deliberate imagery. Such interim way stations between past and present can be precipitous moments of salvation.

By my third year of Lutheran college, when the time came to declare a major, I was eager to avoid the theological guttersniping that seemed to characterize the church all around me. So I opted out of continuing courses in religious studies to major instead in nutrition and psychology. It was a second best and my heart knew it. One day two years later in a large Midwestern college library, as I was finishing up this science degree and bored with studying for a chemistry exam, I wandered restlessly through the stacks into a dusty, rarely visited corner of books on church history, selected at random a nondescript volume, J. G. Davies' *Life of Early Christians*, and immediately fell in love with the early church.

Then, as for many years afterward, I had no one to talk to about it. By that time it was too late to change majors, and I had no background in ancient studies. In our progressive, secular high school, those groomed for college had proudly focused on modern languages and literature, French existential theory, and the sciences; only those who would eventually go to medical school had time for Latin. Constrained by academic focus and circumstance, I followed the path of least resistance. After graduate school in nutrition, I worked as a registered dietitian, practicing clinical and public health nutrition in the inner city. It was a field in which (as my family was fond to remind me) there were real jobs.

It was not entirely a bad choice. I did care deeply about public health, with its commitment to issues of poverty, maternal–child nutrition, international hunger, and health inequities. But the inevitable role of a nutritionist—as clinician and educator—was an occupation ideally suited for natural extroverts, not reserved and bookish types like me. I pursued my passion for the early church as I could, on evenings, weekends, and long commutes on public transportation. My memory of first reading Eusebius's fourth-century *History of the Church* is forever wedded to the peripheral image of commuters' feet on dozens of subway rides; it was a miracle that I remembered to get off the train.

As one for whom thought and talk always seemed to be mutually incompatible activities, I found myself constantly exhausted by the verbal and public nature of my job. Paid to be an educator in a government-funded food program for low-income women and their young children, I was miserable, even though I felt a moral responsibility to mindful empathy and did truly care about those I encountered at work. Stuck in a task for which I was unsuited, eager to avoid endless directive conversation and yet paid to do precisely that, I survived by listening and asking questions and then guiding clients' talk into how they could make practical changes in their food choices. Day in and day out I could not escape sensing need; it adhered to the pores of my skin and lined my nerves. From my desk in the noisy middle of health centers in high-risk neighborhoods, I listened to clients' boyfriends try to obtain their infants' food vouchers when I knew that the state had taken the child into foster care. When a very poor, married, white mother told me how valuable our program was for her two ragged (and happy) preschoolers, I smiled and listened, despite her unwashed stench. The barriers she faced just to survive would have overwhelmed me; I knew that if we even hinted at topics such as budgeting or hygiene she would flee, terrified the state would take away her children. I listened to women who wanted what I could offer but who refused the required (and usually free) clinic visit with a doctor, because they "don't believe in that kind of medicine." I was sensitized to situations of potential abuse. When we met with women who were very religious, or who followed unusual faiths, we took special note, lest their food beliefs be hurting the health of their children.

Growing up in an urban, multicultural community, I had always felt more like a global than a national citizen. So it was ironic when during the years when it was my job to empower many immigrant mothers and children with proper nutrition, I was one day perceived as an outsider and a threat to national food resources. I was standing on a subway platform when a complete stranger, a small and seemingly ordinary woman, approached me. Assuming that I was from another country, she began to scream, repeatedly, "Go back where you belong. You're stealing the children's food!" Her voice echoed down the crowded platform until a train roared mercifully into the station and drowned her out. How curious, I thought (much later), that the threat of the outsider was linked, on such a primal level, to family food rights.

I did what I could at the clinics, day after day, until inner exhaustion overwhelmed my moral guilt. By then I had joined an Episcopal parish and was browsing in seminary libraries to quench my thirst for knowledge of the early church. One Saturday afternoon, engrossed in a nineteenth-century Protestant English translation of Gregory, bishop of Nyssa in fourth-century Cappadocia (modern Turkey), I noticed an editor's note, in tiny print, mentioning that Gregory had also written a sermon titled "On the Love of the Poor." But this text (which is in fact two sermons) was not translated in that book or other books I could find. I began to look more intentionally, searching for the original Greek texts, although I could not read them. Eventually I was to learn that Gregory was only one of several authors from the ancient world who wrote on poverty and social issues in the early church, and that almost none of these sermons had been translated into English. I was hooked. What did such texts say? How might they speak to people like me, who cared equally about human rights issues of poverty and hunger and the academic study of the early church and its social influences? How might they relate to my daily work with poor families, mothers, and children and to my desire to bring my faith to modern issues of human rights and social justice? Eventually I took the plunge to find out. I quit my job, traveled briefly to India, and then entered graduate school—again—starting with intensive Greek in order to decipher these early Christian social welfare ideologies and practices that called to me like rare birds across a marsh on a spring morning. I found that the theological controversies of my childhood had prepared me well; from the first day at Harvard Divinity School I felt as if I had come home.

Yet even in graduate school, finally free for the choice of silence and the contented order of the written page, the voices of those in need continued to echo in the back of my mind. At some unknown point in my child-hood, in spite of myself, my family's very ordinary work ethic, and my adult choice to quit a job in direct social welfare, the problem of poverty, injustice, and relief responses had wedged itself into my moral radar, led me deep into the world of early Christian philanthropy, and would not let me go.

Although I still could not stop listening to need, I could now explore new opportunities for doing it with better integration and more prayer-fully. Throughout these studies in the early church, I continued to live in the same neighborhood and wait at the same bus stops. Children in the nearby housing project matured into troubled adolescents. Rats gorged in the dumpster at the natural food store next door, squeezing now and then into the halls of our apartment building. And one Friday afternoon when everyone was at work, the superintendent's delinquent son broke into six apartments in an hour, but could not find anything to steal. Even as I talked to the police I reassured myself that these things kept me inten-tionally aware of the world's tragic needs. But when the chance came to move I packed a hundred boxes of books with an alacrity that took me by surprise. Moving three miles to a suburban house with a yard felt like a relocation to the country. For the first week I was startled awake, alarmed each morning by ominous clicking sounds, only to realize it was the chat-tering of birds. And though the neighborhood was slightly safer, the poor still wandered by, occasionally stopping at the parish church for its weekly community women's meal and food pantry.

It was during this new journey, immersed in the academic study of poverty in the ancient world and no longer facing the intense and endless daily needs of others, that I began to find space to reflect on these issues as they related to my own heritage of poverties. Like Salvian, who renounced family ties while remaining disturbed at the broader social disintegration, in those years I, too, entered a personal solitude that made me more, not less, aware of the family dynamics that contribute to personal choices. I began to understand the influence of my own family, one that had been profoundly shaped by a subconscious narrative of loss and disempowerment.

Conversations in our family had always centered on stories, most of them about ancestors whose difficult lives seemed to warrant more attention than the morning paper. There were lots of real-life props to these stories. We visited, handled, and talked about these props constantly. They included gravestones that lay half buried in windswept maritime grasslands, reminding us of the Scotsman who emigrated to the Maritimes in the early nineteenth century when the Scottish highlands were cleared of highlanders. Old clothing, jewelry, and photos from attic trunks proved the artistic luxury of the Edwardian age, even as original letters, diaries, and epitaphs reiterated their attendant tragedies. Many of these props had once belonged to our great-grandfather, a physician and "overseer of the poor," one of those early New England town dignitaries who kept tabs on needy families, visiting homes to assess their destitution, authorized (or rejected) welfare distributions, and dispatched hopeless indigents to the local workhouse. Soon after he died, all three of his daughters succumbed to tuberculosis in quick succession. His son, the only surviving child, was also serving his village as an "overseer of the poor" when he too died, suddenly, in the first year of the Great Depression. His widow (our resident grandmother) was left with little more than an apple orchard, two tiny children, and an aging, bitterly hostile mother-in-law who controlled the cash. Meanwhile, just a few miles away the man who would become our other grandfather was watching his first wife and child die in childbirth. He suppressed his grief so deeply that his son was sixteen years old before he learned of his father's first marriage.

These stories and others like them of fatalistic loss, stories repeated at every hint of a prop, seemed to emit a fundamental disempowering poverty of hope that repulsed even as it fascinated me, even as I tried to wrench free from its oppressive shadow. In the summer nights of a rural Canadian field in the far north, whenever my father and I stood in rubber boots and warm jackets gazing into a dazzling darkness while he taught me the constellations and I listened to the screech owls deep in the woods, I knew that only a reality as large as the universe could pull me out of the force field of those stories, those village weights of memory.

COMMUNITY OF SOLITUDE

When I made the move from clinical and public health nutrition to a study of the early church, I also chose to live alone. Much of the liberation I experienced happened within the context of this new and welcome personal solitude. Yet by choosing a solitude that allowed me to think, study, and write, I soon found that I had also entered into, paradoxically, a wonderful world of conversation partners. These were members of the broader academic community, both secular and religious scholars, who studied the early church, who knew what I was talking about, and who provided riveting opportunities to learn more.

Yet not all of the voices in my life during this period were either ancient or new. Despite the welcome solitude, I found myself haunted and challenged by family voices of the present, particularly those of the strong women, such as my grandmother, who had shaped my childhood. They were in many respects admirable women, who valued manual work and believed in doing it well. But they had no place in life for ideological discussion, openly viewing my need for solitude and privacy as selfish, even suspect. Shaped by the view that family and economic duty ought to rule every decision in life, they had never been allowed to value personal happiness. Anchored by the spiritual support and insights of a wise Protestant clergywoman, I began to ride out these voices as they confronted me, layer after layer, from every turn of my deepest inner self. Wasn't social justice, they taunted, all about action? Doesn't love really mean self-sacrifice, giving away those things that you most like and want to keep for yourself, such as personal time, space, and the privilege of higher education? And now that I had all this education, how dare I choose *not* to teach? How would I help the world and support myself by abandoning a good job to live alone and spend hours in the library?

Wrestling for several years like Jacob with his disabling angel, I began a gradual, liberating discovery of others who had marked out time-established models for negotiating this treacherous path between wise independence and what seemed like the cliff to hedonism. And along that path I found that there are, in fact, a whole host of voices from other women—ancient and modern—who have gone this route, pairing deliberate solitude with an ongoing and deliberate community identity and practicing a restrained giving that is nonetheless sensitive to global issues. As I had in Germany as a teenager, so again I found new freedom in monastic and even "Catholic" examples, such as fifth-century Amma Syncletica, who withdrew to live in the desert in silence. We know about her because visitors and disciples insisted on a word now and then. And when she did speak, many of Amma Syncletica's "desert sayings" concern charity, the poor, and almsgiving.[14] Another woman who models a life-giving monastic philanthropy within set boundaries is Esther de Waal, an Anglican scholar on Benedictine monasticism who not only speaks internationally about living the Benedictine Rule as part of ordinary Christian life, even for married people with children, but who also (when she can) practices a lay monastic hospitality in a village near the Welsh border. It was de Waal's book, *Seeking God*,[15] that a modern Benedictine abbess handed me one afternoon in an enclosed garden at Malling Abbey, a few miles west of Canterbury, as I, spinning with jet lag, began at last to resolve the din of these competing voices. Both Amma Syncletica and Esther de Waal (as well as the nuns at Malling) knew the liberating—if obvious—truth that hospitality works well for all only when it includes clear personal recognition of and respect for our own limits and the limits of others. This is necessary advice, especially for women drawn to Christian social action who are trained, as women often are, in utter self-negation.

Karen Armstrong offered another model, with what she calls the transformative "science of compassion" or "spirituality of empathy." After years as a Catholic nun conditioned to self-denial, Armstrong left monasticism (and the Catholic church) for studies at Oxford that led her into a life of solitary religious research, writing, and popular public speaking. It was the solitude that took her by surprise. Struggling as I had to resolve the apparent "selfishness," Armstrong realized that

> The silence in which I live has also opened my ears and eyes to the suffering of the world. In silence, you begin to hear the note of pain that informs so much of the anger and posturing that pervade social and political life. Solitude is also a teacher.... Silence and solitude strip away a skin; they break down that protective shell of heartlessness which we cultivate in order to prevent ourselves from being overwhelmed by the suffering of the world that presses in upon us on all sides.[16]

The monk Martin Laird puts it similarly: "Those who sound alarms regarding the realization of the contemplative path as being anticommunity reveal a shocking ignorance of this simple fact: the personal journey into God is simultaneously ecclesial and all-embracing. This in part is why people who have gone fairly deeply into the contemplative path, become open and vital people (however differently they may live this out)."[17] These contemplative ideals depend, however, on a stabilizing coexistence of community presence and accountability. As one group of English Benedictines concurs in their reflections on the theology of monastic life as it relates to modern society, "No one can mature in isolation."[18] A chosen solitude should be linked, however informally, with a responsible relationship to community, however that is defined.

For Armstrong, intentionally looking outside of herself to enter into an empathy with the pain of others forced her to go beyond herself and to learn how to forgive and better understand those who oppose what she believes in. And Laird notes, "In this depthless depth we are caught up in a unity that grounds, affirms, and embraces all diversity."[19] This sensitivity for the other that is rooted in the solitude that gives true space to the self may also be what the monk Thomas Merton had in mind when he scribbled in his *Asian Journals*, "True love requires contact with the truth, and the truth must be found in solitude. The ability to bear solitude and to spend long stretches of time alone by oneself in quiet meditation, is therefore one of the more elementary qualifications for those who aspire towards selfless love."[20]

PERSONAL NARRATIVE IN A GLOBAL COMMUNITY

Recalling now the first of this book's three paradigms, "sensing need," experiences such as those of my childhood friendships, that were drawn from a wide variety of religious traditions and ethnicities, taught me about the importance of encouraging an empathic Christian "sensing" that is mindful of one's own place in the global community. Experiencing the global community will affect how we think about Christian responses to contemporary human need that draw on narratives from the past. Global awareness allows us to remain ever mindful of models from different faiths and even from those who care deeply about social justice but who profess no religious beliefs. Engaging in issues of social justice is, after all, a form of interfaith dialogue.

Indeed, most ethical systems share similar moral views on these problems of poverty and injustice and the call for a response that is based on ideals of righteousness and compassion. There is much room for dialogue and practical collaboration with other communities of faith and with social justice groups in addressing these issues. Care for the poor and a response to human need have a place in most religions and are sacred imperatives in each of the world's three major religions. In Judaism doing good for another person is a "mitzvah," an act that embodies *tzedakah*, "charity," effecting a righteousness that can remake and heal the world. Obligatory alms, or *zakāt*, is the third pillar of Islam, honored together with witness, worship, fasting, and pilgrimage. In Christian monotheism, caring for the poor is identified closely with the Christian doctrine of the Incarnation, that is, the belief that the one God chose to take on flesh in the singular, unique human body of Jesus, and that the teachings of Jesus affirm that the poor and needy in any age may be (to put it mathematically) equated with but not equal to that very physicality of the Holy One. For Christians, that is, the body of Jesus Christ remains unique even as the poor are icons of it. Returning to Salvian's image at the beginning of this chapter, it is in the bodies of the poor that Christ is the most universal of all needy beggars. For all three of the world's leading monotheistic traditions, the actions done to the poor in this way elide with hands-on service (that is, liturgy or worship) with and/or to God, however the divine is understood. Certainly there are differences in the nuances of Christian, Jewish, and Islamic alms. Yet the physical needs of the destitute poor stand in all three traditions as a signifier for injustice, demanding response even as poverty engages with the sacred.

Living as I do in the wealthy and developed Western world, I spend most days in a culture that is sheltered from perpetual encounters with the most extreme faces of human need. But most people in the modern—and ancient—world were and are not so sheltered. In many towns and villages around the world, stark destitution is—and was—visible at every turn, even a "normal" and apparently immutable fact of life. And even in the West, we love to watch our media stars and heroes as they champion the needy. We define our wars with the language of liberation, and use images of widows and orphans to advertise responses to international poverty, crises, and public health-related diseases such as human immunodeficiency virus/acquired immunodeficiency syndrome (HIV/AIDS). We may judge popes by their social policies and measure the integrity of megachurches by their behavior toward the needy in their own backyard and neighborhoods. Those who once lauded John F. Kennedy's Peace Corps and Lyndon Johnson's "War on Poverty" may now praise their children and grandchildren as new generations seek global justice with a similar zeal, while also often looking to the past for models of faith with which they can rewrite the present and reform the world. Yet often there remains a huge cultural chasm between those in the West who are most motivated to "do something" about global needs and those for whom these issues define daily realities and limitations. What does "sensing" the poor and "empathizing" with human need mean when you do not have a choice? How does it differ from what it means for those of us who can afford what one scholar has called "disaster tourism,"[21] traveling to participate in relief activities and professionally concerned with the amelioration of poverty, yet never truly observing it, remaining ever ultimately independent of the affected communities in terms of our own survival? While this book cannot begin to explore such issues adequately or completely, a quest to understand cultural and locational differences may, I suggest, nurture a perspective that is open to sensing need at a personal level in ways that might make a few small differences in how we engage in the encounter with other persons within our global community.

Both Simone Weil and Mother Teresa offer two extreme examples of practicing voluntary sensing from a social location somewhere between privilege and the fixed boundaries of poverty itself. In 1943 Weil, a Jewish-Christian philosopher, writer, and social activist, chose to embody empathic identification with the poor and oppressed of her Nazi-occupied France to such an extent that she died at age thirty-four from starvation-aggravated tuberculosis. She did not, however, die in a Nazi-occupied country. She succumbed to the effects of self-induced starvation and starvation-aggravated disease as a patient in an English hospital that provided her with plenty of food and the best medical care of the day. Her refusal to eat what she needed for healing and recovery was, in her view, an act of intentional solidarity with the sufferings of her fellow French citizens (whose lives, unlike Weil's, were spent constantly seeking adequate food for survival). Her death raised (and continues to raise) serious questions for many who had admired the spiritual sensitivity to need and the passion for a religious response to political injustice that had characterized Weil's life and her work toward what one scholar has called "a provocative remapping of the human psyche and a reconfiguration of the space of political action."[22] Simone Weil was controversial because the extreme consistency between her convictions and her actions seemed to border on psychological illness.[23] Yet tensions between action and thought can also be controversial. The recent publication of Mother Teresa's letters to her confessor shocked many, revealing as it did the darkness and doubts that tortured her as she emptied herself, while perpetually smiling to the world as she ministered to the terminally ill in the Calcutta slums. For many readers, Mother Teresa's hidden and "true" feelings about her work and herself seemed to make a lie of this otherwise inspiring woman's lifelong, sacrificial, and public face of hope and love for the Christ-poor.[24] Did her depression and doubt invalidate the real relief that she provided over many decades to millions who lay dying? Despite the human failings and rhetorical tensions in the lives of these two very different women, the lives and writings of both Simone Weil and Mother Teresa stirred—and continue to stir—many to sense and act, with full honesty to themselves, in ways that change and improve the world. Truly sensing the poor inevitably invites confrontation with the inner poverty and need issues of the sensing body itself, and one's personal reactions to it.

This perpetual inner dynamic may be one of the reasons that the most effective responses to need and injustice seem to rise organically from within the affected communities in which they occur: organic responses growing from mutual sensitivities. Empathy is, after all, a close engagement with and an entering *in* the pathos of the other, not a distant experience from another place. True empathy is a lateral experience, incompatible with the condescension or "looking down on" others that so often characterizes pity. In fact, early Christian writers, such as the Cappadocians and John Chrysostom's responses to poverty and injustice that will be discussed in Chapter 3, build on these organic lateral relationships by emphasizing that the destitute poor are entitled to relief precisely because they are vital members of the human family on whom the spiritual survival of the rich depends; an honest sensing of poverty is the first step toward social participation in the body of Christ and the kingdom of God.

Yet even if I personally do not, for example, live with the extremes of disabling destitution and injustice that are commonplace for most of the world's needy poor, and even if my attempts at a realistic but "solidarity" level of divestment seem consequently impossible and futile, I do have choices for effectively "sensing" need, both locally and globally. These include engagements that will lead, easily enough, into the second paradigm, "sharing the world." They include choices such as fostering friendships and relationships with those who are physically located in such situations, doing what I can, like Jeremiah's servant, to enact a platform

that allows their voices to reach others, and listening attentively to what
they have to say even as I explore options to do what I can in my own
voice, from my own location. I can learn from others who are members of
these communities, I can listen to those who make and apply policies, and
I can probe their neat boundaries to tease out the effects that their policies
or activities have (or do not have) on ordinary people. I can sense with
brutal honesty my own conscience, gifts, and excuses. I can confront and
counter the prejudices and patronizing assumptions that I may discover
in the depths of my own manner of thinking. I can allow something as
simple as listening to a song, for example, to shake my world.

Some months ago I attended a symposium on the problem of infants
and young children whose lives are affected by HIV/AIDS in resource-
poor communities in sub-Saharan Africa. Hosted by an eminent American
academic medical institution, conference speakers included international
economists, aid administrators from leading nongovernmental organizations, and community health workers from a handful of religious and
medical organizations in representative communities. The focus was on
breaking through existing barriers with evidence-based action to effect
ways that these needy and usually dying children might rather grow up
enjoying the same health and educational opportunities as their Western
counterparts. Speakers included not only well-trained physicians and
social activists with years of experience; many present had also lost parents, spouses, and extended family members to the HIV/AIDS epidemic,
and some were living with it in their own body, as widows and orphans.
My public health background had trained me to be comfortable with professional gatherings such as this, founded on goals to build plans of action
based on statistics, scientific studies, and facts discussed as objectively as
possible. So I was startled by the obvious undercurrent of powerful emotions at play in this particular setting and the sharp economic tensions
evident in each talk. It was not the religious aid representatives who raised
these tensions, but those who were, on the one hand, closest to the household realities and those who were, on the other hand, closest to the money
that might be directed to implement change. From my plush auditorium
chair, taking notes with attentive objectivity, I was literally startled out of
my seat as the conference ended, by what seemed yet another breach of
medical and scientific "manners," when the audience of hundreds rose up
to stand together and hold hands, joining in an African song.

After the song ended I caught my breath as people began to leave the
auditorium. Gathering up my scattered notebook, I smiled politely at the

African health worker next to me with whom my only contact that day had been this touch of hands. But it was obvious to her that my well-trained cool had been broken. "It's how we stay sane," she said to me, kindly. "It's how we keep from going crazy in the situation."

As we parted to our respective exit aisles, I suddenly saw the whole event, and my response, in a new perspective. Despite all the information I had neatly outlined in my notebook, despite the competitive tensions between interest groups, and despite even the rousing song and physical contact, I had not, until this woman spoke, personally and kindly to me, truly "sensed" the human beings who daily live with these social crises, even though I had spent the day in an attitude of openness to listen and learn from each speaker. In her few words, this woman put it all together. The song was not, as it had seemed to me, an out-of-place evangelistic appeal to emotions. It was, rather, the organic expression of a meaning that I had not until that moment even dimly perceived. While my trained objective openness had left me untouched, my neighbor's explanation broke through because it resonated with something that I too shared as part of my own personal story: I understood the power of music. That is, I understood her because I knew firsthand the use of song in religious traditions and its power to release the depth and pain of the heart in ways that rational text alone cannot. Yet it was not the song that broke through to me, but the personal kindness of her perception about me and my need for such an explanation. In that moment when she spoke, through this woman's spontaneous response to my obvious Western cluelessness, I was able at last to "sense" the situation of need far beyond my rational perceptions. Sensing the poor thus begins with the personal and at the intersection of personal stories.

ENGAGING PARADIGMS

The Shape of Early Christian Need

> When you fill His belly, you will find the Bread of
> Life...You drink His Blood—take up and give
> Him to drink, for He is parched.
>
> —Jacob of Sarug[1]

Preaching from a dusty Syrian village, in the district of Sarug near ancient
Edessa around the year 520 A.D., a local bishop named Jacob urged his villagers to view the destitute poor around them as dirt. "The poor are like a
vast piece of land for the purposes of justice," he wrote in a sermon titled,
"On the love of the poor." "The needy are the 'good soil' of justice," Jacob
repeated, using terms that they, as farmers, could easily understand; "The
soul does not have anywhere to sow justice if the poor are not serving as
the soil on which to sow.... You sow here on the land of poverty and your
seed is placed in the hands of the Lord, according to His promise."[2]

For farmers then as now, dirt—or soil—signifies a substance that is
essential for human survival, literally the basic "ground" through which
all food, and with it agricultural wealth and property, is produced. By calling for a view of the poor as dirt, Jacob was not denigrating the poor; quite
the opposite: in his view, they were living opportunities by which those
who engaged with them might turn a heavenly profit through another
sort of action: action for justice.

Jacob's imagery, and the vivid descriptions of the poor in fourth-century
sermons by three bishops called "the Cappadocians," which are the focus
of this chapter, demonstrate how early Christian writers used such dialogue to build a patristic understanding of the three paradigmatic concepts that were outlined in Chapter 1. Patristic texts on poverty—most of
them reflecting sermons that were originally preached to an often illiterate
audience—offer modern readers a view into how the ancients "sensed"
the poor, how they used these sensory impressions to push for the practical

actions of sharing the world, and how they envisioned the ultimate supra-cosmic reality that they called the kingdom of heaven.

In each of his references to the poor as soil, Jacob's word for "justice" is a Syriac term that was precisely the same word that Syriac speakers would have used for "alms." As a Semitic variant of Hebrew, the Syriac word for "justice/alms" has the same linguistic root as the Hebrew *tzedakah*, discussed in Chapters 1 and 2, which means both "righteousness" and "charity." In Jacob's world, that is, people understood almsgiving as an act that effected justice. Such charitable justice is like gardening: it engages with the material world in a manner that makes things grow properly. Certainly many who gave alms and other forms of relief to the poor did so out of self-interested motives (hoping to buy their way into heaven). Yet such acts done toward the poor were viewed as ultimately benefiting the self regardless of inner motives, since such behavior was morally right before God. Doing charity effected social justice because doing charity properly was an act of spiritual justice.

SACRED GROUND

To speak of social justice using images of the poor as dirt may strike the modern reader as hardly a compliment. No one wants to be called "dirt poor." But in the ancient world the survival of a village might depend upon its farming capacities, and modern environmentalists frequently remind urban dwellers that soil is a valuable resource requiring great care. Ownership of land in rural antiquity was valued not so much for its rentable potential as for the land itself, as an inheritance and as a defining feature of one's identity that contained perpetual potential for agricultural life and growth. Community controls tightly defined who had the right to use the land and profit from it. In creating this image of the needy poor as agricultural ground—good earth that promises its sower a rich harvest—Jacob brings the body of the poor into a recognizably positive community image. Through this image, the poor are transformed into a valuable resource by which the rich rewards of heaven are for those who can assert good stewardship of such a resource, appropriating and applying the divine generosity and imitating God who cares for all that He has made. This appeal to heavenly benefits for actions done on one's own turf in this present life is a theme that Gregory of Nyssa (discussed further below) also uses in his Greek sermons on the love of the poor, over a century earlier. On caring for the sick and bedridden poor, Gregory writes, "Don't let someone else treat those in your neighborhood. Don't let another rob you of the treasure laid up for you."[3]

This image—of the poor as soil that one might "seed" with alms that are understood as justice—is only one of the many images used to depict the poor and to appeal for their relief throughout early Christian tradition. Such earthy images are based in the Christian affirmation of the material world itself. Because God took on human flesh in Jesus, Christians argue, believers could affirm the good and even redemptive nature of God's tangible creation. This idea takes special shape in the parable of the sheep and goats at the last judgment, Matthew 25:31–46. Christian writers in the first six centuries (and later) repeatedly refer back to this text as the "real" truth in almost every incident of human need and charitable (or miserly) response.

In fact, Jacob of Sarug develops his sermon on the love of the poor to describe the divine relationship of the poor in exactly such terms; the reference to soil is only a small part of his broad and vivid vision for social justice. Jacob uses an extensive series of analogies and contrasts in his sermon, which is worth quoting at length, to make his point about this equation between the needy poor and the material reality of the divine as described in the Matthew text:

> For your sake He was made a beggar in the streets, in hunger and need along with the poor in this world... The Creator, to whom the entire creation belongs, has abased Himself so as to borrow from you in (the person of) the poor... 'Give to the needy, and I will be as a debtor to you: 'I am the one who borrows from you in (the person of) the poor, 'for on their behalf I will give you great wealth...' although He is God, He has equated Himself with the poor... He is hidden and exalted high above all the ranks of heavenly beings, but when a poor person stands at your door, you see Him! (831) He who has constructed the house of (both) worlds for the races to live in, in the person of the destitute He has no house to take shelter in. He with whom the Creation is full, and cannot contain Him, is knocking to enter your house in the person of the despised and the insignificant... He whom the cherubim convey on their backs with trembling lies smitten on the bed of sickness, along with the sick. Wherever you want to see Him, you will find Him by means of the luminous eye of faith that does not doubt: with the sick, with those in distress, with those who mourn, with the needy, with the

hungered, the buffeted and afflicted...Brought low, wretched, buffeted and afflicted, He has come to you; sit Him down at ease, while
you get up and serve Him, rejoicing as you do so...For the poor person
who has stood at your door is God Himself...In a lowly and despised
guise He has come to visit you, so that when you fill His belly, you will
find the Bread of Life.[4]

This image of Christ in the poor is also explicit in other Syriac texts.
For example, in John of Ephesus's sixth-century account of the widow,
Euphemia, who will be discussed in Chapter 6, Euphemia chides her
neighbors sharply for ignoring "Christ lying covered with sores in the
marketplace." John tells us that in her daily visits to the poor she would sit
beside each person and ask what they wanted for dinner.[5] Such texts demonstrate that, for these early Christian writers, the incarnation of Christ
touched material creation such that the material composition (and even the
food preferences) of the needy mattered because it embodied the divine.

Such views of the poor also suggest a broader image, that of sacred
ground or holy land. This image crosses cultural and religious traditions
and is also a key theme in modern concerns of both the environment and
body. In her tortured memoir about living with mental illness and homelessness, Robin Hyde evokes the ancient image of earth as a holy mother
associated with the destitute when she writes that "We are all of us seeking
for our homes in this earth. I say, may the very need of earth, which we
have wronged but which also we have loved, and which, therefore must
forgive us (like the woman earth is), strengthen all the homeless in their
dark journey tonight."[6] Yet even Christians who would not share Hyde's
pantheistic implications of "earth mother" are not shy to speak of holy
land when referring to biblical places, although discussion of the "Holy
Land" focuses, more often than not, on stories about buildings, events,
and people rather than earth. In fact, throughout much of the middle-
eastern "Holy Land" today visitors sometimes find it easy to ignore the
stark beauty of the natural environment as they look "past" it to imagine
biblical events or to dig through it, in archaeological excavations. Indeed,
in modern Jerusalem it is impossible to find an inch of ground that has
not been covered by the residue of later centuries, confused and conflated
with multiple constructions over long years of war and devastation. Only
a few writers on modern life in the Middle East lament the damaging
effects that endless conflict over holy place has had on trees and wildlife.[7]
More often it is blood that marks the essence of what is considered holy

ground. Martyr relics—bits of earth and bone—are viewed as holy precisely because they represent those whose bloody death planted them like good seed in the ground of holy becoming. In early Christian images of the poor, however, it is ground itself that is sacred, as it symbolically demands not the death of blood and seed, but life and the rich fruitful planting of *tzedakah*, righteous justice.

EARTH, FLESH, BONES: THE CAPPADOCIAN POVERTY SERMONS

Jacob of Sarug was not the only early Christian writer to link the natural powers of the earth with the embodied divine presence, poverty relief, and social justice. Other, better-known examples of early Christian responses to need are found in the sermons and letters of three fourth-century Greek-speaking bishops from the Roman province of Cappadocia (modern central Turkey): Basil, bishop of Caesarea, Basil's brother Gregory, bishop of Nyssa, and their friend Gregory, bishop of Nazianzus. Their writings (sermons, letters, and treatises) contain a wealth of concepts and images related to their responses to poverty and social crises. A close look at these particular texts enable us to begin to understand the complexities of at least one particularly historical context in which the history of religious responses to poverty addresses many of the same issues familiar to us today in our own cultures.

When a severe famine struck the region in the late 360s Basil, bishop of the capital city, Caesarea (modern Kayseri), immediately began to preach on the moral connection between the hyper-retentive lifestyle of the rich and the meteorological retention of a catastrophic seasonal drought that had caused disaster, particularly for the now-starving poor. Although Roman writers caricatured Cappadocia as a backward, rural region famous only for its wheat and horse breeding, Basil, the eldest son in one of the region's leading families, was no farmer. Highly educated in the finesse of Roman diplomacy and urban, civic leadership, he applied the full eloquence of his rhetorical training to these sermons on the practical and ethical topics of poverty and relief, and the indecency of wealth, hunger, usury, and injustice. Basil's ideals had been shaped by classical Greek culture within a Christian framework, and he envisioned social justice in terms of the classical Greek *polis*, that is, urban political dynamics of legal order and patronage. And although members of his family owned large tracts of land, his was not a typical wealthy family. His Christian grand-parents had suffered during the last great persecution (before Constantine legalized Christianity), surviving by hiding in the hills, and his father, a lawyer and rhetorician, had died when Basil was young. Soon after he finished his formal education in Athens, Basil went off to become a monk, most likely influenced by both the example of his older sister, Macrina, and his spiritual teacher, Eustathius, a man who would eventually become a controversial and theologically slippery opponent. Basil retreated to a rural hillside on family property and founded a monastic community; the location of the site was recently identified at a hill in Turkey's north-ern mountain country several miles from the modern village of Sonussa/Uluköy.[8] There Basil lived for a while so simply that he may have damaged his liver. He almost certainly could not cook, and the monastic retreat depended (at least in the beginning) on food packages from his mother. Yet even after returning to the city, where he was ordained a priest and then a bishop (his monastic community seems to have continued to grow), he used agricultural as well as civic images to appeal during the famine to the ultimate measure of God's right ordering of the world. In Basil's view, it was human injustice that had caused the famine, a human violation of the natural processes that had the power to disorder even the weather. For example, preaching to his rich neighbors in 368–369 as they hoarded grain while farmers and their families wept in the fields and wasted away, Basil cries out, "Wipe out the oppressive contract of usury, that earth might bear appropriately.... You and all your wealth will share one death; contrive a way of transporting a few grains [to heaven]; persuade the earth to bear fruit; effect liberation from the calamity by using the arrogance and swag-ger of wealth."[9] Although in Greek the words used for alms are different from those used for justice, Basil, like Jacob of Sarug, assumes an intrinsic connection. He appeals for alms as "justice" to the poor, specifically alms in the form of grain that will transport the spiritual sower to heaven even as they revive those suffering from starvation.

At least four of the sermons on social issues that Basil preached during this crisis survive. These focus on very specific issues related to poverty, justice, and human rights, issues such as hunger, drought, usury, wealth, and stockpiling. We also have the two sermons of Basil's brother, Gregory of Nyssa "On the love of the poor," which concern homeless and diseased beggars; these are the texts that I found many years ago mentioned (but not translated) in the NPNF. After Basil died, his brother also preached a sermon against usury and wrote a funeral encomium that mentions

Basil's response to the famine. Another sermon, even more famous than these, is Gregory of Nazianzus's *Oration* 14, also called "On the love of the poor." Gregory of Nazianzus also wrote a funeral sermon for Basil (*Oration* 43) that describes his friend's philanthropic projects in great detail; this sermon (even more than Basil's) has been the primary source for much that has been written over the centuries about Basil's work on this issue. Some details about these poverty-related crises and responses are also mentioned in letters that survive from all three writers.

While the Cappadocian texts provide an unusually extensive portrait of a crisis as seen by three separate authors in the same time and general region who were in constant communication with one another, other early Christian writers at this time were also expressing substantial and similar concerns for the needy poor. Less than twenty-five years later John Chrysostom, as bishop of Antioch and later Constantinople, preached many sermons filled with references to and details about the mandate of Christian social justice and alms for the poor. Chrysostom's concern for the needy poor is perhaps best known today from his series of sermons on Luke 16:19–31, the parable of the beggar, Lazarus, and the rich man.[10] By the sixth century, the church in both Greek- and Syriac-speaking communities around and east of Antioch was preaching about Basil's famine relief,[11] and celebrated January 4 as a day to consider "travelers and the poor," as we know from the surviving sermons of Severus, Bishop of Antioch, around 519.[12] Together, these sermons and others like them suggest connections among episcopal writers who either knew or would influence each another in various ways. The bilingual Ambrose of Milan (Augustine's spiritual teacher), for example, corresponded with Basil and translated into Latin much of Basil's sermon against usury to include in his own homily on the same topic.[13]

As we set about to read such sermons for what they say about the three models suggested in Chapter 1—sensing need, sharing the world, and embodying sacred kingdom—it may be useful to approach them with certain basic questions in mind. For example, we might begin by asking, simply, what stories do such texts tell and how do they tell them? Next, reading into them more carefully, we may ask: what challenges might we face when we want to draw from such texts, not just for devotional reading, but in the interactive "on the ground" conversations we have with others about modern social welfare and justice? And finally, once we gain some appreciation of both the stories and their challenges, we can ask: how are these texts relevant in building usable conceptual bridges for thinking about sensing the poor, sharing the world, and embodying sacred kingdom across history and across culture?

The second question, that of identifying challenges, was outlined briefly in Chapter 1 and will be discussed further in Chapter 4. The remainder of this chapter will explore the first and third of these questions, the context of the stories themselves, and suggestive reflections on their relevance for modern dialogue.

SAVING THE RICH: FROM CLEMENT OF ALEXANDRIA TO THE CAPPADOCIANS

To best understand the goal of the Cappadocian poverty sermons as a sort of focused "case study," we must first appreciate their broader cultural context against the background of the Christian world of Greco-Roman antiquity. The fourth century was a time when Christian leaders were deliberately intent on using the Christian past, its rhetoric and ideals, to influence Roman civic life and public policies. Much of this effort was driven by two underlying and related concerns: first, to prevent a return to persecution (Christianity had been legalized only recently, in 313), and second, to seize the new opportunities for legal power in order to establish a particular Christian dominance over society and church life. The brief reign of Emperor Julian (361–363) had threatened a return to the suppression of Christian leadership in education and civic life; the Christianization efforts that escalated after his death were at least a partial reaction to this threat. Early Christians (like their Jewish contemporaries and predecessors) had always been very active in bringing to both their own communities and their neighbors a strong social emphasis on caring for the needy poor simply because they were poor, as a moral mandate that both groups based substantially in Old Testament texts. As Christianity became a dominantly "gentile" religion, non-Jewish converts to Christianity were likewise shaped by these texts from the Judaic tradition in addition to existing ethical ideals from their own traditions. Greco-Roman philanthropy, for example, might include individual ideals of merciful giving, but its community and literary expression focused on public civic honors rather than on human need as the laudable motive for beneficence. Nonetheless, classical Greek texts on feasts and on healing frequently mention that beggars and the sick were camping out in or around religious shrines and temples, expecting miracles—and alms. The Cappadocian poverty sermons reflect both the Greco-Roman ideal of civic honors and the adequate worth of need itself as a basis for giving, with frequent references to Biblical texts on justice from the Psalms, Proverbs, Isaiah, and the minor prophets. They also, increasingly, mention the poor and sick who position themselves near churches to beg or seek healing. In making responses to need and the poor a significant element in the deliberate political application of Christian rhetoric, such writers redesigned existing cultural philanthropic ideals in new ways.

With the rise of Christian social action as a part of public politics, dilemmas common in private giving now took on more public discussion. One such dilemma was how to choose who among the poor was worthy of receiving alms. Early Christian authors addressed this issue in several different ways, and did not always agree. The Cappadocian responses continue debates that began much earlier, in Christian writings on wealth and divestment from the second and third centuries as they in turn interpreted Gospel teachings. At the turn of the third century Clement of Alexandria, for example, had minimized the "fleshly poor," those whose needs are merely material, but he admitted that the rich ought to transfer their goods to this group if they have any hope of gaining true spiritual wealth.[14] He pointed to the parable of the Good Samaritan to emphasize that one's "neighbor" should not be limited to a coreligionist, blood relative, or fellow citizen,[15] yet at the same time he also interpreted Matthew 25:31–46 as meaning that one should understand the Christ-embodied poor to mean "those who believe on Christ."[16] He added, "not that you should yield to a request or wait to be pestered, but that you should personally seek out people whom you may benefit, who are worthy disciples of the Savior."[17]

Clement wrote at a time when periodic persecution was still a risk. His focus on the value of keeping one's wealth whenever possible is especially poignant since his immediate audience might have faced state seizure of their property at any time. Yet his focus on supporting needy Christians does not necessarily exclude material generosity to others.

In North Africa just fifty years later, during an equally sporadic but more deadly persecution, Cyprian, the Bishop of Carthage—like Clement a member of the elite—is famously indiscriminate in his view on helping those in need. In the context of praising Cyprian his deacon, Pontius, writing after Cyprian's martyrdom, says that

> Many who, by the straitness of poverty, were unable to manifest the
> kindness of wealth, manifested more than wealth, making up by their

own labour a service dearer than riches, that by both rich and poor in
the church, "what is good was done in the liberality of overflowing
works to all, not to those only who are of the household of faith."

Pontius adds that Cyprian was known for "practicing a clemency which
was like the divine clemency [and he] loved even his enemies."[18] Still
another fifty years later, in Egypt, during the final Roman persecution
of Christians (as Basil's grandparents were hiding in the mountains)
Pachomius, a pagan teenager whom the Roman Army had conscripted
and locked in prison with other press-ganged teens so they would not
run away, encountered the same generosity from some people who
visit his prison to provide essential food and drink. Asking about them,
Pachomius was told that Christians are "merciful to everyone, including
strangers."[19]

The topic of distributions to those in need in a world of limited
resources always evokes the difficult questions of who decides eligibility
and who does the actual giving. Programs rarely have enough resources
available for everyone's immediate needs. In addressing such challenges,
early Christian texts on welfare and poverty relief also contain admonitions to prudent giving even simultaneous with acts of broad generosity,
generally advising people to do as much as they can to the best of their
ability and resources.[20] Basil himself demonstrates how vocation might
influence one's practical approach to these issues. As a young man testing
monasticism in Egypt, for example, he wrote to a correspondent saying
that he believed donors ought to practice charity in person and not dis-
turb monks, who have turned away from fiscal cares to focus on a life of
prayer and contemplation.[21] But as a bishop later running an institution,
he recommended that people channel their donations through discerning
leaders such as the bishops (who were often also monks, now burdened
with public duties) since such authoritative administrators can best assess
legitimate need. Writing to his friend Amphilochius, Basil advised that
"each should limit his possession to the last tunic" but that it was "not
necessary for anyone to take upon himself the distribution of his goods,
but only to commit this task to him to whom the management of the alms
of the poor had been entrusted." Experience, he argued, is "necessary for
distinguishing between the person who is truly in need and the person
who begs through avarice."[22]

Throughout early Christian texts, there is almost universal agreement
that all who are in genuine need merit generous assistance even as there is

almost as much skepticism about those who claimed they deserved such aid. As Christian ideals became increasingly codified into Roman law, "genuine need" had to be tested and proved, for example, by a beggar's willingness to work if he were offered a job.[23] A few bishops, like Leo of Rome in the fifth century, did consistently and adamantly limit church-supported assistance to members of the Christian community. Yet John Chrysostom, writing around 400, expresses the broadly inclusive view that dominates most such texts:

> If you see any one in affliction, do not be curious to enquire further. His being in affliction gives him a just claim to your help. For if when you see a donkey choking you lift him up without inquiring whose he is, you certainly ought not to be over-curious about a person. He is God's, whether he is a heathen or a Jew; since even if he is an unbeliever, still he needs help.[24]

Some early Christian writers were all for unmeasured generosity, even to the point of including swindlers, since God may be using their behavior to test the donor; writers warn that however much one might lose materially in such situations, it is the assured heavenly reward that matters most. And in a number of stories it is the rich who are blessed by choosing (or being forced or tricked into choosing) to *accept* alms from destitute Christians whose lives model a generosity that the rich ought to emulate.[25] Early Christian narratives of medical healing also often contain stories in which the wealthy, suffering incurable ailments, must learn humility from their close contact with the poor before they can be healed.[26]

Once Christianity was legal, Christians could engage more openly with their neighbors, and establish charitable institutions without fear of losing their property or their life by admitting that they were Christians. The fourth century was thus an age in which church leaders and wealthy believers began to establish variants of the traditional Greek *xenodocheion*, "guesthouses" that are already called "poorhouses" (*ptochotropheion*) in the 350s, some years before Basil would choose to build one. Social justice and relief activities were soon operating on a large scale. By the early fifth century, in a claim famous for its fantastic statistics, John Chrysostom boasted that his church in Constantinople was—*daily*—supporting at least 3000 widows and virgins, not to mention prisoners, those in the guesthouses, healthy travelers, the crippled, and people serving in the church in return for food and clothing.[27]

SENSING NEED IN CAPPADOCIA

This background may help us to better understand the context in which philanthropic rhetoric was one response to a famine that struck Cappadocia in 368–369. This particular crisis occurred just as Basil was attaining prominence as a preacher and his response may have played some role in his appointment to bishop in 370. The three bishops' writings on the crisis illustrate how they expressed the concepts of sensing need, sharing goods, and imaging sacred kingdom.

In his sermon containing the most explicit details on the famine itself (*homily* 8), Basil describes poverty and injustice in terms that evoke a direct experience of "sensing" the poor. He speaks of those who were already poor before the harvests failed, and who are now beginning to starve. In this sermon as well as *homily* 6, from the same period, he tells of the rich landowners who are stockpiling their grain and selling it at inflated prices while also reducing personal consumption, tightening their own belts to make it through the shortage with their wealth intact. Vividly Basil's sermons paint word pictures of the poor, as they wander the roads, waste away, sell children into slavery, and weep.

Basil sought to persuade the rich to release stockpiled grain that he would then use to feed the starving. In *homily* 6, he appeals to such land-owners with the challenge,

> Think, you who call yourselves "Benefactor"!... You have been made a servant of the good God; an administrator for your fellow servant.... But you try to lock up [your riches] and keep them hidden using bolts and bars and under seals. You watch them anxiously and think, "What will I do?"
>
> "What will I do?" Offhand, I would say, "I shall fill the souls of the hungry. I shall open my barns and I shall send for all who are in want."[28]

He describes the starving victims in terms that force his audience to "sense need," writing, "Their voice is powerless, their eyes sunken...the empty belly collapsed....Whoever has the power to alleviate this evil but instead deliberately opts for profit by it, should be condemned as a murderer."[29] But starvation resulting from famine is not always so dramatic. Studies of hunger throughout history emphasize that those starving are often characterized by expressions of hopelessness, listlessness, or frantic and secretive food rituals. They may be children with distended bellies, or with skin, bone, or eye ailments due not to starvation itself but to its associated malnutrition, with inadequate protein, vitamins, and/or minerals over a long enough period to induce biological deficiencies and their physiological consequences.

Desperate need in antiquity (as today) was a chronic condition, and living in this way, with one's health perpetually on edge, could spiral quickly into personal disaster. In the ancient world there was, after all, no electricity, high-speed highways, refrigeration, pesticides, preservatives, or antibiotics. Food shortage was a constant fear. Even the stockpiling rich had good reason to worry about famine. People survived through their social connections: to family, community, and rich patrons who held political and economic power. And such power was not always exercised with justice. The Cappadocian texts describe a familiar range of economic fraud and corruption. Even without debt a poor family might need to sell children or essential goods to survive. A small farmer could lose his land if a greedy neighbor took him to court on false charges and bribed the judge.

Criminally high interest rates on loans often threatened to destroy those who dared to live beyond their means. The famine offered greedy landowners an opportunistic chance to profit from such loans. Basil's sermons against stockpiling (*hom.* 6) and on Psalm 14 (Psalm 15 in modern Bibles) contain uncompromising denunciations of such usury. Interest rates in this culture might range from twelve to fifty percent per year, and Basil describes excessive interest as an aberrant or metastatic growth, a natural horror that destroys its victim. In condemning usury, Basil writes that it "involves the greatest inhumanity, that the one in need…seeks a loan for the relief of his life…. While searching around for antidotes, he came upon poisons. It was your duty to relieve the destitution of the man, but you increased his need."[30]

To those who think they need to borrow, Basil offers alternative ways to imagine their difficulties: "Examine your own resources…Sell them; permit all things to go except your liberty…Are you rich? Do not borrow. Are you poor? Do not borrow…Why…yoke yourself with a prolific wild beast?"[31] And he instructs the rich to make loans interest free, not even expecting repayment. Here he defends this practice on the basis of Proverbs 19:17: "He who has mercy on the poor lends to God," and appeals again to the divine nature: "Do you not wish to have the Lord of the universe answerable to you for payment?"[32]

Thus rather than hoarding grain, lending it at usurious interest, or going into debt during the famine, Basil urges his congregation to live simply and imitate God's generosity, since God without distinction gives rain and food to all on the earth, just and unjust. By this divine imitation, Basil suggests, differences between rich and poor could be leveled. Such economic leveling was one of Basil's social ideals. By sharing equally, he taught, the hungry will have what they need, the rich will deflate into healthy and spiritual sanity, and the city will enjoy peace and good political order.

While most of these images and ideas come from Basil's sermons, it was apparently Basil's actions that provide one of the best-known early Christian examples of hands-on aid to relieve the poor in the fourth century. According to his brother, Gregory of Nyssa, Basil sold "his possessions and having changed the money into food, when it was rare even for those who were very well supplied to prepare a meal for themselves, he continued during the whole period of the famine to support both those who came together from all sides and the youths of every [part] of the city…[even] the children of the Jews.…He transferred his entire citizenship from earth to heaven."[33] We are not sure who these "Jewish youth" were, since apparently there were few Jews in Cappadocian Caesarea. In John Chrysostom's sermons the term "Jewish" was sometimes used as a derogatory term for other Christians who sometimes attended Jewish synagogues and festivals.[34] Yet whoever Basil's "Jewish youths" were (and Basil himself never mentions them), Gregory's point is that Basil's exemplary aid to the needy was not restricted to a limited religious group but was extended broadly to include any needy person.

Basil also took the lead in directing the distribution of grain relief, which he mentions in one of his letters (*ep.* 31). Describing this aspect of Basil's hands-on approach, Gregory of Nazianzus writes,

> He gathered together the victims of the famine…men and women, infants, old men, every age which was in distress, and obtaining contributions of all sorts of food…set before them basins of soup and such meat…on which the poor live…he attended to the bodies and souls…combining personal respect with the supply of their necessity…[35]

After the famine, Basil built a poorhouse, in Greek a *ptōchotropheion* (from the Greek *ptōchos*, the very poor, and *tropheus*, meaning to feed or

Basil of Caesarea and Gregory of Nazianzus caring for the poor and sick. *Paris gr. 510, f. 149r.* Paris, Bibliothèque Nationale de France. Used with permission.

nurture). Basil's poorhouse is sometimes called "the first Christian hospital" and was best known to many contemporaries as the "Basileias," or "Basil's Place." It became a popular symbol for the model Christian relief organization. The figure below illustrates how one imperial artist in the ninth century imagined Basil and Gregory together in the Basileias, feeding and washing beggars.

This image, which the artist has titled in Greek letters within the picture itself, "St. Gregory and St. Basil heal the sick," is as far as I know the oldest surviving illustration of the story of Basil's philanthropy. It is from a manuscript of the sermons of Gregory of Nazianzus, where it introduces Gregory's sermon "On the love of the poor."[36] The figure shows only the top frame of the full-page illumination. Under each of the four arches, we see (from left to right): Basil washing a man's feet, giving another soup, serving meat to two at a table, and offering a bowl (which may contain either food or medicine) to a man dressed only in a loincloth who is covered with sores. Where the paint has not flaked away with age, it is possible to see that there is direct eye contact between the two saints (who have gold halos) and the poor (who do not). The ninth-century painter explicitly paired this image of social service inside the Basileias with another painting that fills the bottom half of the page (not shown here and in very poor condition) illustrating the biblical story of Lazarus and the rich man as each faces his respective fate in heaven and hell. This pairing of patristic and biblical stories would remind the reader in no uncertain terms of the costs and benefits of imitating Basil's philanthropic model.

The Basileias was completed around 372 and was part of a complex of episcopal dwellings that also included a church; some of Basil's letters mention other church-run poorhouses in the region as Basil lobbies for their tax exemption.[37] He defends his institution using the ancient Greek image of the *xenodocheion*, or guest-house for strangers, as well as traditional Roman terms of good social order, writing to the local governor that he is providing "hospices for strangers, for those who visit us...for those who require some care because of sickness, and extend[s] necessary comforts, such as nurses, physicians, beasts for traveling, and attendants...[and] occupations to go with these people."[38]

Despite all of this detail from both the original narrative and later hagiographical depictions, there is a great deal we do *not* know about the Basileias. The sources lack specifics, for example, on how various administrative or distributive activities actually took place. Basil never describes the "job training" or "occupations" he mentions in his letter to the governor. The site itself is long lost, its ruins probably rebuilt into the cellars, walls, and homes of modern urban Kayseri. Nor do we know where Basil got his nurses or physicians. It is often believed that they included members of his monastic community, but there is no proof of this for Basil's particular endeavor. Gregory of Nyssa mentions people who "devoted their lives to the sick from their youth to their old age, while remaining entirely healthy themselves."[39] But he does not identify them with any formal church or monastic roles. Basil had studied medicine as a young man in Egypt during his visit to monastic communities, but most of his letters speak of his own ailments rather than those of others. Gregory of Nazianzus's brother, Caesarius, was a court physician whose belongings (and books) Gregory inherited when Caesarius died in 368. In the will he wrote in 380, Gregory of Nazianzus appointed two deacons and a monk (two of the three had been born as slaves and were now freedmen) as "agents to care for the poor," but this reference is not linked to any specific hospital or poorhouse so one can only guess where and how such agents worked. Given this lack of specifics, Basil's poorhouse remains an enticing model but cannot be used to argue for any explicit administrative practice of healthcare since we simply do not know precisely how it operated from one day to the next. Nor do we know how it managed to serve the needs of both the hungry poor who worked and traveled and also—as both Gregories attest—the afflicted who suffered from that terrifying category of illness known as "leprosy." Whatever these "lepers" actually suffered in medical terms, the Cappadocian sermons illustrate that people preferred to avoid them and ostracize them from normal society. Yet Gregory of Nazianzus called the poorhouse "the new city, the storehouse of piety...where disease is regarded in a religious light, and disaster is thought a blessing, and sympathy is put to the test.... Basil's care was for the sick, and the relief of their wounds, and the imitation of Christ, by cleansing leprosy, not by a word, but in deed."[40]

Nor do the Cappadocian texts provide us with any evidence that Gregory of Nazianzus helped to serve at or raise funds for Basil's hospice, although this has long been a popular belief, as the presence of both Gregory and Basil in the figure attests. Gregory's own sermon "On the love of the poor" says nothing about Basil's project and dates some years after its foundation, when he and Basil had fallen out and Gregory was having problems of his own. Gregory's famous description of the project was written as part of a memorial sermon after Basil's death and again does not mention that Gregory had any role in the project. The three men clearly shared a concern for the issue of poverty and social welfare and an acute awareness of community beggars, but it is likely that their individual sermons on these topics were (at least during their lifetimes) first targeted exclusively to the problems in their own locale, some miles apart from one another, and then shared, as written texts, with other learned Christian bishops and colleagues.

Although details about nursing and medical care in the early years of Basil's hospital are lacking, there is better evidence for how things worked fifty years later in the hospitals for the poor that bishop Rabbula founded in Syriac-speaking Edessa. Rabbula is famous for his commitment to poverty relief at the expense of church finery. He established several hospitals, and the administration of Rabbula's hospitals was entrusted to church deacons, deaconesses, dedicated church virgins, and "trustworthy brethren appointed to minister."[41] In at least one case, he appointed a deaconess as head of a women's hospital. Rabbula also had at his service another group of lay ascetics distinct to Syriac communities, dedicated celibate men and women called "sons" (*bnay*) and "daughters" (*bnat*) "of the covenant" (*qyāmā*). These individuals were not monks or nuns, nor were they members of the diaconate. The women of this group might be very broadly compared today to dedicated lay women such as the medieval *beguines*, who lived disciplined lives of religious celibacy but retained their own property and personal autonomy. "Sons of the covenant" might serve the bishop in roles similar to that of deacons, and "daughters of the covenant," also closely identified with parish administration, routinely served the poor and sick. Rabbula's "Rules" or "Canons" contain several hints about how they lived. "Daughters of the covenant," for example, sometimes wove garments for both priests and deacons (Canon 3), lived with others like them of the same gender or else in their family homes (Canon 10), had power over their own income, which Rabbula forbids them to lend out at interest (Canon 9), learned psalms and metrical hymns that they performed in church choirs, and were forced to join monastic communities only if they "fall from their rank" (Canon 29). Everyone who was bound to obey Rabbula's canons (that is, priests, deacons, deaconesses, and sons and daughters of the covenant) "shall persevere in fasting and be diligent in prayer; they shall take care of the poor and demand justice for the oppressed so that they do not show favor" (Canon 11).[42] Thus "daughters of the covenant" were among those who did actual hospital labor, nursing, medicating, washing the sick, and changing their sheets.[43] Rabbula was not the only early Christian leader to write a job description for such women; another Syriac text from the same period tells us that the occupation of the daughters of the covenant was to care for the poor.[44] We know that sons and daughters of the covenant were among the church orders with administrative responsibilities, because Rabbula allows secular laypersons to assume administrative roles only when a community has no members of the *bnay qyāmā*.[45]

John Chrysostom, growing up in Antioch and serving its church for years as its bishop, also knew of young girls who provided nursing care and whose roles are described in very similar terms as those of the "daughters of the covenant," although Chrysostom, writing and speaking in Greek, does not call them this. His thirteenth sermon on Ephesians describes teenage girls who, raised in wealth and comfort, with slaves to meet their every need and desire, now chose to dress in coarsely woven garments, go barefoot, sleep on leaves, spin, eat one meal a day (flour, legumes, olives, and figs), and "work harder than their servants at home." Their work, according to Chrysostom, was to "wait upon women who are sick, carrying their beds and washing their feet. Many of them even cook. So great is the power of the flame of Christ. So far does their zeal surpass their very nature."[46]

Most of the poor whom Basil evokes in his call to "sense" their need are those whom we would identify as "the working poor." In contrast, the three sermons "On the love of the poor" by the two Gregories describe the homeless and sick beggars at the edge of society. The Gregories' sermons are at least as powerful as Basil's for their metaphorical imagery and evocative appeal to the senses. Like Basil, Gregory of Nyssa describes situations that he expects the audience to recognize. Preaching some years after the famine, Gregory can still write that "We have seen in these days a great number of the naked and homeless." He describes them as victims of war, political unrest, and economic crisis. They are lying in the alleys, hands stretched out, or hiding in the cracks of walls like owls. They drink from cupped hands and use their knees for a table. They include the sick who may be hidden in tiny rooms or else out wandering the streets in all weather. Some of the sick, missing limbs, parade their deformities in order to get attention and alms, surviving on scraps. Many of these beggars are treated worse than animals, Gregory says. The deeds done to them cry out to heaven, for they are the beloved of Christ. Preaching from Isaiah 58, a text on God's "true fast," Gregory exhorts his audience to "starve to death your greed for Mammon. Let there be nothing at your house that has been acquired by violence or theft. What good is it to drink water while plotting to drink the blood of your neighbor through dishonesty?" After all, Judas fasted, Gregory adds, and even Satan and his demons don't need food; yet they are constantly oozing bitterness and jealousy. Rather, Gregory continues, quoting Isaiah, we must loose injustice, free the oppressed, untie bonds, share our bread with the hungry, and house the homeless poor. Recommending that people get directly and physically involved, he writes,

> Let no one say...[to] send them off to some frontier...[Instead] become Christ's beast of burden; strap on love (*agape*) for those who are in need...Do not despise those who are stretched out on the ground as if they merit no respect...They bear the countenance of our Saviour...If we wish to heal the wounds by which our sins have afflicted us, heal today the ulcers that break down their flesh....[Truly] it is hard to master the loathing that most people naturally feel in the face of the sick....Will we give up hope of blessing because it is incompatible with comfort?...Sympathy toward the unfortunate is, in this life, profitable for the healthy.[47]

And Gregory of Nazianzus describes the poor in similar terms, writing that "There lies before our eyes a dreadful and pathetic sight: persons alive yet dead, disfigured, a wreckage of what had once been human beings.... and we are so derelict in our obligation to look after our fellow man that we actually believe that avoiding these people assures the well-being of our own persons... He is part of you, even if he is bent down with misfortune."[48]

Basil and Gregory's sister, Macrina, shared this vision for empathic relief. She and their youngest brother, Peter, had a monastic community separate from Basil's and during the famine Macrina and Peter distributed grain at their own initiative and from their own storehouse. Influenced by egalitarian monastic ideals that some contemporaries viewed as extreme, Macrina's home-based monastic community shocked even her own mother, who was forced to eat at the same table with their household slaves.[49] According to Gregory of Nyssa's treatise describing his sister's teachings and death, some of the nuns in Macrina's house were women she had found starving by the roadsides and carried home. While Gregory does not mention the children of such women, it was not unusual as early as the third century to place young orphaned children into the care of monastic women. Indeed, as the oldest in the family, Macrina had helped to raise her own siblings after their father's death. Nor were Macrina, Peter, and Basil the only family members caring for those in need. Another brother, Naucratius, had lived as a Christian hermit in the woods for five years, where he and a servant, Gregory says, "cared for a group of old people living together in poverty and infirmity"[50] and would "go hunting to procure food for them."[51] Maybe these old people were some of the social outcasts described in the various poverty sermons. Naucratius died in a fishing accident, literally giving his life for those he served. Scholar Anna Silvas suggests that this very retreat site was, a few years later, the hillside where Basil launched his earliest monastic experiment.[52]

APPLYING THE PARADIGMS

How then did the Cappadocian poverty sermons express the three cross-cultural paradigms of sensing need, sharing the world, and embodying sacred kingdom? Some of the imagery is obvious from the passages that have been quoted. These and certain other elements of the texts are explored in the following sections as they may be read constructively in light of each of these three conceptual relationships to the poor and their need.

Sensing the Poor

The Cappadocian sermons on the poor are rich in appeals to the senses. The authors repeatedly demand, for example, that the audience (or readers) "see" what the preacher is describing, if not in everyday life then at least imaginatively, through hearing the sermon while in church. In addition to Basil's physical description of the starving body, we also find Gregory of Nazianzus introducing the mutilated leper with the phrase, "There lies before our eyes." The texts are often intentionally emotive with skin-crawling detail. In both sermons, Gregory of Nyssa alludes to the Matthew 25 image with first-personal visual language. In his first sermon he says, "I have seen the Son of Man descend from the sky." That which he "sees" is "a court of justice painted so precisely" that it might teach beneficence. He contrasts this with that in the immediate neighborhood of the church, where (he describes) gourmands and drunken feasts proceed while "a myriad of Lazaruses sit at the gate." These are also, he adds, scenes that "God sees." In his second sermon, he appeals even more explicitly to sensory reactions. He begins, "Again I hold before my eyes the dreadful vision of the return of the kingdom," an image that he says makes him quake in terror. To avoid judgment, he points to the lepers. "You see these people" who have wood instead of fingernails; "listen to the rasping wheeze that comes from their chest." Their feet are eaten away and "their begging repels you." He calls for a deliberate appropriation of new sensations: "Why aren't you moved by the diseases you perceive happening to other people?" "Do you listen to their plaintive songs?" The preacher confesses that they alarm, overwhelm, confound, and upset him, "these scenes that force one to tears." But which is worse, Gregory asks: to have a body that is rotting like carrion or to have one that has lost all neural sensations? "Where is their sight? Their smell? Their touch?" They display their bloated abdomens, their useless faces, their gangrenous remains. Are you repelled, he asks his audience, by the "oozing of the rotten humors and blood infected by pus and flow of bile?" Did his listeners fear contagion from touching them? There is no reason for concern, he insists, arguing that in such cases only health is contagious. It is difficult, he agrees, to overcome physical repulsion to such bodies, but God teaches that "the way to life is difficult." What is a little hard exercise compared with eternal glory?

Gregory of Nyssa is quoted and paraphrased here at length because his sermons contain the most extensive sensory language of the three bishops.

But other texts contain similar images. In his sermon against stockpiling, Basil argues for merciful divestment by describing the mental agony of a poor workman who must decide which of his sons to sell into slavery so the rest of the family might survive. In another passage, he paints the tragi-comic image of a debtor who panics and hides under the bed as the credi-tor approaches. John Chrysostom similarly appealed to visual and visceral language in his series of sermons on Lazarus and the rich man, writing, "Paint this parable, you rich and you poor: the rich, on the walls of your houses; the poor, on the walls of your hearts. If it is ever obliterated by for-getfulness, paint it again with your memory."[53] The parable is a lesson for the ears: "Let the poor man hear and not be suffocated by discouragement. Let the rich hear and change from their wickedness."[54] Chrysostom often depicted life as a theater, with "players" judged according to their works once the play comes to its end and the masks are removed.[55]

These preachers also appeal to internal intellectual responses. "Are you poor?" Basil asks, chiding those who readily agree with the reminder that "There is one poorer." "Do not say to me, 'My mother is an almsgiver,'" John Chrysostom scolds those who wish to evade philanthropic respon-sibilities, adding, "What does that have to do with your own inhuman-ity?"[56] Chrysostom ends his final sermon on Lazarus using sensory images that turn to heavenly irony, as he writes, "Flee the spectacles of Satan and the harmful sights of the racecourse." Rather, find virtue and by it enjoy "those ineffable good things which eye has not seen nor ear heard."[57]

Sharing the World

Such texts also have much to say to potential donors about what to do: how to handle and release their material goods. Advice includes actions such as giving food to those who come to the door; giving away that second or "spare set" of clothing in the closet; forgiving the interest on debts (and if possible even treating the principal as a free gift); using funds that belong to and are returned to God; and assisting in direct bodily care of those who are sick, homeless, wanderers, or afflicted with repulsive deformities. The texts also give examples of "sharing the world" through their references to charitable institutions and their call for welcoming the needy into one's home (as Macrina does, long term, or as Chrysostom urges, at least for a meal or two). They offer examples of meeting needs "where they live," as Naucratius did in serving his elderly and destitute neighbors in the woods. Such texts also allude to sharing through the way they use language of goods as gift, goods as neutral but heavy dross, and goods as temptation to grieve and to sin through avarice.

The material dynamics that these authors outline are merely part of a larger vision about sharing the world. The needy are understood, first and above all, as "human beings like ourselves" who share God's image, God's natural goodness, and all the same "rights" as everyone else to earth and heaven, including the right to justice in protecting what few earthly possessions they might own. Not all of the poor are obviously "other," that is, people outside of the social group or immediate audience. We find frequent allusions here to those in the congregation itself who willingly view or class themselves as among the "poor" and some "lepers" are identified as former community members whose close relatives now reject them. Thus the "poor" share both church and marketplace with the rich and are part of the homiletic appeal to think about ways to live and do justice.

Embodying Sacred Kingdom

Finally, both poor and rich in these texts embody the image of a God-given cosmos. The imagery that constructs them in this model consists of frequent and deliberate paradoxes. Both Gregories argue that lepers who have physical deficiencies are uniquely able to effect spiritual healing for those who minister to them in the present. Those who ought dare touch the sick are bodily well, but spiritually diseased. The earth itself may mirror the miserly and stingy with famine, drought, or flood, yet the earth is capable of responding to spiritual liberality with a change of weather.

Both rich and poor also take on the face of the divine. The rich do this by imitating God's mercy and justice, God's model of patronage. The poor do this by their basic needs for food and water, thereby imaging Christ. Service to the poor is treated as a liturgy; in other words, it is just as important for true worship as is going to church. Even inert goods take on sacred value, and the human body is a holy thing indeed. Beneficence is not ultimately about meeting the basic needs of the body, since those can never be fully and eternally satisfied in this life. Beneficence is rather an act of obedience between fellow travelers on a journey that functions to lighten the load so that each party can attain a safe and manageable homecoming at their final destination. Beneficence "embodies" sacred kingdom when it treats the human body in this way, when it asserts social justice in the face of economic corruption, and when it focuses on healing, liturgy, and global restoration.

CONCLUSIONS

The Cappadocian responses to need in the fourth century, explored in detail in this chapter, demonstrate a particularly well-documented relationship between religious text and action. These texts—like Jacob of Sarug's later poetic homily on the same subject—are rich in sensory images intent on evoking an inner awareness of the ethical mandate to do something about poverty and injustice. These texts attest to a specific "sensing need" even as they describe ways that the audience might then "share the world" in concrete action and relief. Each of these texts envisions such ethical responses in terms that "embody sacred kingdom" as they identify the destitute with the body of Christ and as they construct meaning for philanthropic responses using the language of the cosmos, the heavenly kingdom, and engagement in and with the sacred.

And yet these stories remain worlds apart from our own contemporary culture, systems, and many modern images for relief and social justice. How do we handle stories and texts such as these when we come to discuss the place of religion in modern social welfare issues? How might we sort out what of the ancient world is unhelpful or hopelessly different from the present and what might be usefully similar or applicable? What might we learn from others in history, closer to our own time, who were obviously helped or inspired by texts such as these? These are the questions explored in the next chapter.

FROM TEXT TO LIFE

Crossing the Gap

"Stories alter our lives as we return from text to
action."

—Richard Kearney, *On Stories*[1]

In his essays *On Stories,* Richard Kearney reflects at length on the relationship between living and telling. As he considers the bias that we as readers
inevitably bring to a text in our own assumptions, as well as the bias that we
inevitably encounter through the author's (often unstated and sometimes
unrecognized) agenda, Kearney reminds us that "narrative memory cannot afford to be naïve, for stories are never innocent."[2] Indeed, he adds,

> Life can be properly understood only by being retold mimetically
> through stories. But the act of *mimesis,* which enables us to pass from life
> to life-story introduces a "gap" (however minimal) between living and
> recounting. Life is lived, as Ricoeur reminds us, while stories are told.[3]

In our own journey of reading Christian texts on poverty, as we seek to
read the past in the context of present social action, we too are constantly
challenged to make a critical attempt to negotiate this bias and the "gap" it
creates between text and life or, in this case, between text and action. Such
an attempt requires more than simply understanding the ancient sources
in their original context, the focus of Chapter 3. If we believe that stories
from the past can have positive effects on present action—or, as Edith
Wyschogrod and Carl Raschke put it, "When the past speaks, it speaks
as an oracle to the future"[4]—we may need to live with a creative risk, not
only the risk of narrative bias but also the prismatic teasing of multiple
meanings that come with texts such as oracles, prophecies, and sometimes
strange snippets of the past.

One path by which we might negotiate such a journey between past and present meaning is that of identifying interim "stepping stones," reference stories along the way that invite us to measure our response against the voices of other writers who have read these texts before us with similar concerns, and who tried to apply them to their own age. This chapter offers three such encounters: one from the sixteenth-century Protestant Reformation, one from mid-nineteenth-century Catholic France, and the third from late nineteenth-century England. These three stories offer examples of patristic application to later social issues that may provoke us toward an informed, creative philanthropic *mimesis* in our own religious responses to human need today.

Reading how others tried to cross the "gap" between text and action through using these several pasts can lead us to a particular appreciation of four interpretive issues that are discussed following the three stories, at the end of the chapter. These four interpretive issues—language, exegesis, social power relationships, and an understanding of human rights—are directly relevant to the challenges of bias and action, particularly in reference to social welfare. Biases may be more visible when we are on unfamiliar ground, or considering different worlds from our own. Thus weighing the present in light of the multiple "pasts" of these accounts challenges us to think through and from these unfamiliar relationships in order to build a constructive response to poverty and need for the present.

GREGORY OF NAZIANZUS AND THE PROTESTANT REFORMATION

One of the earliest examples of how patristic social texts influenced the Protestant reformers begins with a man named Johannes Oecolampadius (1482–1531). Oecolampadius (who, incidentally, helped Erasmus with Hebrew for his New Testament[5]) was a Swiss Catholic scholar whose bishop appointed him to the German-speaking city of Basel to preach against the Protestant reformers. To the bishop's dismay, Oecolampadius joined their cause and by 1529 was the city's leading reformer.[6] As a new "Protestant," he brought to the movement his fascination with patristic social texts on poverty and their relevance for the destitution of his own time. In 1519, Oecolampadius translated Gregory of Nazianzus's *Oration* 14, "On the Love of the Poor," from Greek into Latin. A subsequent German translation of Gregory's sermon was circulating in Basel by

1521. Deeply influenced by this particular patristic text, Oecolampadius then published his own treatise on poor relief, *De non habendo pauperum delectu*, in 1523; by 1524 this, too, was available in German.[7] We know that these works influenced his friend and fellow reformer Ulrich Zwingli. Zwingli also wrote treatises on the poor and used patristic texts in shaping his social reforms at Zurich.

It is likely (but not certain) that any or all of these texts and translations may have reached Martin Luther. Despite being a Greek scholar, Luther does not seem to draw on any of the Greek patristic texts on poverty and social relief—either the Cappadocians', John Chrysostom's, or any other examples in various Greek church histories from the fourth and fifth centuries. Luther used patristic sources chiefly to support his argument against papal primacy;[8] he regarded patristic examples as "useful historical witnesses"[9] to practices that (in his view) had authority only if they were also clear from his reading of scripture. Whether or not he knew the patristic texts on poverty issues, there is no evidence that Luther would have disagreed with their views of the poor. He certainly drew on Latin patristic writers, such as Ambrose of Milan, in writing about social issues of poverty and hunger.[10] In 1522, Luther called the poor "living images of God,"[11] expressing a view identical with Zwingli, who wrote that "The poor are true images of God."[12] Zwingli used this argument to support his case against church art, arguing that God "turned all visible cults from himself to the poor."[13] Oecolampadius and Zwingli were among those who opposed Luther's view on the eucharist in the 1520s, and the three were physically in the same space at the same time, together, to sign the Fifteen Articles on Evangelical doctrine at the Colloquy of Marburg in early October 1529; there they were part of a group of reformers that agreed on fourteen of the articles and left unresolved their differences on the eucharist.[14] Luther's sermons were printed in Basel, and it is no stretch of the imagination to guess that Oecolampadius's translation and treatises on the poor may have reached Luther (who held more moderate views than Zwingli on church art) despite their sharp disagreements about the eucharist.

It is also possible that Oecolampadius's patristic translations and writings on the contemporary poor, together with other influences from John Calvin (1509–1564), may have reached the Anglican divine, Thomas Cranmer, who wrote the *Book of Common Prayer* and steered England through its early Reformation. J. Todd Billings has noted recently that "Calvin was self-taught as regards most of his knowledge of patristic theology."[15] Although Calvin warned that it was "necessary to decide prudently which among the fathers to imitate,"[16] he deliberately used patristic texts to reform and redesign sixteenth-century social welfare issues in Geneva. In discussing care for the poor and controversies over property and divestment, Calvin appealed to Jerome along with "Chrysostom, Ambrose, Augustine, and other bishops like them" (*Institutes* 4.4.6), popes Gelasius and Gregory the Great (*Institutes* 4.4.7), and stories about Cyril of Jerusalem and Acacius of Amida taken from Sozomen's and Socrates' fifth-century church histories (*Institutes* 4.4.8). Calvin based his teachings about the diaconate on his reading of John Chrysostom.[17] In his commentary on 2 Corinthians, Calvin prescribed moderation and cheerful giving in terms similar to Jacob of Sarug's and the Cappadocians' emphasis on alms as justice: "Indeed when we heap up riches for the future [Calvin says], 'We *defraud* our poor brethren of the beneficence that we *owe* them.'"[18] Billings notes Calvin's affirmation that anyone in need should be helped, with a focus on enacting this justice among coreligionists:

> While there is a special obligation to those in need generally, this obligation has particular application to members of the church.... Participating in the body of Christ means cheerfully giving of heart, mind, and finances. In Calvin, this process of "participation" is profoundly congruent with notions of duty, justice, and equity—giving a person their due, even when their circumstance of need increases the obligation that is "due" to them.[19]

Calvin's respect for the patristic writers may have helped strengthen their influence on those for whom Calvinism influenced early Anglican reforms. Thomas Cranmer, influenced by both Calvin and Luther, also claimed that "I have seen almost everything that has been written and published either by Oecolampadius or Zwingli."[20] It would be Anglican churchmen who would establish the Elizabethan Poor Laws, legislation that was to replace the historically Catholic charity systems with a state structure based on geographic parish membership in England, as Zwingli also did in Zurich.[21] Another example of Calvin's influence on Anglican reforms is that of Isaac Casaubon, originally a Calvinist and professor of Greek in Geneva. Casaubon held a high view of patristic authority that conflicted with the way the Reformation at Geneva appeared to be developing. Moving to England to join the new Anglicans, Casaubon became a close friend of Lancelot Andrewes. Andrewes was a leading member of the group that produced the King James Bible and a scholar eminent for his extreme devotional piety who shared Casaubon's respect for patristic authority.

Andrewes is an ironic example of how not every reformer steeped in patristic scholarship was willing to heed John Chrysostom, Basil, and the Gregories in their demand to help the sick poor through direct, sacrificial contact. When the Great Plague struck London in 1603, worst hit was the parish of St. Giles Cripplegate, a tenement neighborhood of poor people who died and were buried forty to fifty in a pit, week after week. By the end of that terrible year, three out of every four people in the parish were dead. But Andrewes, who was the parish vicar, left town as soon as the plague struck. He spent the following year in a country retreat along the Thames, not only surrounded by his students but also enjoying the services of a butler, a cook, a scull for pleasure rowing along the river, and a rower.[22] When the activist Henoch Clapham, engaged in ministry in London when the plague struck, published a tract condemning the "divine" Andrewes for abandoning his parish in its most heartrending time of need,[23] Andrewes had Clapham put in prison for libel. Clapham argued that Andrewes' flight was all the more inexcusable since Andrewes himself taught that the plague, while having some element of natural cause, was also a sign of God's wrath and thus nothing its chosen victims could do would save them. If he really believed this, said Clapham, why run? Alas for Clapham, it was Andrewes' political influence that prevailed. Clapham went to prison and Andrewes wrote the recantation that Clapham would need to sign for his release. Clapham signed it, then published an objection to the recantation. The hubbub eventually settled down and Clapham was released from prison around 1605.[24] It may be easy for a modern reader to condemn Andrewes as a coward and hypocrite, even if we admire the devotional anguish found in his little book of *Private Prayers*. The quarrel between Clapham and Andrewes reminds us that we are not alone in our reactions and our personal limitations. To meditate on the issue of need, poverty, and response is to open the self up to tensions that are not neatly resolved.

FROM PARIS TO PRINCETON: PATRISTIC PHILANTHROPY IN NINETEENTH-CENTURY FRANCE

The French Catholic Felix Martin-Doisy (1795–1878) belonged to a world very different from that of either Oecolampadius or the early English reformers. Nineteenth-century France was politically and socially tumultuous in its own way; the city of Paris was tense with extremes between rich and poor as social experiments and Republics rose and fell.

The fifty years that followed the French Revolution of 1791 were rife with conflicts between religious and secular forces. Another revolution gave birth to a short-lived "Second Republic" (1848–1852) characterized by a socialism that was dominated by Catholic writers.[25] This was the age of the abbé Jacques-Paul Migne, a pugnacious and shamelessly self-promoting priest-entrepreneur in Paris who single-handedly funded and engineered a new Catholic press to publish his 384-volume *Patrologia*, an edition of all known Greek and Latin patristic texts in their original languages. The 218-volume *Patrologia Latina* (PL) rolled off the presses between 1844 and 1855; the *Patrologia Graeca* (PG; 166 volumes) followed between 1857 and 1866, as did another 85 volumes of the Greek fathers in Latin.[26] In this monumental endeavor Migne "borrowed" every patristic edition that he could find and published them quickly, typographical errors and all, giving full credit to himself and short shrift to his sources. Disaster struck the project at a scale equal to that of its creator's zeal when in 1868 the press burned down, reducing 500,000 plates of typesetting to molten lumps. All that remained were the printed volumes. Migne's *Patrologia* became the standard patristic resource of research libraries and divinity schools throughout the nineteenth and twentieth centuries. Today available online by subscription, the series continues to serve as the only known edition of many obscure texts.

Several years before the abbé Migne's ascent to fame and infamy, the Catholic "Société d'Économie charitable" published an inaugural volume in its new series, Annales de la Charité, the series a brainchild of the Catholic nobleman and philanthropist Armand de Melun (1807–1877).[27] The book, titled (in French) "History of charity in the first four centuries of the Christian era," was written by an otherwise little-known layman named Felix Martin-Doisy.[28] Weighing in at over 600 pages, it was available in bookstores just days after the 1847 Revolution.

Martin-Doisy—who likely had access to the same sources as Migne, and certainly would have known of the patristic venture—had an explicit political agenda. He wrote within the immediate context of political crisis and he hoped that the new French government would use his work as a resource to reform social welfare practices. The introduction makes this quite clear. Here, the author provides a detailed summary of centuries of French social policies and practices. He describes how French Catholic charity hospitals had historically cared for orphans and he reviews laws against begging. Drawing from the early church itself, he alludes to almost every patristic example of social relief known in his day, including the Cappadocians. The book was meant to be a call to his own generation for heightened awareness of the hordes of desperate poor throughout France and for new political social action based on Christian ideals. Defining this action in terms of the post-Revolutionary vision in France for equality and fraternity among mankind, Martin-Doisy concludes that

> The life and death of the incarnate God was the proclamation of an absolute and sovereign truth. Renunciation of wealth out of love for the poor, love for humankind to the point of death, are the supreme elements of human perfection, the only true principles, the only solid foundations of equality and fraternity among men. Renunciation of wealth and renunciation of life are also the most solid foundations of liberty, for it is by them above all else that man is free.[29]

In describing early Christian responses to poverty, Martin-Doisy says outright that his goal was to offer "la plus sur moyen de frapper les esprits et de toucher les coeurs," that is, the surest means of impressing souls and touching hearts.

It might have surprised Martin-Doisy very much to learn that among those hearts and souls that his book impressed and touched was an American railway magnate and Presbyterian trustee of Princeton seminary, Stephen Colwell. Like Martin-Doisy's sponsor Armand de Melun, Colwell was a wealthy layman who took very seriously the social responsibilities of his religious beliefs. Colwell dedicated his life not only to the practice of Christian philanthropy but also to supporting and promoting research on its history. In 1851, not long after he obtained Martin-Doisy's book, Colwell published *New Themes for the Protestant Clergy*, a lengthy treatise that criticized his fellow Protestants for their failure to take charity seriously as a foundation of Christian theological practice.[30] As one of Colwell's biographers observed, "Because he was in a very remarkable way open and receptive to the new possibilities of interpreting the Bible and Christian tradition on the one hand and to new social and political reality on the other, Colwell challenged uniquely the conventional wisdom of his generation."[31]

Although a staunch Presbyterian, Colwell encouraged a universal poverty relief that practiced no confessional bias:

We must not turn our back upon those who are suffering from what
we can give them. But are we not equally bound to exert ourselves to
afford permanent succour—to raise our suffering brethren to the same
level in comfort with ourselves? We owe a duty not only in every particular case, but we owe a debt of love to every individual; and we are
bound to pay that debt, not only in special acts of kindness, but in general efforts, not merely for the benefit of individuals, but of the whole
human family.[32]

Yet Colwell's book, like Martin-Doisy's, clearly reflects an agenda that was
based on the author's personal cultural history and bias. Raised in West
Virginia, Colwell's "proslavery" stance has been well recognized,[33] and his
book demonstrates his support of the rich American Southerners in 1851
in their defense of slavery.

In fact, Colwell says very little about the patristic period. He acknowledges Martin-Doisy as his primary source for this era, but his selective use
of the available stories is striking. A full third of Colwell's short chapter
on the early church defends the idea that the "light of Christianity" may
hasten the end of slavery but only "in that mode which is best both for
master and slave; both being bound to love each other until the door of
emancipation is fully open without injury to either."[34] Among patristic
sources, Colwell mentions 1 Clement 55, in which Christians are said
to have sold themselves to feed others, and the story of a fifth-century
redemption of captive Vandal slaves by the bishop of Carthage. Among
his cited sources that do not relate to slavery, he recognizes material
divestment as a first step in monastic charity, narrates Christians' medical care for plague victims in Alexandria, and quotes both the emperor
Julian's praise for Christian philanthropy and Eusebius's reference to
Constantine's patronage. He concludes the chapter with a popular tale of
a Roman deacon who, told to hand over the church's treasures during a
persecution, gathers and displays the city's poor. These stories likely were
new to his audience of American Protestants, who perhaps shared little of
John Calvin's patristic curiosity. What is not new in Colwell's approach,
however, is his use of these examples to condemn medieval Catholicism;
nineteenth-century Protestants who studied the early church commonly
defended it as an exemplary era that, alas, "sank gradually into all the
abuses of Roman Papacy."[35] Despite his anti-Catholic bias, however,
Colwell thinks more highly of Martin-Doisy than he does of his Anglican counterparts who were then engaged in the "Oxford Movement"

(discussed further in the next section). Intent on urging American readers to new social awareness and action, Colwell writes of Martin-Doisy that "although the Catholic Church is greatly lauded by this writer, we do not hesitate to recommend his work to Protestants, as calculated to humble their spiritual pride, and possibly goad them into paths of charity hitherto little trodden by their feet."[36]

Colwell did more than goad. Capitalist to the bone, he was determined to influence and encourage American religious scholarship on social issues. He funded an English translation of another French Catholic book about early Christian charity.[37] He also wrote extensively on the credit system, condemning the American poorhouse as "the stigma of Protestantism." After his death, he was praised for "cultivating political economy as a theory of beneficence." He donated his library of eight thousand books and pamphlets to the University of Pennsylvania, requesting that both it and Princeton establish academic chairs in his name. One (promised but not delivered at his death)[38] was to be in social science; the other, in ethics, is now the Stephen Colwell Chair in Applied Christianity.[39]

BASIL'S SOCIAL ACTION: FROM THE OXFORD MOVEMENT TO MIDDLE AMERICA

Stephen Colwell dismissed the Anglican church of his day as "shaken to its basis, and certainly in danger, if not already crumbling."[40] And indeed, the Church of England was then in the midst of a long and nasty "high church"/"low church" controversy over the use of liturgical elements such as vestments, incense, chanting, and confession. Although this had never been a settled issue in Anglican tradition, the immediate debate took shape in the early nineteenth-century "Oxford Movement" whose leaders (for the "high church" position) included the Oxford cleric-scholars John Henry Newman, E. B. Pusey, and John Keble. The relevance of this controversy for patristic social ethics began with Newman, whose subsequent conversion to Roman Catholicism in 1845 seemed to many of his contemporaries to shake the very walls of the Protestant–Catholic divide.

During the 1830s, Newman published several literary "sketches" of early Christian writers, among them Basil and Gregory of Nazianzus. These biographies, which first appeared in 1833, were so popular that they are still in print.[41]

In Newman's sketches of the Cappadocians, he briefly mentions Basil's famine relief and his hospital, largely paraphrasing Gregory's funeral sermon. Newman seems to be unaware of or unconcerned with Basil's own sermons about social issues. His study of Gregory says nothing about Gregory's sermon on the poor. Indeed, Newman focused much more attention on the history of church politics, particularly the correspondence and controversies between various bishops. This focus is typical of the interests that ruled the Oxford Movement itself. Despite the views of Anglicans, Episcopals, and Protestants such as Colwell, who condemned the Movement for corrupting the Reformation by introducing "popish" practices, Newman's *Church of the Fathers* had a tremendous impact on many English-speaking Christians. For the first time, ordinary people— clergy, divinity students, and seminary teachers—had immediate access to the patristic world in English translation. Newman's translations and "sketches" sparked a renaissance of patristic translation efforts in both the United Kingdom and the United States. One important but little-known priest who played a role in bringing Basil of Caesarea to the ordinary reader is the Rev. Blomfield Jackson (1839–1905).

Probably during the 1880s, Jackson agreed to produce an English translation and introduction to the volume on Basil of Caesarea for the then-new Nicene and Post-Nicene Fathers (NPNF), a twenty-four-volume series, under the general direction of the American theological scholar Philip Schaff. Schaff's NPNF was a logical extension of an earlier series, the *AnteNicene Fathers* (ANF), which largely reprinted texts from the earlier nineteenth-century "Oxford Library," a series that Newman and his colleagues had launched in 1837. Schaff's NPNF, however, was to include many new translations of texts that were not already available in English, and Jackson's volume was one.

Jackson's formal task was simply to translate Basil's treatise *On the Holy Spirit*, his *Hexaemeron*, and his letters. He was not asked to translate any of Basil's sermons on social issues. Newman, after all, had never mentioned them. What Jackson does with this assignment is therefore all the more surprising. In the introductory essay to his translation, published in 1894, Jackson outlines and describes almost all of Basil's sermons, including those related to poverty, famine, and social justice. Jackson's introduction remained one of the few sources in English for nearly a century that described Basil's social agenda in the context of his own homilies. And, as I discovered during my own journey to these texts, the ANF/NPNF was one of the very few patristic sources that an interested Protestant layperson could easily locate in English as late as the 1980s.

Little has been published on Blomfield Jackson's life, but what we do know may begin to explain his obvious sensitivity to the tensions of class issues and the problem of poverty that would logically contribute to his interest in Basil's social agenda. His views were likely informed by his Victorian high church appreciation for social welfare based in patristic history. They were also likely shaped (although this is a guess) by his personal relationship to his childhood parish, a community split down the middle by an extended theological squabble within a neighborhood that was characterized at the end of the nineteenth century by its increasing contrasts between rich and poor.

The oldest son of Thomas Jackson, a colorful, charismatic, and controversial "high church" clergyman, Blomfield was eleven years old in 1850 when his father's career ambitions seemed to be realized with an episcopal appointment as one of New Zealand's new bishops. The grand dream quickly fizzled. Soon after Blomfield's mother disembarked in the new land dressed to the hilt in "silks and ostrich feathers," and his father launched his ministry by pressing for social and fiscal rewards proportionate to his exalted ecclesiastical ambitions, the New Zealanders had enough of the Jacksons and sent them back to England. The fiasco cost their London sponsors £3000. Salvaging the wreckage, when Blomfield was thirteen, the bishop of London appointed his father pastor of St. Mary's in Stoke Newington, now a northeast London suburb, where Thomas remained rector for thirty-four years, but not without further controversy. In the midst of his tenure, the Stoke Newington parish underwent an acrimonious schism, with the historically "low church," Old St. Mary's, worshiping literally across the street from the new "high" church (also called St. Mary's) that Thomas had built. Blomfield could not escape; as soon as he was old enough, his father appointed him curate of Old St. Mary's. It is not likely that he spent much time there, since at age twenty-six he was appointed Classical Master and then Fellow at King's College, and spent ten years as tutor to Queen Victoria's children. Yet Blomfield did continue to live in Stoke Newington, where his children were born between 1868 and 1875. The schism roared on until the bishop of London finally agreed, in 1886, to remove the aged rector. But Thomas died first, and Blomfield's appointment as curate came (not surprisingly) to an immediate end. By the 1890s, when he was translating Basil, Blomfield was rector of St. Bartholemew's in Moor's Lane, London.

Church schisms usually indicate determined (and often numerous) contingents on both sides of a conflict. And indeed, the Stoke Newington parishes were both very large, and the Jacksons saw a period of rapid building as well as increasingly stark social contrasts. By 1900, for example, the church (which remained a technically single parish) had forty district visitors (that is, church-sponsored social workers who visited the needy) and one hundred mission workers, in addition to various clubs and guilds for working class men, girls, and troubled youth. There is as yet too little published about Blomfield to say whether he was active in any of these support or relief activities. Despite his parents' love for wealth and finery, and his own social eminence, it is unlikely that he was entirely detached from the active social welfare and relief activities, since they characterized much of the high church movement during his lifetime. This heightened sensitivity to the role of ostentatious wealth, greed, and liturgical disagreements in social action for the London poor of his own day may very well explain Jackson's extraordinary and unprecedented commitment to describe Basil's social action for his English-speaking readers. The footnotes in his translation of Basil's sermons make it clear that he also, like Colwell, was reading late nineteenth-century French texts on patristic social issues. Citing one French author's praise of Basil's "poorhouse" as it fed the needy and distributed alms in obedience to the gospel, Blomfield allows himself a rare personal outburst, noting, "A high ideal! Perhaps never more nearly realized than in the Cappadocian coenobia of the fourth century."[42]

ENGAGING PARADIGMS: TOOLS FOR
EMPATHIC REMEMBERING

The shapes that patristic texts took in each of these three very different historical situations illustrate some of the interpretive challenges outlined in the previous chapters. Although these stories do not tell us how specific passages in specific authors were enacted—that is, how later writers behaved toward individual poor persons because of something written in one sermon or another—they do display various examples of how immediate context, background, and other agendas biased their limits and uses. In these texts we find indications that the journey across the "gap" from text to action might be influenced by any of four particular issues: terminology, exegesis, social power structures, and one's views on human rights. Because these four represent aspects of relationship, and because they happen inevitably in any reading of a topic that might be "applied" to the real-life present, these issues are especially important in our own measured use of such texts. How we are influenced by these four issues may determine whether our use of patristic readings of social welfare perpetuate problems or empower thoughtful dialogue toward healing the world.

Terminology

All discussion begins with vocabulary. The vocabulary that English speakers use to discuss issues of human need is extensive and complex. Given that early Christian texts on these issues were written in a world that was dominated by at least four different languages (Greek, Latin, Syriac, and Coptic), and that many of these communities spoke other languages as well, we begin to see the problems. *Tzedakah*, discussed earlier, is just one example. Terms means different things to different audiences, even when they speak the same language. There are important differences in English, for example, between the nuances behind the words charity, philanthropy, justice, and love, and yet all of these are used, sometimes interchangeably, in talking about relief and poverty issues. Each of these multiple terms has its history of misuse, and many imply nuances of denigration, discrimination, and other bias. For example, most English-language discussions of "charity" are based on the Latin word *caritas*, which actually means love or dearness, but has no real roots in "philanthropy" as it relates to those in real need. Nor, as a Latin word, is *caritas* relevant to the Greek sermons of the Cappadocians and John Chrysostom or their Aramaic or Hebrew sources. A deceptively similar Greek word, *xaritas,* is the accusative plural form of *xaris*, grace, and can imply gifting ("graces")—and indeed redemptive alms assumes aid conceptually similar to pre-Christian ideals of gift exchange in patronage-based societies. But *xaris* is not a term that occurs frequently in these sermons, nor is it linguistically associated with poverty relief. "Alms," from the Greek *eleemosyne*, has its root in the meaning "acts of mercy," but not all relief to the needy took the form of alms, and mercy was a Greek word quite distinct from terms used for "justice." Gregory of Nyssa's common use of *euergetism* (literally "good works," but in context also implying patronage) is helpful, but even among modern Christians "good works" may have different nuances, for example, for Calvinists and Roman Catholics. *Philanthropy*, from the Greek *philanthropia*, love of humankind, is also a common patristic term for social action, but its modern meaning often suggests large institutional granting foundations, or else the patronage of the demeaning handout. Words translated "love," such as *philia* and *agape*, are also found in the ancient texts on the poor, but the English word too easily elides with other meanings, most of them evoking emotions that were not necessarily associated with alms or even "mercy" in the ancient world, nor necessarily related to the ethical enactment of social welfare. Even the phrase "social welfare," which I have frequently used for want of better alternatives, is rooted largely in modern concepts about particular views of public good. Yet public good itself was another common appeal in early Christian texts; Basil uses the word *koinopheles*, "common good," in several places to mean exactly this greater good for the broad civic society. But *koinopheles* and other words translated as "common good" did not always refer to relief of poverty nor to righting social injustices. Despite these many problems with meaning and nuance, we usually find ourselves employing all of these terms, since most of them can in some way express concern for enacting an ethical Christian response to provide material *justice* for those who cannot obtain it through their own limited resources.

The challenge of terminology is even more complicated than this, however. It is not just about how we translate individual words; it is also about the differences in words and phrases we use to associate ideals that are not exactly the same across cultures. We see this starkly when we compare ancient and modern "catchwords," those terms in any extended discussion of a topic that may illustrate what a speaker thinks is most important about the central theme. For example, the Greek patristic authors on poverty relief tend to dwell on the following terms: sacred, holy, image of god, patronage, mercy, begging, brother-and-kin, Christ-in-the-poor, redemptive alms, and kingdom of heaven. But these are not the prevailing images we find in modern human rights, where different cultural focus often lead to using different sets of words entirely. These include words such as political power, government versus volunteer intervention, immigration, health insurance, equitable, disease prevention, fair trade, working conditions, social class, liberation, gender disparities, and education. Such a difference is particularly obvious in the way that Martin-Doisy structured his arguments for using patristic examples: he used words that reveal his political framework of ideals shaped in the eighteenth-century French Revolution and his own equally political vision for new policies. The use of such radically different word sets and their contrasts emphasizes how differently ancient and modern societies, including Christians within these societies, regard these issues in terms of different priorities, motives, and aims.

Exegesis

Exegesis, meaning the way a text is interpreted, is a common theme in describing different approaches to the interpretation of religious scriptures. There were different interpretive approaches in antiquity just as there are today. For example, most of the patristic sermons that advocate care for the poor take quite literally Jesus's parables about the poor and rich. The Christ-poor in Matthew 25 is one of the most frequently cited examples.[43] We also find frequent reference to the story of Lazarus and the rich man in Luke 16:19–31, a biblical association that (as we saw in the discussion of the figure in Chapter 3) continued in patristic exegesis and application for centuries. Early Christian texts preached that alms and justice literally and directly influenced one's personal, heavenly benefits or lack thereof. Alms were thus understood as guaranteed-return investments in the stock of heavenly and eternal wealth, and the poor were considered heaven's gatekeepers and court witnesses before God. This was as true in the Syriac- and Greek-speaking east, in places such as Edessa and Cappadocia, as it was in the Latin-speaking west of Ambrose, Augustine, and Salvian.

But even if the Christ-poor of judgment day were taken literally, patristic exegesis was far more circumspect and generally more moderate when it came to interpreting gospel teachings about material divestment. The fourth-century noble Roman woman Proba, for example, shared Clement of Alexandria's earlier view that it was acceptable to retain wealth as long as the rich person practiced detachment and a reasonable compassion.[44] Others, like Basil of Caesarea, condemned surplus goods (including extra clothing), but still supported their rights of ownership over land, goods, and even slaves. One of the few early Christian texts that does recommend complete impoverishment as something required for Christian living is a treatise "On wealth" that is attributed to the Pelagians, and was dismissed by opponents at the time as heretical.[45] This variety of views and hesitations is one that has characterized these issues for centuries; modern Christian writers are similarly "all over the map," preaching views that range from a literal judgment day to genuine waffling about material divestment, or to a "health and wealth gospel" in which godliness is frankly defined by personal prosperity. Cultural rhetoric can be used to evoke many different responses. The ways that different Christians might interpret and exegete texts such as the parable of the sheep and goats, the story of Jesus and the rich young ruler, or even the "poor" who are blessed in the Beatitudes, will vary, often regardless of shared beliefs in the incarnation, redemption, a last judgment, and a kingdom of heaven.

Paradigm crossing requires an understanding of how the two reference points are alike or different in their exegetical style. We cannot compare two interpretations without some appreciation of other obvious differences that might exist between the two sources. Exegesis is like bias: it happens inevitably. But it is also different from bias in that it has the potential to encourage new possibilities in creative practice.

Social Power Structures

Another challenge is the way that social power structures actually *cause* many of the "blind" biases in the texts, or use them to promote injustice. Stephen Colwell, for example, was apparently biased in his selection of patristic texts on social welfare by his personal views on slavery. Post-Reformation sixteenth-century social structures may have determined how politics influenced the shape of both Elizabethan and Zwingli's "poor laws." Both John Henry Newman's Oxford Movement and Blomfield Jackson's childhood parish in Stoke Newington refused to give up issues of liturgical practice and authority and this apparently affected their chosen focus on the patristic texts they considered worthy of study, translation, and publication. Care for the poor is historically depicted in art and imagination by a (literally) "large" and powerful person bending down to offer some assistance to a correspondingly small or weak, dependent supplicant, and this is not an exclusively Christian artistic construction. The earliest known painting of almsgiving within the Christian era (though there is no evidence that it is a Christian image) is a fresco from Herculaneum that dates prior to the eruption of Vesuvius and depicts a wealthy woman (accompanied by a female servant) who towers over a diminutive beggar holding his hand out to receive the coin she offers.[46] The most famous twelfth-century manuscript illustrating Gregory of Nazianzus's sermon on the love of the poor shows the bishop in exactly the same pose with the same marked difference in size; the powerful bishop is standing straight with his hand prepared to give aid, while the smaller, ragged, handicapped beggars bend before him in clear expressions of supplication.[47] In ancient Roman sculpture, slaves and subordinates are often proportionately sized down so that they often appear to the modern viewer to look like children.

In any cross-cultural comparison, we must remember that the entire social structure of the ancient Greek and Roman world was organized in terms of patronage, and the relationship between patrons and clients was an interdependent one, something viewed as acceptable and ideally good. This contrasts radically with the modern Western ideal of democracy and equality for all; it contrasts with the corresponding capitalist ideal that hard work pays off in the present life. In the ancient world there was, despite a certain level of "free trade," no real democratic equality. Many sought and some attained upward social mobility, but it was generally discouraged by laws such as those in the fourth and fifth century that ordained what colors people in certain social classes and occupations were allowed to wear and also limited or forbade occupational changes, even if someone wished to become a priest or a monk within a now presumably Christian society. Patronage almost never included educating the children of the poor. "Good" relief was understood to mean assistance that is fair and not corrupt, but the poor remained servants to the rich. It is, after all, the poor who are expected, *as* poor, to carry that hazardous material of wealth (received in the form of alms) into heaven on behalf of the rich. The poor remained objects of aid, not agents or leaders. Their existence gave bishops a preset group of political contingents that could be used to showcase or assert the bishop's leadership in the new political systems of the fourth and fifth centuries. While Basil's views on divestment and rights were radical in some ways, he himself served as a very traditional patron. His community equity is largely invested in his ideals for monastic "voluntary" poverty, as reflected in his monastic "Rule," and his monks who lived in moderate but adequate circumstances. He did not apply it, as his sister Macrina did when she insisted on treating household slaves as social equals, to publicly overturning social norms. We may say the same about someone like Martin-Doisy, who outlined his vision for social welfare in terms of the New France, but who himself was an elite layman immersed in politics. When structures of social power remain unchanged, the involuntary poor remain distinctly different from those who give to them and who have the power to choose self-divestment for monastic (or political) ends.

Human Rights

Finally, cross-cultural interpretations and uses of social ethics will be influenced by how both the original text describes and the readers understand "human rights." Modern western culture considers rights to be intrinsic "givens," something that people innately deserve by nature of their basic

identity as human beings. Although rarely practiced, equal rights are, at
least in theory, considered to be fixed and not relative "truths." For example,
the Universal Declaration of Human Rights (UDHR), signed into international law by the United Nations in 1948 in reaction to the Holocaust-
related violations of Nazi Germany during World War II, based its thirty
articles on a common recognition that "the inherent dignity and...the
equal and inalienable rights of all members of the human family [are] the
foundation of freedom, justice, and peace in the world."[48] This Declaration, spearheaded under the diplomatic leadership of Eleanor Roosevelt,
is by no means incompatible with Christian ideals. Indeed, it was meant to
serve as an effective moral and social mandate across religious boundaries, its wording shaped by deeply religious contributors to the dialogue,
including the Catholic philosopher Jacques Maritain, and others.[49] As
the founders of the document included nations whose philosophical ethics were based, for example, in Marxist atheism (the USSR), Buddhism
(China), and other divergent religious views, a consensus document necessarily required a certain distancing from specific religious claims about
God. Nonetheless, the rights so granted by such declarations are only as
solid as the human consensus that brings them into being. In contrast,
for early Christian (and Jewish) writers, as for Oecolampadius, Zwingli,
and Luther, human "rights" were ultimately relative to the nature of God.
Their permanent existential identity was assumed to rest in divine, not
human, attributes. Because they were not viewed as existentially "absolute,
self-evident givens" (that is, in and of themselves apart from any external
creator) but were innately understood to be relative (that is, to a divine
reference point), "rights" in ancient societies might better be equated
with what modern economists call *entitlements*. That is, they are viewed
as something to which each member of the human race has, on the basis
of some relational concept, received "title."[50] The validity of an entitlement depends on the nature of its source. For the Cappadocians, the poor
were understood to be entitled to justice and equal rights because of their
identity as God's creation, their value further defined and affirmed by the
eschaton imagery of Matthew 25 and its identification with the physical
body of Christ. Early Christian texts define rights and equality using the
language of body, family, household, kinship, and citizenship in the kingdom of heaven—all terms whose meanings are, by definition, relational.
The poor also have a cosmic identity since they are part of creation; they
are essential agents in healing toward a new heaven and a new earth and
a restoration of the natural world. This relational dependence does not in

itself limit the early Christian understanding of rights or freedoms more than do our modern concepts (though social biases hindered the liberations that we might expect would follow from certain assertions). But it does assume that God is the ultimate arbiter. The conceptual relativity of rights language as "entitlements" with distinct human limits still rules in many nonwestern nations, challenging those of us who have been raised on Jeffersonian "self-evident" truths to find a way to discuss these differences in a manner that "does justice, loves kindness, and walks humbly" with those who may view rights differently than we do.

The Cappadocian sermons contain explicit language on human rights and equality based in human nature. Gregory of Nazianzus asks his congregation to imitate the equality or evenhandedness of God, which one translator interprets as "the justice of God."[51] Gregory uses a word that can mean either "equity" or "equality of rights" when he describes how relationships at creation ought to continue to serve as a model for the present. "I would have you look back to our primary equality of rights," he says, "not the later diversity.... As far as you can, support nature, honor primeval liberty, show reverence for yourself and cover the shame of your race, help to resist sickness, offer relief to human need."[52]

Gregory also uses these terms to make an appeal that is based not on issues of identity such as ethnicity or politics, which might suggest exclusion, but rather on broader definitions that would include most, if not all, needy persons. Describing the homeless destitute as including wandering strangers who were victims of natural or political disasters, Gregory does not identify them by geographic or religious origins; they are not called Cappadocians, Greeks, or even Christians. Gregory of Nyssa argues that such people deserve social justice simply because they are "human persons."[53] Both of the Gregories as well as their contemporary, Asterius, the bishop of Amasea, define the needy using terms that deliberately bring them into close identification as members of an all-inclusive "race" and "kin." In both his sermons, "On the Rich Man and Lazarus" and "Against Avarice,"[54] Asterius argues against those who claim that economic inequalities reflect qualitative differences in human nature. In his sermon "On the Rich Man and Lazarus" he writes that if "the nature of things were such that our life was truly represented by the inequality of [the beggar Lazarus's] career with that of the rich man, I should have cried aloud with indignation: that we who are created equal, live on such unequal terms with those of the same race!"[55] And in "Against Avarice," he condemns covetousness precisely because it creates a "marked disparity in the conditions of life between human persons created equal in worth."[56] Asterius understands inequality as an abnormality, explicitly using the Greek word *anomalia,* writing that "covetousness is the mother of inequality, unmerciful, misanthropic, cruel. Because of it human life is full of *anomalia*."[57] Yet the way that Martin-Doisy, for example, would have understood such social anomalies in light of his experiences during the 1848 Revolution in Paris may not have been quite the same as those Stephen Colwell would have imagined from Virginia just before the Civil War.

CONCLUSIONS

These first four chapters have set out the challenge that readers face who read early Christian sources on poverty and social welfare responses and wish to make them relevant in their own particular culture and time. Chapter 1 considered what "empathic remembering" might mean in such a journey. Chapter 2 explored the inevitable role that personal stories have in all that we may bring to such tasks. Chapter 3 plunged into the ancient world with a detailed examination of the Cappadocian responses to acute poverty and crisis in the fourth century and related texts that enable us to better understand their immediate context. This chapter began the decompression process of carrying them forward in a turn toward the present with a look at stories about people near our own time who have tried to do something with these texts. Together, these chapters have offered various conceptual tools we might use to enter the more deliberately interwoven stories that follow in the second half of the book, in which examples from past and present are layered together in a narrative that is less theoretical and more creatively suggestive. Chapter 5, on poverty and gendering, brings us back to the initial focus on "sensing need," particularly as it affects women and children. Chapters 6 and 7 explore what it means to "share the world," which might be defined and perceived differently depending on whether we begin in the past (Chapter 6) or in the present (Chapter 7). And by moving into a different realm entirely, Chapter 8 concludes by considering how such texts on religious responses to the needy poor in this present world relate to the paradigmatic image that so often defines what is "ultimate" in Christian theology: embodying sacred kingdom.

POVERTY AND THE
GENDERING OF EMPATHY

"O Firstborn One who was a weaned child and
familiar with children...hearken to my lambs who
have seen the wolves, for lo, they are crying."

—Ephrem of Edessa[1]

In modern Badakhshan, a province of Tajikistan and part of the former
Soviet Union, women are routinely bleeding infants and children in a
"healing" practice that cuts their back, arms, and the roof of their mouth
with razors. The women "healers" in these desperately poor, remote, and
rural mountain communities at the easternmost edge of the ancient Persian
empire practice two kinds of incisional bleeding on these newborns, tod-
dlers, and young children. One they call *qum*, which cuts the roof of a
baby's mouth to release "dirty" blood in a sick infant. The other, *pilé,* is the
practice of slicing their skin open on a regular basis, sometimes monthly,
as a prophylactic believed to promote good health. The affected infant or
child is bled until the initially "dark" blood flows bright red. After the cut-
tings, healers mop up the flow with clean cloths while the infant cries. It is
a sign of "health," say the healers, when the baby eventually quiets down
into a peaceful "calm" after losing "a few spoonfuls" of blood.

This unusual medical practice, here done by women to children they
value and love, within a setting that is marked by other risks of life-
threatening poverty, offers a vivid image for the theme of this chapter:
the role of gender issues in global and community injustice as it touches
on human need. These bleeding and scarred children are extreme examples of how, in any culture, women and children are both the ultimate
victims of poverty and sometimes the victims of its targeted relief. Their
examples demonstrate how poverty can influence women and their children. It reminds us that a perceptive "sensing" of those in need is likely
to engage us in encounters with issues related to gender discrepancies and

distinctions. Statistically poverty is characterized largely and most acutely by women and those who are most dependent on them: their infants and children. The choices that I and others make for (or against) empathy in the context of human need will inevitably be nuanced by our views on gender and how we habitually act on these views.

Dr. Salmaan Keshavjee, a Harvard-educated physician-anthropologist who encountered the infant bleeding practice during his humanitarian work in the region, found it deeply disturbing. He interviewed the "healers" to learn why they engaged in this practice.[2] They told him that it was an effective way to clean out the poison and curse of a "dirty" womb and "bad blood." It corrects and counters damage from jinns (demons), they said. It treats an inherent and even genetic disease, they carefully explained. This disease, aggravated by the social environment, is on the rise, they warned him. It is not a clinically straightforward blood disease, but results from the broader conditions of worsening regional poverty. While poverty aggravates the polluting factors, bleeding is said to release the excess, the "poison." Bleeding babies makes them healthy, the healers assured this American doctor.

The women described the pathology in "medical" terms by saying that those born with the "infant's disease" have "more blood than they should." The first symptoms they use to diagnose it are cramps and diarrhea. These are in fact symptoms pandemic to any area in which children are undernourished and sanitation is poor. Other signs that clue them in to symptoms of disease include blue circles around the mouth and runny eyes, also common enough in undernourished or anemic children challenged by various infections. The "jinns," they say, make the parents' blood "dirty," by feeding the babies jinn-produced milk *in utero*. The "healers" also admit that common microbes play a role. The parents' "polluted" blood is blamed on "bad" post-Soviet social conditions and behaviors, including alcoholism, theft, and rampant poverty. The disease—considered contagious—is on the rise "because the town is dirty and rubbish is not removed for a long time."

One health worker, who lives several miles from the nearest water supply and whose granddaughter had died of dysentery, emphasized to Dr. Keshavjee that bleeding is a very careful, precise process that releases only a few spoonfuls of blood and has no bad effects if done "properly." And yet, as both her granddaughter's death and Dr. Keshavjee's detailed descriptions of the community emphasize, the children who endure this practice are already at extremely high risk. Between 1990 and 1994, in the economic collapse that followed the fall of the former Soviet Union (of which Tajikistan was part), maternal mortality in the province of Badakhshan doubled, from 41.8 to 87.6 mothers dying for every 100,000 live births. Infant mortality in 1994 was 42.4 deaths for every thousand infants born. This rate is nearly ten times that of the United Kingdom and Canada, where the infant mortality rate is 4.8 per thousand.[3] Lacking essential medicines, heat, food, and clothing, thousands of mountain people would have died without humanitarian aid. But even with aid, infant and child malnutrition skyrocketed. The rates of newly reported childhood pneumonia more than doubled between 1990 and 1994, from 2,747 to 6,752 per 100,000 children, and at the time of Dr. Keshavjee's research in 1996, both adults and children were nine times more likely to have a diarrheal disease than they were in 1990.

A young child's body is acutely sensitive to fluid imbalances and the child can die very quickly if diarrhea is not promptly and properly treated. Water that contains bacteria can devastate a baby's gut, making it less able to absorb essential nutrients. This is a risk in poor countries no matter how women feed their babies, since even breastfed infants are often given water or small amounts of other substances for various reasons. Thus, illnesses that are socially attributed to "dirty blood" or "bad milk" may in fact be fatal as a result of something as simple as dirty water or diarrhea induced by malnutrition and increased risk of infections.

Dr. Keshavjee knew that his own discomfort about these practices was not going to change the situation. As a first step toward doing what he could, he set out to understand the cultural significance that bleeding babies and children has for the people of Badakhshan. The cuts of *qum* and *pilé* leave scars that serve, he found, "as a marker of a specific ethnocultural and religious identity and as the embodiment of self and difference." Unlike male circumcision, a form of infant cutting that we in the West view as normal and even healthful, the lines of visible scarring on these young children's bodies in Badakhshan are "scars that transcend gender." They are also scars that mark poverty. "On some profound level," Keshavjee writes, "the bloodletting of sick infants simultaneously represents and exposes the social realization of material deprivation.... Like folk piety elsewhere, infant bloodletting literally and symbolically occurs at the interstices of the social world, in which experiences of marginality—like illness, death, and misfortune—are often addressed." The social and health problems that a crumbling social system cannot address are "treated" in living substances that can be controlled: the body and blood of children.[4]

Like Dr. Keshavjee, we may also find ourselves deeply disturbed by this scenario. Reading accounts such as this may awaken our own senses to the discomforting realities of poverty in other parts of the world. Such a narrative invites us to enter an empathic engagement with the children and infants who are the helpless victims of their family and community poverty. Such images remind us that stark poverty affects people of every age in a society, but it is the children who are most often irreparably scarred.

Societies have, throughout history, localized the disorders and "pollutions" of poverty in women's body products: not only blood but also other products of childbearing, including breast milk. Oozing definitions of gender, these substances connect easily to ideas about pollution that often determine the self-image of women faced with the challenge and shame of poverty.

Medical writings from antiquity suggest that the Badakhshan example is not something entirely unique and unprecedented. The Roman writer Celsus echoes the Badakhshan healers in explaining why his contemporaries might also bleed babies for their health. In his chapter "on bloodletting by incising a vein," Celsus argues that children who are "weak" should not be bled, "but a strong child in good health may be so treated with safety."[5] This might sound reassuring, except that in Celsus's view, thin children had more blood to spare than their chubby peers, who had more flesh than blood. Therefore it was the thin babies who most likely faced "therapeutic" bleeding. Celsus's reasons are very similar to those of the mountain healers: "If the harm is a copiousness or the material has become corrupted, there is no better remedy" than a good bleed.[6] We know that infant mortality in the ancient world was very high; it is not hard to imagine that infant bleeding would have statistically increased this risk.

Celsus's views on infant bleeding did not represent the majority of surviving medical texts from the ancient world. Most physicians in antiquity were against bleeding infants or children. Galen in the second century, for example, said that bloodletting should never be used in cases of diarrhea or respiratory distress, which are in fact the two conditions that kill most children in Badakhshan.[7]

ON DIRTY BLOOD—AND MILK

The thread that leads us deeper into the role of gender in poverty in this story of knives, blood, and screaming babies is its theme of body fluids.

In the therapeutic scheme in Badakhshan, there is a direct relationship between blood and milk. The jinns that invade the womb feed their polluted, demonic milk to the fetus, polluting the mother's blood. Affected children are treated with *qum* and *pilé* from the ages of six or seven months to a year; this is in fact the same window of time in which infants depend on milk for their primary nourishment and the period of time when they start adding other foods to the diet. Even in cultures in which babies are not bled, there has historically been a deliberate association between maternal milk and the ritual "purity" (or pollution) of maternal blood. Clement of Alexandria, a late second-century Christian intellectual writing in Egypt, illustrated just how elaborate this association might be in the literary imagination and as a metaphor for Christian nurture when he wrote in his treatise, *On Pedagogy:*

> Milk is the product of the blood; and...milk has a most natural affinity for water, as assuredly the spiritual washing has for the spiritual nutriment....And such as is the union of the word with baptism, is the agreement of milk with water....And it is mixed naturally with honey also and this for cleansing along with sweet nutriment. For the Word blended with love at once cures our passions and cleanses our sins....Furthermore...milk is curdled by wine, and separated....And in the same way, the spiritual communion of faith with suffering man, drawing off as serous matter the lusts of the flesh, commits man to eternity, along with those who are divine, immortalizing him.[8]

Macarius, the bishop of Magnesia in the fifth century, provided (or perhaps repeated from an earlier source) an argument similar to Clement's when he said of the newborn infant:

> except it eats the flesh and drinks the blood of its mother, it has no life...it is true that the nourishment comes in the form of milk, but milk is really the same as blood; it is only its proximity to the air that gives it its lighter colour. Even so frost will make water white, without changing its nature. Just as the Creator makes the foul waters of the abyss trickle out in a clear fountain, so do a woman's breasts, by an elaborate mechanism, gather blood from the veins, and send it forth in a palatable form. If then even children tell us these things with persuasion...what is there that seems to you disturbing if the Gospel saying of Christ [John 6:53] may be set beside them?[9]

This association of infant food and ritual purification is so important in many religions that it is often a standard image in initiation rites, sometimes associated with references to ritually "pure" blood. Clement's North African contemporary, Tertullian, says that the "baby foods" of milk and honey were normally given to the newly baptized.[10] Another early Christian writer, Procopius of Gaza, commenting on Isaiah 55, directly associates milk with the eucharistic "blood" in his description of liturgical practices: "long ago [milk] was carried to the enlightened with the body and the blood. And in certain churches they say that the custom is still observed."[11]

The "purity" (or "pollution") of blood (and milk) in the ancient world, as in many cultures today, did not make a clear distinction between bodily and spiritual issues. Both sensory reactions and spiritual factors played a role in standard explanations about disease, healing, and food. As in Badakhshan, these "impurities" were often blamed on disordered "natural" or social processes and not solely on physiology or on individual moral behaviors. For example, ancient physicians who wrote about breastfeeding, such as Soranus in the second century, assumed that the quality of breast milk was influenced not only by the blood that produced it but also by the disordered or internally "upset" state of the woman. During the first few days after she gave birth, Soranus argued, a mother's milk was "unwholesome ... produced by bodies which are in a bad state, agitated and changed to the extent that we see the body altered after delivery when, from having suffered a great discharge of blood, it is dried up, toneless, discolored, and in the majority of cases feverish as well. For all these reasons, it is absurd to present the maternal milk until the body enjoys stable health."[12]

To a modern reader conscious of the biological value of giving infants their mother's breast milk as soon as possible after birth (since the first milk contains unique components that help protect infants from infections in addition to providing essential fluids and nutrients), Soranus's advice sounds disastrous for any woman who does not have safe feeding alternatives. In the ancient world, as in any modern but resource-poor society that cannot guarantee its infants clean water, healthy food, and proper vitamin–mineral supplementation, infants deprived of mother's milk in the days after birth are likely to die. "Stable health" is a luxury for most women (and many men as well) in such cultures, and in parts of the world today infants still face the risk of malnutrition and even starvation because of popular beliefs about body fluids as moral barometers and "bad blood" causing "spoiled milk."[13] Maternal human immunodeficiency virus/acquired immunodeficiency syndrome (HIV/AIDS) presents a complex catch-22 in resource-poor countries because there is clear scientific evidence that even if mothers obtain appropriate medical treatment, the virus can and does transfer from maternal blood to maternal milk (though the risk varies depending on when treatment begins, how consistent and appropriate it is, and other factors), putting infants at increasing risk of becoming HIV positive the longer they breastfeed.[14] Yet the countries with the highest maternal HIV rates are also countries in which ensuring clean water is a constant challenge and women are too poor to buy formula, diagnosed and treated late and often suboptimally, and are often already malnourished. Must such women choose between losing their child to HIV/AIDS or losing it to malnutrition and starvation? Further, a child's potential to learn and to develop normally, to build its society for the next generation, is also undermined by poor health, malnutrition, and the social and behavioral consequences of parental illness and death.

Thus mothers' blood, milk, and social disorders are as closely related in the modern world as they were ritually related in early Christian texts. As the most vulnerable members of society, women and the young children they feed have historically suffered most from the problems of poverty and messages of social blame that are commonly traced, one way or another, to taboos about female body products. Some early Christians barred menstruating women from the eucharist, expected postpartum, bleeding, and lactating women to stay home until they could be ritually "churched" by a priest, and traditionally used menstruation to argue that women could not serve the altar as priests or deacons (although there is evidence that some women did[15]). The miracle of Mark 5, the story of the hemorrhaging woman who is healed after touching the hem of Jesus's garment, in a certain measure supports this taboo: the miracle is not that her blood was purified, but that it disappeared. Touching Jesus stops her bleeding; therefore she ceases to emit pollution. And men, too, might be viewed as ritually impure and disqualified from priestly service due to emissions of seminal fluids. Fluids must, thus, be controlled. And if a woman's flow is, like poverty, associated with shame, then practices that control bodily fluids, such as the imposed and deliberate cutting and bleeding in Badakhshan, may be used in an attempt to assert power—even if through a potentially risky practice that is maintained with the best possible intent by those with little power to alter their social and economic destitution.

Poverty always affects a society most deeply in the human bodies and human dignity of its weakest members. In his sermon on the famine and drought, Basil of Caesarea alludes to infants who were being brought to church in numbers. He identifies their bawling with a sort of inappropriate "confession, even though they have no grounds for grieving nor the knowledge or ability to pray."[16] It is the rich and greedy in the congregation who ought to weep in repentance, he says, and who ought to act out of compassion for the agricultural laborers weeping in the fields over the absent harvest and their starving wives and children.

Driven into debt beyond hope of solvency, parents in the ancient world often had to sell their children or, faced with a complex mix of social choices, abandon them to either death or slavery. Ancient documents frequently express the distress and shame of parents who had to make this choice. Children thus sold lost their inheritance and ties to their natural family, becoming property with not even their bodies at their own disposal for free moral choice. As the work of scholars Bernadette Brooten and Jennifer Glancy has highlighted, girls sold into slavery lost all power over the right to control their sexual choices. Even under purportedly Christian slave owners, a slave woman might not be able to follow the Christian teachings to obey parents or husbands, who were often unavailable or equally enslaved. A girl might find the Gospel passages about obeying even a coercive and unjust master at direct odds with biblical moral teaching to avoid fornication and adultery.[17] The tensions between being (not) a legal person and being legal property were inherent in a poverty and negation of all one's rights, even if slaves were not considered "poor" since they often had access to essential physical resources such as food, clothing, housing, and medical care.

Even free children in the ancient world faced a life fraught with health risks. Orphans as well as abandoned and donated children account for the many we hear about who, by the fifth century, lived in monastic institutions throughout the Christian world. Of the 15,000 human bones examined from the crypts of St. Stephen's monastery in Jerusalem, for example, 3,004 belonged to infants and children, the youngest being a prenatal seven-month-old fetus. Most of the bones belonged to children who died between age two and three, a common age for weaning.[18]

A few early Christian writers do speak positively about maternal blood and milk, although usually as a spiritual metaphor. Gregory of Nazianzus, for example, refers to both in the fifty-one epigrams that he wrote after his mother, Nonna, died of old age in church in the very act of prayer, her dead body found physically gripping the altar.[19] "The blood of the mother boiled for both her sons," Gregory writes in *epigram* 30, "but mostly for him whom she had suckled," that is, himself. In *epigram* 33, he identifies "her suffering flesh" with the martyrs' blood, in *epigram* 53 "dying at the place of sacrifice." By such a death, he says, "Nonna rose, a great sacrifice" (*epigram* 73), concluding, "This altar sent god-like Nonna to God" (*epigram* 74).

Nonna's physical association with the sacred altar is logical in light of the common early Christian association of widows with an "altar" for alms-offerings. But these positive references to blood and milk are associated with her "god-like" character rather than her specific female gender. When gendering of women's bodies is more explicit, the imagery of blood and milk flowing from them is rarely positive, even in stories of martyrdom. For example, when the married Roman noblewoman Perpetua and the slave woman Felicitas were martyred around 200 and fed to beasts in the arena, Felicitas's naked body evoked public comment because it was obvious that she had just given birth, as her breasts were still dripping milk. Her martyrdom is admirable in spite of this detail in the story, not because of it. Perpetua, also a new mother, is allowed to retain the honor of her class—at least by the storyteller—in that she enters the arena with a more "controlled" body: by the time she is forced to appear before the crowds, her milk has "miraculously" dried up. When women bleed in early Christian texts, their blood is ritually and socially "pure" only as it is linked with the meaningfully different flow of Christ's sacrifice.[20] Women's blood, unless it is a consequence of martyrdom, might be the stuff of kinship and nourishment, even that ultimate and divine nutritive kinship at the center of Christianity—engagement in Christ's blood—but only when it was clearly processed by exposure, whitening, a functional purification that distanced it from the producing body and made it suitable for the other body, the young, innocent "clean" infant and catechumen properly prepared to receive it.

BEYOND BLOOD: NUMBERS AND CASES

Just as in Badakhshan women and children's ritual "pollution" can be traced, historically, to maternal substance and the transfer of fluids, so children's poverty throughout the ages and in modern society continues to be inextricably linked with women's poverty, whether or not a supportive (usually also poor) father is present. "Sensing" need in these circumstances is not as easy as encountering homelessness on the city streets. Poor women and poor children are not always obvious among us, and they do not necessarily provoke (or want) voyeuristic pity and a soup-kitchen-style line with handouts. Because such need may hide from public view in the domestic corners of low-income households, low-paying jobs, and "safe" women's shelters, we may need raw statistics to begin to understand the extent of this problem.

Many of these statistics are global; one example is the "gender-related development index." This is a measure that shows, through annual demographic figures usually intended for economists, that the greatest disparity between men's and women's economic development, based on income, education, adult literacy, and life expectancy, is in the world's poorer countries. Men and women are more equivalent in these areas in more wealthy nations.[21] And yet the truth is not quite so straightforward. Most of the world's very poorest nations are in Africa; these countries have such dismal human development indices that, between war and starvation, there is little room for much measurable difference in deprivation between men and women. And in a world where life is short, men may spend a third to half of their lives as boys, that is, as children, within that very group at highest risk for suffering from poverty's lifelong effects. Further, in any culture there are obviously a significant proportion of men who will fall far below the poverty line even if they do earn more than many women.

Yet it is clear that women cannot assume that they enjoy economic equality simply because they live in a nation in which wealth and power are more available. In a famous study conducted in Sweden—a country in which we might expect economic gender equality—investigators demonstrated that the publication record, work profile, and accomplishments of women who were applying for science fellowships needed to be an average of two and a half times better than those of the male applicants before the (all-male) review committee perceived their applications as having equal funding merit.[22] This finding—and it was a very careful study—identifies a power bias that is especially troubling because it is apparently unconscious. If, as it seems, such a bias is a "natural" reflection of the way men view women, how then might those many men who are truly concerned about gender equities and who hold positions of power work to create the systems necessary to break the cycle perpetuating such bias? Given that most women earn less than most men, such a bias in the everyday marketplace directly contributes to perpetuating the poverty and deprivation that handicap women and children. As a logical *consequence* of such an imbalance between gender and economics, coupled with single parenting, related health expenses, and often a low self-image resulting from years of such pressure, even "ordinary" working women (and their children) can experience a loss of dignity and self-respect and spiral down the social ladder into the fragile and often violent world of poverty, destitution, and homelessness.

Women experience poverty, even shared and extreme poverty, differently than men. Celine D'Cruz, a founder of Slum Dwellers International, says, "housing is something that's very important to women. A man can come to a city and live under a bridge, a sheet, anywhere. But if a city can't provide for a woman, she's extremely vulnerable." When it comes to securing housing rights, "Women have much greater stamina for dealing with the complexities."[23] That is, women are more likely than men to persist through the red tape, shame, and administrative "hoops" of obtaining social assistance since they also face a much higher risk than men of suffering violence, victimization, and life-threatening abuse if help fails. Because it is not safe for women to live alone in many societies, women's poverty may also be related to a history of abusive relationships, early childbearing, and fear of reporting abuse. As Southern feminist writer Dorothy Allison puts it, "Behind my carefully buttoned collar is my nakedness, the struggle to find clean clothes, food, meaning, and money. Behind sex is rage, behind anger is love, behind this moment is silence, years of silence."[24]

The intersecting effects of poverty, women's lack of self-respect, and the violation of innate dignity also increase women's risk for stress-related diseases.[25] For example, my experience of living in a high-risk neighborhood, described in Chapter 2, fostered such a subconscious anxiety that for a few weeks after I moved to a safer apartment the sound of birds chirping in the early morning was startling enough to set off my inner alarms and increase my heart rate. Yet living in that neighborhood had been my choice, and I had the resources, energy, and opportunity to change my circumstances. Those limited by extreme poverty or denied such choice face physical stress without similar choices and healthy alternatives. This was true for many of the women I counseled during my experiences in nutrition clinics. Some of their stories so unsettled me that, like Dr. Keshavjee, I took notes simply to try and understand how they coped.

There was, for example, six-month-old Tommy,[26] whose mother and siblings lived in a low-income apartment in high-risk Roxbury, on welfare. When I saw Tommy, he had recently been hospitalized for salmonellosis, a dangerous bacterial infection that his doctors had traced to polluted tap water that his mother used to mix his formula. Without a car, she now had to add the expense and labor of buying water to the other challenges of living poor. She told me that her slum landlady and the Board of Health were not doing anything to address the problem.

There was Joan, whose two-year-old daughter, Peggy, had Prader-Willi syndrome, a genetic condition of mild mental retardation in which the affected individual is incapable of knowing when or learning to stop eating. The only way to prevent extreme morbid obesity in such individuals is to lock away and tightly control any access they have to food. Joan was a normal, loving mother who could not imagine such a prison-like environment for her daughter. She was also afraid, she said, that if she didn't give Peggy the food she wanted, Peggy would eat the many cockroaches that she enjoyed chasing around the apartment.

Little Yolanda, recovering from rickets, would never remember her mother's best housing choice when she was born: a slum apartment with drug-dealing neighbors. By the time I met her and her mother they had been forced to move to an emergency housing motel after one of the other tenants set the house on fire after a fight with the landlord. Yolanda's mother was too ashamed to tell me that she was effectively homeless; I learned about it later from a clinic worker who lived nearby.

Abe and Debby took me by surprise because they seemed so out of place, or perhaps because they seemed so much like me. A married white couple from England and Iowa attending a predominantly black inner city clinic, they needed supplemental food because Abe's promised job fell through soon after they moved their trailer east with all they owned. With one child and another on the way, they were moving from friend to friend every few weeks, and looking for a good church. "Boston sure has a lot of weird churches," Abe told me. "Right now I'd be happy to find some nice dead Lutherans."

And I will never forget Luella Mae from Mississippi. Twenty-one years old and in her first pregnancy, Luella Mae was four feet seven inches tall, weighed 75 pounds, and could not read. A victim of fetal alcohol syndrome, her mother's perpetual drunkenness before Luella Mae was born had left her with mild retardation as well as many congenital abnormalities that required surgery. One of her siblings, born without legs, died. Luella Mae came north to live with a foster "aunt," but she had been sexually active back home, her aunt said, "for food." Luella Mae had few choices about the situation life dealt her. People always told her she would die if she got pregnant, she told me, because she was so small. But she wanted to live, and she wanted to keep her baby. Because Luella Mae did not drink, her baby had a chance of being normal. But social services took her child.

The health risks that these women faced were often very extreme. A much more common and pervasive health risk associated with women's poverty, however, is obesity. In the United States, the poorer and less educated a woman is, the more likely she will be obese.[27] Low income and low education levels are consistently and directly associated with higher obesity rates among women but not among men.[28] Obesity increases a woman's risk for diabetes, heart disease, certain cancers, and other health problems. Yet these are the very same women who cannot afford to take time off from a low-paying job to see the doctor, and who often lack health insurance even if they could. To retain your health insurance benefits you either have to keep your job or be able to continue to pay the premiums.

Research suggests that poor women tend to be obese not because they are more often hungry, but because of what is called "food insecurity." "Food insecurity," an economic concept developed by the United Nations' Food and Agricultural Organization, means "limited or uncertain availability of nutritionally acceptable or safe foods."[29] Households with children are twice as likely to report food insufficiency; this is found most commonly in single parent families, in families without health insurance, and in households in which the parents did not finish high school. Poorer families said that "the most important factor in choosing and preparing foods was to ensure that no one would complain they are still hungry."[30] Human rights attorney Rebecca Cook distinguishes between women's *practical* health needs—those related to reproductive care—and their *strategic* needs, which she identifies as the need to play a human role in "the economic, political, spiritual, professional, and cultural life of communities."[31] Poor women and the children who grow up in such families often suffer both practically and strategically.

Shame is another common element in poverty for both men and women; men may express it through violence whereas women are more likely to turn it against themselves. In American and much of Western culture today obesity, as well as its related disempowering health problems, feeds the shame. As writer Dorothy Allison puts it, "Poor white trash I am for sure. I eat shit food and am not worthy."[32] A poor self image is a disability in the job market, and makes it that much harder to learn and keep a job. And though such problems are not limited to women, women's lower-paying jobs are more likely to reinforce this message.

WOMEN'S POVERTY AND THE EARLY
CHRISTIAN PAST

How does such a collection of neat facts and statistics relate to the history of poverty and the religious responses to poverty in the ancient world? After all, poor women in antiquity were probably far less likely to face the modern risks of obesity even though food insecurity was a constant fact of life for the ancients, rich and poor. The Roman and later Byzantine grain "dole," which addressed food insecurity only incidentally, was not meant for the poor. It offered supplemental food to homeowners (implicitly benefiting all their dependents, including slaves and favored clients) in only two cities—Rome and Constantinople—and included a few programs for upper-class or otherwise privileged orphans. When the dole ran short, people rioted. Many texts suggest that Christians were generous with food handouts, but state- and church-sponsored doles were never practiced broadly with very long-term consistency; practical relief varied from church to church, and town to town, most commonly dependent on an ever-changing range of available resources. Religious feasts—pagan and Christian—might offer food benefits to the whole community at some level, but these were not daily events and surely there was never enough for everyone. Even today, if a rural third-world village with a poor water supply and no more than a few hours of electricity each day sponsors a feast, hunger remains a perpetual risk once the leftovers (if any) have spoiled. In the ancient world, survival depended on patronage and a community identity. The nutritional status of women and children depended on their place within this broader structure. Dignity, then as now, was "a distinctly social (sometimes spiritual) concept...a distinctly subjective experience grounded in social and political relationships."[33] Even today, sociologists say that "levels of religiosity are significant to the well-being of individuals residing in high-poverty neighborhoods."[34] "Always find a church," a woman advised Barbara Ehrenreich when she traveled incognito to experience firsthand how the working poor in America survive.[35]

Some characteristics of poverty for women and children are timeless, although we may need different cultural "filters" to member their shapes with empathy and hold their images in mind as we turn to the gendered poverty of our own society. Class is relative, and so is culture, economics, and security. We cannot measure the past against modern "gender-related development" factors by assuming similar meaning for education level, literacy rates, income, and life expectancy, statistics that are simply unavailable for the ancient world. What we find instead are stories and enticing hints about widows, garments, holy women, prostitutes, and poor children.

Widows and Garments

Women were the recipients in one of the earliest organized Christian assistance programs in the church after Pentecost. The office of deacons was originally created solely to prevent ethnic discrimination and to ensure justice in the food distributions for Jewish and Greek Christian widows (Acts 6:1–6). Although the first deacon-administrators were men, wealthy women also served widows through private donations. The best early example of this is Dorcas/Tabitha in Acts 9:36–42, who was devoted to "good works and acts of mercy;" when she died, a group of gathered widows show Peter the "tunics and other clothing" Dorcas had made for them.[36] Early Christian texts such as the third-century *Didascalia* prescribe the very specific care that the church was to provide for widows, with the bishop serving as the intermediary between donors and recipients. We know that churches distributed relief supplies such as food and clothing in the early years of the fourth century because church inventories have survived that list the items seized from the churches during the Diocletian persecution. Some lists suggest the existence of a parish thrift shop or storehouse of supplies for the poor. For example, when state officials seized the church at Cirta in Numidia (modern Constantine in Algeria), the deacons handed over lamps, pitchers, kettles, candles, jars, and barrels, along with "82 women's tunics, 38 veils, 16 men's tunics, 13 pairs of men's shoes, 47 pairs of women's shoes, and 19 crude thongs."[37]

Church officials also wrote "orders-of-provision" (which survive on Egyptian papyri) that instructed stewards and administrators in the various churches to dispense a stated quantity of grain, wine, or clothing to the bearer; many of these orders concern widows. One, dated January 27, 480, instructs an administrator named Peter to "Provide to Sophia, widow, from the coats that you have, one coat for good use, one only."[38] Some lists identify these widows by their home church or as having children. Certainly not all church supplies were for the poor; tunics and veils could also have liturgical uses; a "veil" was among the "sacred ornaments of the church" that Cyril of Jerusalem sold in the mid-fourth century to buy food for famine victims, and this sale included an elegant length of fabric that the donor had intended for "the altar."[39] But the list of items in the church at Cirta on the day of its legal closure, when surely most Christians stayed at home, together with other evidence about standard clothing distributions to the poor, suggests that these were inventoried alms. Cirta is on a high plateau and the winters are very cold. Church donations of clothing were not limited to widows. John Chrysostom appeals for aid to homeless and wandering beggars as people who "need more nourishment, a heavier garment, a shelter, a bed, shoes, and many other things."[40] Basil also refers to thieves who, during a church gathering, stole "the cheap clothing of poor men" (*ep.* 286), although it is not quite clear whether these robes belonged to his assembled parishioners or if they were in a storeroom for the poor (which would have been part of the poorhouse) opportunely raided during the event.

Church widows were not always content with what they received, and they rarely received it without some implied expectations. Texts often speak of widows as functional church "employees" whose job it was to pray for their supporters. The *Apostolic Constitutions* 3.7.3 condemns some church-supported widows, discontent with their fixed income, who were making extra pocket money by loaning out funds at interest. But lending was not always discouraged. In the archives at Jeme, an Egyptian village from the Christian era, we find women lenders in about one-third of the texts concerning loans.[41] Though most of these were loans to men, the records show that women were more likely to borrow from women.[42] Widows at Jeme appealed to the church for help even when they clearly retained property or other resources. They were also at liberty to remarry. Such documents tell us that even widows not technically "on the church welfare rolls" could in certain cases request and expect assistance from the church.

Holy Women and Prostitutes

Homeless women have always been at greater physical risk of suffering personal violence than homeless or wandering men. Recognizing this, the early church came to direct, and even occasionally force, women into monastic alternatives. Macrina, for example, took starving women off the streets to join her ascetic household. Maura, one of the rare examples we have of a woman administrator in an early Christian hospital, in Oxy-rhynchus, may have done the same.[43] There are many stories of Christian women who disguised themselves as men in order to live safely alone in the desert, their secret often kept throughout their lives and revealed only when they died. Such "transvestite saints" are rarely encumbered with children.[44] Many of the stories of holy men describe how male ascetics shed not only goods but often wives and children, shuffling their dependent women into the care of nearby nuns. St. Antony did this when he adopted monastic life as a teenager after his parents died. At first keeping some of the family land to support his younger sister, he gave her to a convent of virgins and gave away the land once he chose to retreat more deeply into the desert.[45] Orphans might also be entrusted to individual nuns. One Egyptian papyrus is a letter from the nun Maria to Kyriakos, "the anchorite," requesting prayers on behalf of an orphaned boy whose father had left him with her.[46] And in the fifth century, we find a young ascetic boy who was put into the care of a holy woman, Hicelia, in a particularly interesting case.

Contrary to most ancient gender expectations, Hicelia was not only "building the church" (probably funding and apparently also directing the construction) of the Cathisma of the Mother of God on the road between Jerusalem and Bethlehem, but she was also leading liturgical reforms. Cyril of Scythopolis tells us that Hicelia "led the way" in celebrating the Feast of the Presentation (February 2) with candles. She took the young Theodosius under her wing because he could help her perform the church office; later he became a steward in the church she "built."[47] She disappears from the record as the story turns to Theodosius who, like most holy men of his day, left town to avoid the responsibilities of church leadership. Hicelia may have been a woman of wealth and aristocratic social rank, since a number of such women in the fifth century funded building projects and founded churches and hospitals. But few are so openly praised for liturgical construction, for teaching men, and for leading reform. Her disciple-assistant, Theodosius, founded the largest monastic community in the Judaean desert, a complex containing hostels, hospitals for monks, for visitors, and for the poor, a home for the aged, a special enclosure for monks with mental illness, and four churches.[48] As discussed in Chapter 3, other fifth-century hospitals also cared for both poor men and women. When Rabbula, bishop of Edessa, instituted church-funded healthcare reforms, he made sure that the sick poor in his hospitals received good food, soft beds, and clean linen, with deaconesses (dedicated virgins) appointed to minister to women for the sake of modesty.[49]

Although male monastic solitaries rarely cared for young children, let alone young girls, we do have at least one story of such a relationship from the Egyptian desert tradition, in which a seven-year-old orphan, Maria, is adopted by her paternal uncle Abraham, a solitary hermit-monk who lived in the village. After giving away Maria's considerable inheritance "to the needy and orphans" so that she "might not be entangled in the affairs of this world," the monk established boundaries—literally. He built the girl a room attached to his hermitage, and limited his access to her to a small window that he created in the wall. Through this window he could teach her (and share food), but they could not see one another. In this way, the story says, Maria lived with her uncle for twenty years, learning his monastic way of life.

But Uncle Abraham was, like many monastics intent on prayer, not very attentive to his young disciple. When Maria was eventually tricked into leaving her cell and was violently raped by a visiting monk, she blamed herself and fled the village to become a prostitute. It was a few days before Abraham noticed that she was gone, and "two years" before he left his cell to look for her. Finding her in a city brothel, Abraham cunningly rescued her from the female brothel keeper, and the two returned to their adjoining monastic cells in the village. There, after continual weeping, strict asceticism, modesty, and prayer, Maria was graced with the gift of healing. Where her uncle had combined his monastic solitude with a social role in the village that included his choice to care for his young kinswoman, Maria's village identity as a repentant "holy woman" goes even further. She returns to her cell but not to the solitude of her childhood. Her repentant tears at first break everyone's heart as they pass by her cell until, eventually "crowds of people came to her daily and she would heal them all by her prayer for their salvation."[50] Outliving her uncle, she spent the next decade serving the community as a monastic authority known for her therapeutic social action. Her story is narrated by a deacon who was a devoted friend or disciple, and he ends the tale with a long lament about his own personal unworthiness when faced with the holiness of such lives.

Maria's story illustrates how early Christian monastic care for the poor might have affected orphaned children and women. Abraham, despite his inattention, offered Maria an unusual but protective support structure. Their reputations were safe because of their kinship and the architecture of the cell. Maria's provisions were as secure as her uncle's, and those in the community who revered and provided for the hermit would likely have shown similar interest in the child. Maria was clearly capable of leaving the cell; and how many children in antiquity had a room of their own and constant proximity to their guardian? Unlike Antony, Uncle Abraham does not see Maria as any threat to his life as a hermit, either before her rape or after her return, when she begins to draw crowds. The cell that was for twenty years a place built to remain unseen now became a site that drew the needy; the place of her violation, self-blame, and despair became a place of redemption for the whole village. Maria's role is transformed from that of a dependent under her familial patron to a patron herself. It was to such holy men and women and to saintly shrines like theirs that parents in the ancient world often came when their children were ill. We find such stories in the lives of women such as Macrina and the fifth-century *Life and Miracles* of St. Thekla.[51] Some ancient healing shrines, such as that of St. Artemius, specialized in afflictions such as inguinal hernias that were common in young children, and Christian healing sanctuaries dedicated to other saints or martyrs who healed "for free" often drew the poor and desperate, including mothers with young children.

Women who face the extremes of poverty and violence sometimes prefer to remain socially "invisible," indistinguishable, and even "normal" to the rest of us, as if safety in all areas of life requires the same invisibility that offers protection against private abuses. Women who "hid" in men's disguise in the early Christian desert knew this instinctively. Even women who today have the courage to proactively flee domestic abuse find it necessary to hide, to act in silence, to lie low, as incognito as possible. Yet in encountering such women, it is often obvious, even to those of us who have never faced such extreme threats, that something is very wrong.

This aspect of "sensing the poor" and its call to an empathy for women's needs was emphasized to me in a particularly poignant way early one Easter morning several years ago during a monastic vigil. A local Episcopal men's monastery sponsors this annual Easter vigil; the doors open at 4:00 AM and the service lasts for three hours. The monastery is very small, with three distinct worship spaces—the rear nave, the side chapel, and the choir—each progressively farther from the outer door and closer to the altar. About 4:30 AM, after all of the coveted choir seats were taken and moments before the service began, a woman entered the choir area, searched about almost frantically for a seat, and then insisted that she would remain there despite the crowds, sitting on the floor, although there were still open seats elsewhere in the sanctuary.

After her entrance, which happened in silence but seemed dramatic in the otherwise total stillness of the chapel, it was hard not to study her, and yet there was nothing unusual about her except her behavior. She was clean, not obviously homeless, in her mid-twenties, and dressed very simply. Yet somehow she was emotionally vacant, very alone. She was obviously literate, intent to follow the order of service, and otherwise polite. Why the urgent compulsion to worship so near to the altar that she was willing to spend three cold predawn hours on the hard marble floor? Those who were watching her very closely found out soon enough. One unguarded moment, during that sudden doze that threatens any sleepy participant who rises in the dead night hours for a candlelight vigil, her grip on her trench coat slipped and it became evident that she was wearing almost nothing underneath. Immediately she woke up and took tight hold again, and all the watchers in that place were ready to forgive. For it was then clear that she might indeed have good reason to seek out the safest enclosed location in the chapel, as close to the altar as possible, as far from the door as she could go without actually entering the monks' enclosure. Although those in the sanctuary were startled by her choices and did not know her circumstance, her affect was clearly that of a woman facing poverty at its most desperate limits, forced to keep her mind emotionally vacant, as far as possible from her body.

After the service was over dawn came, the candles were put out, the hymns were at their most festal, and all the bells were rung; the congregation then dispersed. I never saw her there again. But she reminded me of other women I had known, like those in the Roxbury clinic who lived so close to perpetual crisis that they were not always entirely present, as if poised to instantly disintegrate and disappear at the slightest threat of their carefully gripped shame being exposed.

Few people who deliberately choose poverty for religious or social reasons find it necessary to react to perceived threats with such obviously public behaviors. Such reactions are usually conditioned by chronic destitution and a lifetime of risk and stress. Choice, after all, implicitly denies victimization. Choice is about doing what is within one's power and one's possibilities. Choice can be measured only within the subjectivity of the one who chooses. We can choose freedom, choose to perpetuate victimization and violence, choose independence, or choose codependency. All choices are limited by certain constraints that are beyond our control, with some being more difficult than others. Christian women eager to obediently submit themselves to "God's will" may too often find themselves trapped into what appears to be a voluntary poverty, but which may in fact be disempowering subservient dynamics to authorities who are all too human, progressively undermining the self-confidence needed to make wiser choices.

Gender and Class

The narratives from the ancient world about women who chose poverty and a life of monastic philanthropy, almost always written by men, commonly contain a subtext of sexuality that deliberately appeals to the interests of the male (albeit monastic) audience that saves and reads such stories. This subtext may come at the expense of what poor women "really" thought, since it is the monk who tells or writes the story. In most cases only rich, elite women who chose monastic divestment had the power to force other details into their life story. Melania the Elder and her granddaughter, Melania the Younger, were two such women. The writer Palladius called Melania the Elder "that female man of God." Widowed at twenty-two, Melania had a passion for reading Origen, and practiced hospitality for nearly forty years, each year donating more of her immense wealth "to churches, monasteries, guests and prisons."[52] She was viewed as "holy" even though she essentially abandoned her only surviving son, Valerius Publicola, leaving him to be raised by rich relatives while she took off on her long pilgrimages. It may be no surprise that Publicola was not impressed when his own daughter, Melania the Younger, decided to emulate her peripatetic grandmother. Relieved when both of her young children and her father died, the younger Melania and her husband, Pinian, adopted monastic celibacy and traveled across the empire. As exuberant as the older Melania in philanthropic practices, the couple used their wealth to lavishly help the poor and needy, freeing those who were in prison for debt, visiting the sick, and selling property to fund monasteries and hospices. Fluent in Greek and Latin, the younger Melania was a prodigious reader of canons (church rules), sermons, and the lives of the Fathers; she also copied both the Old and New Testament for her friends and monastics.[53] These two Melanias and Basil's sister, Macrina, are only a few of many women from this period in Christian history whose stories demonstrate the self-confidence and relative autonomy that rich women might enjoy. Hicelia, mentioned above, was another, as was the fifth-century empress Eudocia, famous for her theological support for and funding of churches and monastic hospices, and also Olympias, a fantastically wealthy widow who seems to have supported John Chrysostom's charities almost single-handedly.[54] Upper class women usually retained sexual honor in the monastic life whereas lower class women, such as the converted harlot Mary of Egypt, were understood to be entering Christian life without it, their religious practices gaining them (often very briefly since they frequently died soon afterward) a dignity that was not viewed as socially theirs by rights. Regardless of an ascetic's former state, however, voluntary poverty was consistently regarded as admirable, just as involuntary poverty was recognized as inhuman and unjust. Poverty and class intersect in stories of such choices for men as well as for women, in the ancient as well as in the modern world.

Yet across all classes in these stories we may be occasionally reminded that neither abuse nor victimization is limited to the behaviors of one particular gender; injustice is a human experience. Violence against the poor in the ancient world, as in the present, cannot be blamed solely on men with power, nor can its effects be limited to one's destitute peers. It was well recognized that the powerful rich—both men and women— often exercised the greatest degree of violence against those in need. It was, after all, the rich who had the funds to lend out at exorbitant interest rates and the servants to turn the screws on their victims. Violence could even be cloaked in good intentions. Jerome tells of a very rich Christian woman distributing alms in the Basilica of St. Peter in Rome. Flanked by household servants, she distributed one coin to each beggar in a line, "with her own hand to increase her reputation for sanctity." But when "an old woman, full of years and rags, ran in front of the line to get a second coin...she got no coin but the lady's fist in her face, and for her dreadful offense she had to pay with her blood."[55]

A social service administrator from the fifth or sixth century tells the story of a similar dilemma between two men. Distributing linen garments from Egypt to the needy in Antioch, he noticed one man who stood in the same line three times. When the beggar presented for his fourth piece of clothing, the supervisor scolded him publicly and, taking the fourth garment, the beggar went away in shame. Yet that night Christ, wearing the four garments, appeared in a dream to the supervisor and said, "Do not be dismayed; inasmuch as you provided those things for the poor man, they became my raiment."[56] The administrator repented and thereafter gave "to all who asked." In both stories donor and recipient share the same gender; in both the recipient suffers publicly for presumed "greed"; and in both the moral of the story encourages righteous generosity.

CONCLUSIONS

Not all women who live with poverty face victimization or abuse. Many do the best they can within close-knit families and warm and intricate social networks, even when they find themselves facing extreme life challenges. Carolyn was one such woman. I met her in our health center when she came in with her four-year-old granddaughter, Tina. Black, sixty-one years old, and head of a household of single women, Carolyn still worked full-time while taking care of her eighty-three-year-old mother as well as her daughter and granddaughter. Judy, Tina's mother, had sickle cell disease, a seriously debilitating and incurable genetic blood disorder that often requires hospitalization for acute and painful blood platelet crises and that shortens its victims' lives. Carolyn brought Tina along to our visit because Judy was in the hospital with kidney failure. Tina had inherited her mother's condition. But Carolyn took it all in stride, even though she had to take a day off from work to attend our clinic and she was the only wage-earner in the home. As we said goodbye after Tina's appointment, Carolyn joked, "Do you know anywhere I can go for a vacation?" We both laughed; it was all we could do. She was just one of many women I met who faced seemingly impossible hurdles with apparent good cheer as they tried to meet their family's most basic needs.

Yet while poverty is a "normal" condition in many countries and cultures, women and children are ever at risk of paying for poverty with their life blood. In Badakhshan, poverty literally cuts the flesh. In the modern West, the external scars are often visible in other ways, manifested in obesity, low self-image, violence, shame, and exhaustion. One of the comic tragedies of working class women is that they sometimes feel guilty if they are not exhausted. The poor in antiquity, faced with seasonal and often extreme food insecurity, high energy output in walking and manual labor, and different food choices, manifested poverty in more obvious ways, such as malnutrition, compromised living conditions, the risk for slavery and child mortality, and a shortened lifespan. Shame echoes across cultures, however, often expressed in self-denigrating observations and laments, and is found in the ancient world in stories of poor women more frequently than in stories of poor men. Then as now, shame is closely linked to sexual vulnerability, with the risk (or actuality) of violence and abuse. In "the suppressed history of class," writes one author, a key theme is "how low class status, and especially downward mobility, produces shame."[57] Indeed, women's shame today is so closely linked to a lack of self-confidence that the Episcopal church suggests that women reflect on whether their passive submission and self-denigration may be sinful. "Certain temptations are typical features of many women's lives," wrote Martin Smith in his guide to preparing for confession. "There is less temptation to disobedience and rebellion, but more of a tendency to give in to victimization, an unholy exaggeration of turning the other cheek, self-suppression and taking the blame. Some women (and also a significant number of men) may want to search their hearts with special attention to these areas."[58] Such attitudes are not only spiritually unhealthy, but also foster and perpetuate the dynamics of poverty. Poor men, women, and children are often forced to use different currencies to barter for rights that most of us take for granted. In his memoir on being homeless, *Travels with Lizbeth*, the writer Lars Eighner muses that "the rich, of course, know that rights are bought and sold, and the poor know it too. Those between them live in an illusion."[59]

When "beggars" assert the right to make choices, they may shock or even anger donors who expect them to behave as passive and receptive objects. Diane White, a columnist for the *Boston Globe*, described one such experience.

One day on a busy city street corner, White met an old woman who was dressed in a medley of pink rags, her hair white and tangled, her face dirty except for a smear of bright pink lipstick. The woman approached White more brashly than most panhandlers. "Can you spare a dollar?" she demanded. White writes, "I could spare a dollar—several dollars in fact." And she usually gave to the elderly who asked for handouts. But unwilling to open her purse in public to search for dollar bills, she offered the woman two quarters she found in her pocket. Seeing the coins, White wrote, the woman "recoiled from them theatrically, as if they were poisoned. She stepped back from my offending hand and waved away my inadequate offering. She looked down her nose at me with a disdainful, disgusted expression." Embarrassed, White laughed and said, "That's an interesting approach." And the woman replied, "Don't knock it. I make a living this way."

Watching afterward from a distance, White saw the woman repeat the performance to other pedestrians. Reflecting on the encounter, she wrote, "I was angry at her for making me feel small, for taking me by surprise, for not living up to my notions of how she should behave, for cheating me out of an easy way to feel good about myself for a few seconds."[60] When we give expecting nothing more than a grateful "Thank you. God bless you," the joke may be on us.

Sensing the poor with an empathy that is attuned to gender dynamics such as those outlined in this chapter is not always easy or simple. Assumptions about gendered expectations may influence how we perceive such experiences in our own firsthand encounters. As an educated, North American woman raised in a family that assumed gender equality and a woman's right to economic independence as a vital component of responsible maturity, I may see the world very differently from women in other cultures, classes, and even Christian communities. Yet my own extended family's experiences—firmly within the working class—may also color my own perceived limits and expectations. For example, my innate sense of entitlement—to dignity, privacy, respect, and free speech—may also influence how I practice or think about philanthropy. It is always sobering to fall short of our own ideals and good intentions. Yet as doctor to the poor Paul Farmer put it, emphasizing the inherently endless and obvious irony of philanthropic sharing, "All the great religions of the world say, love thy neighbor as thyself. My answer is, I'm sorry, I can't, but I'm gonna keep on trying, *comma*."[61]

MARIA'S CHOICE

Empathy seeks truth, and along its difficult way, it
makes the discovery of compassion as well.
——Patricia Hampl, *I Could Tell You Stories*[1]

Jacob of Sarug, the bishop whose image of the poor as fertile soil is explored
in Chapter 3, died in November 521, his own aged body returning to the
ground. His followers buried him in the Church of St. Mary in the city of
Amida, modern Diyarbakır in Turkey. Amida is still enclosed by the three
miles of dramatic black basalt walls that were built to protect it in antiquity, entered through four gates, and marked by the remnants of eighty-
two watchtowers, on a hill overlooking the Tigris river.

In the year that Jacob died a traveler along the Tigris might have
glimpsed, hurrying through one of the gates, another Maria, not the
repentant prostitute of Chapter 5, but a young virgin who was, with her
mother, Euphemia, fleeing the city in perhaps the first journey away from
home in her life. Whether she knew it or not that day, Maria of Amida
was an expert in the wide range of options and tensions that follow anyone
whose life is dedicated to philanthropic giving and sharing the world, the
second of the three paradigms this book explores.

Options and tensions over how best to share the material gifts and
resources of the earth and society are perpetual challenges to any philanthropic discourse. This is especially true when the needs of those with
whom we desire to share are aggravated by their suffering within unjust
systems. Such systems tend to destabilize individual access to the necessary goods and services that donors and friends hope to empower them
to use. Most of the world's economic systems in both the richest and poorest nations inevitably contain elements of injustice in one form or another,
and early Christian texts have much to say about giving, sharing, divesting, and redistributing—whatever we call that kinetic motion of material goods that does not fit into an organized market economy—in such

environments. Philanthropic examples and critiques of various systems for addressing the causes and effects of poverty more often face human need as an urgent emergency, with responses running in kneejerk-like humanitarian response through the popular media, in international economic rhetoric, even as such response may be defended by an appeal to the texts of early Christian history. Yet the problems of human need remain ever among us, perpetually open to the real change that is possible for individual people, families, and communities in need. The ideals of material redistribution that affect global justice may influence the choices made every day by bank presidents, stock consultants, politicians, coffee traders, and any two-year-old child faced with another child holding a desired object. Effective sharing is as complicated and nuanced as any other human relationship. One way to examine these responses without being overwhelmed by the needs and pressures of supply and demand is to take time for measured considerations of individual stories, such as that of Maria of Amida.

In discussions about options informed by deliberate religious ideologies, early Christian texts offer a range of models that readers can (and often do) order to fit their own neat assumptions about personal property and ownership. But such texts are, like the problem of poverty itself, not as simple as they might at first appear. When we examine these texts to compare their issues and suggested solutions, we may find that they offer a variety of views and ways to interpret the biblical sources on issues such as ownership, alms, divestment, gender behaviors, and moral life choices. Some of the theoretical issues of difference were discussed in previous chapters. This chapter looks at such differences in the context of one specific story. The story of Maria of Amida and her family offers a narrative that illustrates a few of these nuances and the tensions of choice that face anyone seeking to make a place and a difference with that fabric of our material world in which we hold a certain measure of control.

It is a Syrian monk from the region, known to posterity as John of Ephesus for his late-in-life episcopate in that city, who tells all that we know about Maria of Amida.[2] In John's *Lives of the Eastern Saints*, her story is the first among several stories of holy women he has known personally. He introduces her in his description of her mother:

> Euphemia had been wed as a girl and she had a daughter to whom she had given religious instruction since she was quite small. When her husband died this Euphemia and her young daughter had arranged their life so that Euphemia came to move away altogether from a secular existence,

turning to the inner world and the example of her sister [whose name was Mary]. [Euphemia] took up a regulated life of devotion and wore the garb of a religious, while learning the psalms and teaching them to her daughter, who had been thoroughly instructed since her early youth in psalmody, the Scriptures, and writing.... Euphemia set herself fixed times for reciting the services and for prayers, both night and day.... [S]he served two orders together—asceticism and relief for the afflicted.[3]

Euphemia and her daughter Maria supported themselves, John says, by a small weaving business at home. Each day they wove a fixed quantity of goats' wool yarn for the noblewomen of the city; they lived on half of the income and used the other half for Euphemia's charities. John knew Euphemia personally and probably lived for a time in the house she hired for his monastic community when the monks were driven out of their monastery during a period of religious persecution. John, Euphemia, and Maria were Syrian Christians who suffered oppression for their views about how to describe the relationship between Christ's coinherent human and divine natures. In fact, it is now recognized that both these Syrian Christians (whom their opponents called "Monophysites") and the Roman church leaders from Constantinople who opposed them (called "Chalcedonians") actually shared very similar views, but differed in their descriptions and emphases. Yet even in Constantinople loyalties to these two viewpoints were divided, with the emperor, Justinian, supporting the "Chalcedonian" position and his wife, Theodora, actively patronizing Syriac "Monophysite" bishops and monks such as John of Ephesus.

Among the opposing parties in the city of Amida there was no such friendly differing, only open persecution. Christians in Amida such as John and Euphemia, who resisted the Chalcedonian position, formed a close community, supporting one another in times of trial. Yet despite all that John tells us about Euphemia, Maria remains a curious enigma, her personal choices obscured by her deliberate seclusion in her mother's house. John says only that she

was working day and night singlemindedly and without complaint. If one of her companions or someone else said to her, "Your mother leaves you at work by yourself all day," she would say, "My mother's labor is greater than all labors, and God strengthens me through her prayers." So the blessed woman [Euphemia] was freed a little from worry since her daughter worked for their needs.[4]

Maria's defense of her mother's absence while she labored at home is the only direct dialogue John allows Maria in his narrative. It is Euphemia who does all of the talking; until the end of the story, Maria remains silent and hidden, sitting in an inner room and weaving until she and her mother are driven out of town. It is not until they return to Amida after five years of wandering together with Euphemia's older sister, Mary, that Maria, daughter and niece of John's two more dominant heroines, is finally freed to follow her own heart. Yet because her mother and aunt die within a few days of one another, even at the end of the story her choice remains a mystery.

While living with her mother and then wandering with her mother and aunt, Maria encountered a wide range of philanthropic activities. Indeed, between Euphemia and Mary her life was affected by practices that included (at different times and circumstances) all of the following options: living with wealth; living with poverty; holding a steady job in order to give away a portion of her income; living wholly on alms; living a Robin Hood–like life by openly seizing neighbors' wealth to help the poor; living as a wife, as a widow, or as a virgin ascetic; virginity contained; virginity lived in public wandering and public prayer; living alone; living with family; living in a monastic community. Indeed, these encompass the full range of giving, receiving, being accepted and praised by neighbors and fellow Christians, and being persecuted and driven out of town. In other words, Maria would have been familiar with most of the options discussed in Christian dialogue about material exchange today. Because she spent her life in the shadow of two very different models and did not (at least in the story as we have it) exclusively choose one lifestyle over another, Maria's silent, active awareness offers a background against which we can explore these issues, a lens through which the empathetic reader might appreciate the tensions and options she faced living with her mother's and aunt's choices, and perhaps how such tensions and options might inform modern religious responses to human need.

EUPHEMIA'S CHOICE: SOCIAL ACTIVISM

A modern reader might easily identify Euphemia with Dorothy Day, the twentieth-century politically radical, theologically conservative founder of the Catholic Worker movement. Like Day, Euphemia was a social activist who intentionally lived in close and direct contact with the poor, forcefully working for their benefit with no fear of either law or government authorities. Like Day she had a small daughter when she chose to abandon her "secular existence" and took up the "regulated life" of Christian devotion and appearance, reciting the daily prayers and psalms of the church without entering into a formal association with a monastery or pledging the usual monastic obedience to a religious superior. While clearly following Christian disciplines in every aspect of her life, she was, in her neighbors' eyes, a law unto herself.

In her social activism, Euphemia remained in her own house, made her own independent decisions, and refused all charity that was offered for the benefit of herself or her daughter. All of the alms she received she spent on others. Daily, Euphemia sought out direct, personal contact with the city's poor, sick, and prisoners. Each morning found her walking the streets and combing the squares for the homeless needy, asking for news of destitute widows and orphans. She would sit down beside each in turn, John tells us, to learn about their situation and ask what they wanted to eat that day. She spent alms and half of her personal income on this food and medicine for the poor, delivering it to each in person. Every evening she went home to weave for a few hours and to recite prayers and psalms. John adds that she often took beggars home. Predictably, the demand for her services soon outstripped her resources. As it did, the reader learns how she stretched her income to generate additional aid for the poor. She might, for example, pawn household utensils for small change to give away. And when the Chalcedonian Christians began their persecution in an attempt to force religious conformity, Euphemia took in the homeless monks. She hired and furnished large houses and obtained the supplies needed for a new monastic chapel. She took over kitchen duties, ensuring that the monks always had fresh bread, hot cooked lentils, and vegetables. Faced with these new expenses, she launched more aggressive visits to her rich neighbors, boldly commandeering whatever she needed if any were reluctant to donate voluntarily. Meanwhile, she continued to scour the roads, inns, and other monasteries in the region to find any who remained poor and sick, now with particular concern for persecuted monastics. She carried them to the local hospitals where she gave the necessary orders for their care. John describes her physical presence as predictably intimidating, her tongue effective at getting results, and her bare feet perpetually bloodied and blistered. He was clearly fond of her, writing, "We, too, said to her many times in a joking manner, 'Don't kill yourself so violently.'"[5] The sectarian opponents considered her power a threat, treating Euphemia and her daughter as a pair when they objected that "the citizens revere and honor them more than the bishops!"[6]

Everything that we know of this persecution at Amida comes from John, and he was undoubtedly a biased witness. He describes terrible force, even to death, exerted on those who refused to take the communion of the church from Constantinople, the standard method of inducing theological conformity in the intra-Christian theological controversies of the fifth, sixth, and seventh centuries. Euphemia was as particular about whose eucharistic bread she would take as she was about alms. Just as she ate only the bread earned by her own labor, so too she would commune only with those whose Christian position she trusted. Communing with the "enemy" was viewed as a serious betrayal of one's own position in such debates at this time. Forced eucharistic communion was, in fact, used, just as earlier pagan Roman persecution of the Christians in the first three centuries had tested loyalties by forcing sacrifice to the emperor. For her refusal to concede to the political pressure in sixth-century Amida, Euphemia—but apparently not Maria—was imprisoned around 521. Only when "the whole city" objected was she released, and her best option even then was to leave town.

EARLY CHRISTIAN VIEWS ON PROPERTY, GIVING, AND HOSPITALITY

Euphemia and Maria were both literate women, living in a city that was at that time ruled by the Roman empire. Their social connections included the very rich, various communities of monks, and the very poor. Euphemia had access to written Christian sources, including scripture and other manuscripts that would have circulated among this population. Her social choice to address the needs of the poor was not unique to her particular time, theological context, or place. Although the way that these women lived might seem severe to a modern reader, their activities were well within the range of realistic options that early Christians understood when they practiced material giving and sharing. Euphemia's choices demonstrate that she shared particular views on property, on "right" giving, and on hospitality that are also found in other early Christian practices and teachings on these topics.

She clearly knew, for example, the biblical injunction to identify the poor with the body of Christ, repeated so frequently in the sermons of Jacob of Sarug, the Cappadocians, and John Chrysostom. She appeals to this image as she chides her resistant neighbors, scolding that

> It's all very well for you to sit, with your servants standing around attending you, bringing you successive courses of delicacies and wines and the best white bread, and very fine rugs, while God is overcome in the market, swarming with lice and fainting with hunger. Do you not fear Him? How will you call upon Him and He answer you, when you treat Him contemptuously in this way?[7]

Her lifestyle also models that suggested by Bishop of Rabbula of Edessa's Canon 24, which reads, "All those who have become disciples of the Messiah shall not be covetous to possess more than their needs, but they shall distribute it to the poor."[8]

Euphemia's practice also demonstrates, for example, that she believed that it was acceptable for Christians to retain ownership of at least some personal property. She owned her house and her household goods, and she had or could obtain the resources needed to rent other houses for the displaced monks. She might have agreed with Clement of Alexandria, who around the year 200 pointed out the obvious problems with living as a Christian for someone who practiced total divestment. If having "given up the use of wealth, but now being in difficulties and at the same time yearning after what he threw away," Clement writes, the foolish self-styled ascetic "endures a double annoyance, the absence of means of support and the presence of regret."[9] It is one's attitude, not the level of one's goods, Clement says, that requires a real change. Possessions and wealth are, rather,

> to be welcomed ... because they have been prepared by God for the welfare of mankind.... An instrument, if you use it with artistic skill, is a thing of art; but if you are lacking in skill, it reaps the benefits of your unmusical nature, though not itself responsible. Wealth too is an instrument of the same kind. You can use it rightly; it ministers to righteousness. But if one uses it wrongly, it is found to be a minister of wrong. For its nature is to minister, not to rule.[10]

Clement's treatise is unusual among early Christian texts on charitable divestment because it deliberately defends wealth, even though that defense is part of a call for a simple generous life in which the individual is entirely detached from the inner pull of possessions. Many authors recognized that Clement's views reflect a reality common to many of his other early Christians contemporaries, emphasizing the good effects that generous giving can have even if the donor cannot attain the "ideal" of more sacrificial economic divestment. The *Shepherd of Hermas*, another second-century text, also assumed a certain status quo of wealthy Christians, describing a salvific symbiosis between the wealthy who enabled the poor to live and the poor who saved the rich by their prayers.[11] Justin Martyr described church-funded aid to the needy in Rome in the mid-second century that was generated by weekly donations to help "orphans and widows, and those who are in want on account of sickness or any other cause, and those who are in bonds, and the strangers who are sojourners among [us] and, briefly,...all those in need."[12] This acceptance of Christian ownership persisted despite the radical call to asceticism; Basil of Caesarea begged his audience to give at least a portion of their wealth for the well-being of their soul, even if they insisted on keeping back funds sufficient to serve the basic needs of their more transient physical bodies.[13]

Euphemia's choices also demonstrate her deliberate distinction between donor and recipient, even as she models a close personal engagement between the two. She retains—with great effort—both the power she has to give alms or gifts and the right to refuse them for herself. She is always the active agent in transferring donations from her rich neighbors to the poor whom she serves. It is Euphemia who buys the food, carries the sick to hospitals, rents the monastic houses, directs her daughter's education, strict enclosure, and worship, and is in charge of the weaving, even though Maria does most of the work. This focus on "clean money"—charitable funds generated by just labor practices—is yet another common theme in early Christian stories. A popular sermon "On Mercy and Justice" from the fourth or fifth century, for example, taught, "Show mercy from your own earnings, not from injustice,"[14] and "Combine justice with mercy, spending in mercy what you possess with justice."[15] This sermon distinguishes between Christ's "perfect" followers, those who give up all of their material possessions to dedicate their lives to prayer and holy asceticism (in other words, those who adopt the divestment practices that Clement discourages), and the "rest," that is most people, for whom Christ "ordained allotment and sharing of what they have, so that in this way they might be seen as imitators of the kindness of God, showing mercy and giving and sharing."[16] This same theme—of helping the needy only with income earned by "honest labor"—is also evident in another early text, the *Didascalia*. This text, usually considered to be the product of a Syriac-speaking community in the second or third century, prescribes liturgical relationships that ensure that anything given to church-supported widows comes only from honest work.[17]

Not all Christians shared such scruples. Some early Christians are condemned for lending money at interest rates as high as twenty-four percent and then seeking heavenly credit by giving alms to the poor whom they themselves have created.[18] And the apocryphal *Acts of Peter* defends an immoral woman's gift of gold, even praising her for it, "because the afflicted could now be relieved" and because she gave it out of a sense of debt to Christ.[19] In the *Acts of Thomas*, the apostle has no qualms about building a heavenly mansion for the unbelieving king by using the king's more earthly building funds to alleviate the suffering of his poorest subjects. Thomas never seems to question how the money he is spending came into the royal coffers. Rich misers are sometimes cleverly "tricked" into almsgiving by appealing to their more self-interested motives.

Euphemia's choice also demonstrates a particular model of hospitality. Generous as she is, she is highly selective about her use of personal domestic space. Within a culture in which young girls were expected to stay out of men's company, Euphemia closely guards her daughter's enclosure in the home. And although she herself visits the needy once or twice a day and carries them to shelter and medical care, even sometimes into her own home, her home seems somehow to remain largely a place set aside for private work and worship. Euphemia's hospitality more closely resembles an outdoor ministry than one regularly welcoming strangers at home, until the monks arrived. Even then Euphemia carefully separates her private living space from that of the monks. She supplies them with every inanimate object they might need: "with icons, pictures, chests, and all sorts of things—even the eucharistic vessels [and] liturgical books...great mats and curtains and rugs."[20] But once her shopping (or neighborly raiding) is over, she and Maria retire into their own space and, except for Euphemia's cooking, leave the monks to manage for themselves. Even when, John says, "the work she and her daughter did became insufficient for the men's needs [and] she was forced for the sake of the men to accept what they needed so that she could relieve their sufferings," he makes it clear that "she herself refused to eat with them from this source."[21]

Euphemia's hospitality is different from that of Basil of Caesarea, who actively built and staffed an episcopal poor house and who was directly involved in its administration. Euphemia may have known of the model that Rabbula's Syriac Canon 16 from Edessa advises, that "in every church that exists a house shall be known in which the poor, that come there, shall rest,"[22] but she did not make her house in Amida into such a place. Nor does Euphemia use her money and her services to aid the many hospitals that were connected to the churches in this period, although she does add to their patient load by carrying there the sick poor she finds in the streets. Loud and dominant as she is, Euphemia does not try to do everything. She zealously uses both her own resources and the system itself to benefit as many of the city's needy as possible. She has her limits, and considers it more important to defend her theological beliefs, even at the expense of being banished from the city and the needy she so passionately serves.

Throughout John's account of her social activism, we do not find a single instance of either Euphemia or Maria attending church. In fact, the church is mentioned only when the religious opposition tries to drag them in and force them to receive the eucharistic elements. The two women probably participated in communion with the monks, since John so explicitly includes eucharistic vessels among those supplies that she provides for his community.

MARY'S CHOICE: ASCETIC CONTEMPLATION

Euphemia's older sister, Mary, whose lifestyle (John says) influenced both Euphemia and Maria, chose practices that were yet again very different from theirs. In fact, John begins his biographical note of the women by describing Mary's choice at length: "Mary was a pure virgin, and from her childhood she chose for her part quiet abstinence, great feats of fasting, many vigils, constant prayers, exertion in charity, and wandering." This wandering led her to Jerusalem, where

> For three years Mary went about praying, without entering anyone's house or speaking with anyone; nor did she pass a night outside the church, or ask anything of the people. Instead, she sat amongst the poor and spent the night with them, in the church or wherever else it might be.[23]

Like Euphemia, Mary controlled the amount of money she would keep, enough for a small amount of bread, green vegetables, and seeds, and she gave away anything over this amount. For days at a time "she would sit in silence, with her thoughts engrossed in heaven."[24]

After she had lived this way in Jerusalem for three years, visitors from home found her there and revealed that she had a lifelong reputation for holy asceticism. When people realized that she was not just a crazy, poor old beggar, they began to treat her with respect. Dreading such attention, Mary fled the city to begin an annual cycle of wandering, returning each year to worship again in Jerusalem.

Although Mary influenced Euphemia's choice of a religious life when her husband died, the contrast between the two sisters is marked, with Euphemia's attitude to material possessions, sharing, and divestment radically unlike Mary's. Euphemia's voice is dominant; Mary chooses silence. Euphemia married; Mary chose celibacy from childhood. Euphemia's outreach was based at home in a walled city; Mary spent her life in public wandering, although she regularly returned to what was perhaps family property in Tella d-Mauzlath, modern Viransehir, about twenty-five miles north of the modern border between Turkey and Syria and about fifty miles southwest of Amida. Euphemia aggravates her bloody blisters hurrying, barefoot, among the destitute; Mary takes long solitary walks in the hot season to and from Jerusalem, several hundred miles away. Euphemia refuses alms; Mary exists on them. Yet both sisters follow a private discipline with prayer and fiscal control: Euphemia and Maria limit what they will earn in a day; Mary limits the charity she will accept. Like another famous ascetic beggar, the "Man of God" (named Alexis in some Christian traditions and discussed further in Chapter 8), both women gave away their extras, "from alms making alms."[25] Mary follows a recognized ascetic model of wandering holy beggars that is found in many texts from Christian late antiquity.[26] Unlike Euphemia's flagrant publicity, Mary cultivates anonymity. Neither Euphemia nor Mary sought to alter social structure on a broad scale; theirs was not that kind of world. Mary's lifestyle, which may seem stranger than Euphemia's to the modern reader, was in its time viewed as an admirable, selfless model, part of that broad structure of the person whose very existence was understood to serve society by his or her very holiness. Her contemporaries apparently admired Mary even more than Euphemia, and as a woman whose mind was set wholly on heaven, "in due course," John says, "many powerful miracles were worked by her presence, not by her will or her word."[27] By identifying with restorative justice that exceeded what political authorities could offer, holy persons embodied very practical righteousness for the everyday

here and now of those around them, but are often characterized, as in
Mary's case, by an intentional hiddenness and physical distance. If the
poor wanted something of Euphemia, for example, she came to visit. But
if anyone asked anything of Mary, "he never saw her again." There could
hardly be a greater difference.

It may be difficult to imagine Mary's choice as offering anything positive to our modern society. Her choice depended on a culture that tolerated homeless wandering and practiced an almsgiving that was sufficiently
indiscriminate and unstructured to allow the voluntary "secret" ascetic to
survive unrecognized. Homeless women in modern society are those at
greatest personal risk for harm, yet John glosses over any hint that these
independent sisters had anything to worry about beyond religious persecution. Yet we know from other sources that religious women (even those
closeted in family cells, like Abraham's niece) were not necessarily sheltered from the social and personal violence that are characteristics of the
perpetual political unrest and injustices of human nature that manifest
in any society. While John is as close a biographer as one might wish for
the three women in his narrative, we must be mindful that his narrative
is at best a small piece of their story, seen through his own assumptions
and his own concerns. Reading between the lines, for example, we know
that Mary was not always alone, either in Jerusalem or on the road. When
Euphemia and Maria left town, they found her and joined her in her travels for five long years. When Mary died, around 526, someone knew them
well enough that "a man came bringing a letter" with news of her death,
finding Maria where she and her mother (who had also just died) had
been hiding in Amida.[28] The text presumes a close social network of companions and relationships that allowed women like Mary to maintain an
internal "solitude" that coexisted with religious communities. It also presumes the existence of an urban environment in which people were giving
alms and an ever-present marketplace in which small quantities of food
could be bought each day.

Even the sisters' names suggest their respective choices. Although she
was popularly called Dorcas, for her devotion to good works and charity
like the Dorcas of Acts 9:36, "Euphemia" can mean either "prayer and
praise" or the use of good and auspicious words. And indeed words domi-
nate the way she enacted her material redistribution. Mary's story, in contrast, may suggest Martha's sister in the gospel story, the Mary who "chose
the good things," perpetual meditation on the Lord, which precluded her
from taking part in her sister's busy food services.

WHO IS THE BEGGAR THAT SHALL
BE SAVED? DIVESTMENT CHOICES

One conceptual issue that commonly plagues any discussion about sharing the world's goods to help those in need seems to be missing from the
story of these generous holy women. This is the issue of how to determine
which people are worthy of help. In contemporary conversation, the first
question that often arises in any discussion about responsible sharing is
how to identify the "worthy" recipient. Ought one give to all who ask
or only to some? If to all, how much? If only to some, which recipients
do we choose and by what criteria? What is "effective" giving and how
does one target giving that will produce "effective" results? These are
questions that plague any funded program, whether charitable or not.
They are basic concerns in good business practices, especially those that
invest in social or educational programs. Yet such problems do not seem to
have worried Mary or Euphemia. The challenge of selective or universal
benefits assumes limited resources, and certainly the resources that these
women received and earned were acutely limited. Why are modern concerns so much more focused on such questions?

Perhaps one difference is that these women understood charitable sharing of the world's resources as a moral mandate; it was required behavior
for any "true" Christian life, and was unrelated to any concern about reap-
ing benefits or seeing "results" in the here and now. Each woman practiced
a fixed discipline within her fixed income and did not concern herself with
demands beyond the goals of her individual sense of calling. Euphemia
was a natural fundraiser, but she apparently immediately used the funds
she raised to address the specific needs of those she encountered each day.
Neither Euphemia nor Mary seemed to share the modern cultural commitment to effect broader social changes that require programs carefully
planned in advance.

Yet not everyone in the early church shared these women's apparent
lack of concern about choosing the most appropriate recipients. This was a
controversial dilemma for many early Christian writers. While Euphemia
and Mary focus on the immediate needs at hand, others—particularly
bishops who had administrative and distributive responsibilities—leave
evidence of a concern similar to our own for establishing practices of good
stewardship that will have an ongoing social existence beyond the personal activities of one individual. By the sixth century, Christian poorhouses, hospitals, orphanages, foundling homes, and homes for the aged

had become standard establishments that (at least in the capital of Constantinople) received a certain measure of political and economic support. But the stories of these women stand as perhaps helpful reminders that sharing the world, even today, need not be limited to a cautious and "prudent" support for structured programs and fixed institutions. Certainly wise stewardship is a Christian ideal and careful investment is more likely to result in consistent potential for ongoing divestment. But what may sometimes rule the legislative fences we put up to ensure what we call "wise giving" is perhaps nothing more than raw fear: fear that if we do not stake down the borders of our limits from the start, the needs of the world will overwhelm our best intentions and destroy all hope we have of doing good. Christians may be especially prone to stake these borders by making "Christian" claims that do not in fact reflect Christian texts.

One fallacy that I have heard repeatedly over the years is the assertion that Christians are economically responsible to support *only* fellow Christians. The texts discussed in Chapter 3, of the Cappadocians, John Chrysostom, Cyprian of Carthage, and others, illustrate quite plainly that this was not the dominant Christian view in late antiquity according to most Greek and at least a few Roman authors. Another common claim—more often a subtle assumption that is rarely stated explicitly—is that bodily aid is "Christian" only when it is delivered with an equal or greater, and usually obligatory, dose of "spiritual" teaching—evangelism or at least a particular moral attitude in various forms. The modern poet-philosopher Wendell Berry illustrates one danger of this approach when a character in his novel *Jayber Crow* remarks on becoming an orphan, "And so I went out of the hands of love, which certainly included charity as we know it, into the hands of charity as we know it, which included love only as it might."[29] Although we can certainly find early Christian texts that may appear to contain elements of these narrow views, we find many more that do not support them. One biblical example is Galatians 6:10, "So then, whenever we have an opportunity, let us work for the good of all, and especially for those of the family of faith;"[30] the concern suggested by the word "especially" is not the same as it would be if the word here were "exclusively." This text hardly suggests that fellow believers deserve all the available aid. The injunction to help them sets merely a minimum standard. In fact, the broader model of risky generosity seems to have ruled most Christian ideals. Early Christian texts on giving more often condemn those who limit aid as being misers, stingy, people without faith, and people who need to learn from the poor themselves. Gregory of

Nazianzus said of such people that they "feel obliged to watch their pennies and bully the helpless."[31]

Certainly the poor who are familiar, those we perhaps know best within our own faith communities, must not be neglected. Perhaps charity begins at home, but if it remains limited within this sphere it breeds discrimination and fear of any outside needs that might threaten its security. And certainly my call to engage personally with those I help implies that I will bring my whole self to the task, including honest, sensitive conversation that may include talking about a wide range of things that I believe to be true. But this is very different from viewing "evangelism" as an essential ingredient in any effective "Christian" aid. In fact, the common idea that in our divestment it is the poor who "need saving" directly conflicts with the differently nuanced theme found in early Christian texts: that the needy poor—even destitute beggars—have a much better chance of understanding religious truth and making it to heaven than do the rich. According to the gospel story, the only hope that the rich have in sharing Abraham's bosom with the beggar, Lazarus, is by a more faithful, active response in this life to the Creator they share in common with the beggar and all that the Creator calls them to do with their available resources and their life. The only soul that the rich person is expected to improve, by thoughtful "righteous" material divestment and redistribution, is her or his own. Those who cling covetously to personal wealth, however eloquent they may be at evangelism, are, according to the patristic writers, more likely to be guilty and at risk of practicing injustice and impurity than the poor, even the poor whose motives or lifestyle might not quite fit our criteria for assistance. Euphemia gave to street beggars as to Christ. Pilgrims in Jerusalem gave alms to Maria because they saw her as a needy old woman and for the personal heavenly blessings they expected from God for their beneficence. The enemies in the story of both women are those who tried to force religious conformity.

ON BLANKETS AND THE COMMON GOOD

Perhaps Euphemia avoided the problems of choosing "worthy" recipients by her dedication to meet each individual exactly where they lay in the street and by talking with each at length before buying the specific food and other items that they desired. Perhaps Mary avoided this problem because she lived as a destitute woman, in close contact with others as poor as herself. The problem of selective giving is most acute when we act from some distance. This was most evident to me personally in an incident that occurred a number of years ago while I was visiting friends in India. We spent one day with an Indian Christian social worker in a New Delhi slum that had been built up on some acres directly adjacent to the city's finest and most technologically advanced medical center. A handful of Indian Christians were running a health center in this slum, supplied by volunteers and donations. None of these resources, the Christians told me, came from the hospital next door; in fact, the hospital wanted the slum to be bulldozed out of existence.

The social worker took the January day of our visit as an opportunity to selectively distribute some donated blankets. He chose to limit his distribution to a few people who attended the clinic whom he judged to be in the greatest need. Certainly he had to make a choice. There were not enough blankets for everyone in the clinic that day, let alone the thousands whose only home on earth was in the muddy acres around it, where they subsisted in makeshift shanty huts without electricity, running water, or toilets.

But despite his good intentions, the effect of his selective generosity was chaos. Within an hour the clinic was under siege, with word of free blankets spreading fast. By the time we left the clinic to visit a few of the families in their homes, the crowd outside the clinic door had grown into a very vocal throng of women who heard the rumor of free blankets and demanded theirs on the spot. By then the supply was gone, and community resentment began to fester against those particular individuals who had received a blanket. That chaos remains my first stunned lesson in what can happen when even an experienced aid worker does his best in the judicious distribution of limited goods.

In modern social ethics in the Roman Catholic tradition, social justice is closely related to action that works for "the common good," that is, the greatest good of all within the social order, however it is defined. Was our friend's distribution of blankets an act of social justice? On the surface, it appeared to cause no common good, but rather seemed to further social disruption and resentment. Those who did not receive a blanket (that is, most of the people in the slum) could not (understandably) view the social worker's decision as fair; who was he to say that the few among the small percentage who attended the clinic that day needed blankets more than anyone else? Given the limited supply and the stark deprivation, illness, and semistarvation of most residents, what form of distribution would have best served "the common good" in this situation? Years later, I still wonder. And yet those few who did receive a blanket truly needed one.

Early Christians faced similar issues and held similar views. For ordinary people such as Euphemia, Mary, Maria, and the social worker in India, what mattered in the end was not the rhetoric but the material exchange itself. Whether it did (or did not) result in a perceived benefit to the physical body in the community, the act of sharing available resources was understood as a moral mandate for immediate action, despite being fraught with all sorts of risks and problems, inevitably resulting in ongoing inequities within the community.

While some donors choose recipients cautiously, with very selective care, others choose to leave the moral question of who deserves aid to the recipient. A passage in the first chapter of the early Christian manual, the *Didache*, seems to nod at both options. It begins, "Give to everyone who asks, and do not ask for anything back," arguing that the recipient, not the donor, is accountable for determining whether the need is legitimate. The recipient, however, is also sternly warned:

> For if anyone receives because he is in need, he is without fault. But the one who receives without a need will have to testify why he received what he did, and for what purpose. And he will be thrown in prison and interrogated about what he did; and he will not get out until he pays back every last cent.

Yet the passage ends by returning to a focus on the donor, advising the donor to act thoughtfully with a selective care, "for it has also been said concerning this, 'Let your gift to charity sweat in your hands until you know to whom to give it.'"[32] The intended gift is supposed to result in a certain discomfort as the donor is forced to hold onto it, literally unable to use that hand for anything else until deciding how best to distribute the gift. These texts with their various messages emphasize that sharing our world with others in need is not an optional activity. They suggest that the Christian has certain responsibilities about selecting the process of giving, but, beyond that, the responsibility for honest use lies with the recipients. Worrying to the point of miserly or extended retention, perhaps meanwhile "bullying the helpless," may suggest that one values material goods more than they are really worth in the universal breadth of all that is real.

WHAT WAS MARIA'S CHOICE?

Returning now to Maria of Amida, what do we know about her own personal choice? Did she in fact have any choices and do we know what they were?

Born most likely between 480 and 500, Maria lost her father when she was very young, perhaps during the calamities of locusts, famine, disease, earthquakes, floods, eclipses, and tumbling city walls that took place between 499 and 502, or perhaps during the Persians' violent siege of Amida between 502 and 505. Despite all of her mother's best efforts at protection, Maria's world was a violent one and it is no wonder she obeyed her mother and stayed at home.

Even before she is invited to make an active choice, Maria's life differs radically from both her mother's and her aunt's as they negotiate through this same world. Unlike theirs, hers is a life of willing seclusion and regular daily work of a "traditional" kind. She did not need to make any choices about which poor person to feed, what to buy in the market, how to bargain with the vendors, or even how to order her private religious duties. Euphemia controls and guards Maria's chastity from childhood, perceiving her as fundamentally more vulnerable than her sister, Mary, who had chosen the same chastity from her own youth and lived it out in public, with "great feats of fasting, many vigils, constant exertion in charity and wandering."[33] Quietly subordinate, Maria accepts her mother's food choices and limits and her abhorrence of alms; she also shares her fate at refusing the persecutors' eucharist. When the monks move in, Euphemia,

> for herself and her daughter—prepared an inner chamber since, wise in all things, she gave herself alone to the service of the blessed men. But her daughter, because she was young, she kept carefully inside day and night, lest she harm one of the men by her sight, or herself be harmed seeing one of them.[34]

It is possible that John rarely saw the girl. The mother's extreme protection is maintained to her deathbed. Although by then she and Maria had spent five years on the open road with Mary, Euphemia's final dialogue with her daughter is, as John describes it, a list of imperatives with "many strict injunctions."[35]

Yet in the end John lets slip what Maria really wanted. As her mother lay dying, he says, Maria's "whole mind had been set on going to her blessed aunt and sharing her way of life until her death." When the messenger arrives with the news that Mary too has died, the wealthy friends in Amida, where Maria and Euphemia were hiding, "prevented her from hearing and being overwhelmed with grief." Even at the end, Maria is hemmed in by selective communication intended to control her responses and choices, so that we, the readers, never actually know if or how she learns of her aunt's death. For John, whose purpose is to praise Euphemia and Mary without concern for their differences, Maria's fate seems simple and obvious. Euphemia's "blessed daughter still remained," he writes, "fortified by the power of her blessing and her prayer; following in the footsteps of these holy women, she began the vigorous course of their practices after them."[36]

But was it so simple? Unless the wandering Mary's practices were quite different from what their monastic friend, John, has described, it is difficult to imagine any one person practicing both sisters' choices in one life. They are simply too different. John of Ephesus is known for being an inexact writer, and his purpose in writing these stories was not to tell us exactly what we want to know. Perhaps he had in mind as their common "footsteps" the last five years when the three women were together, though he does not describe how they lived during that time. Did Maria begin to visit the poor in the streets like her mother, or did she flee anyone who asked her for help and choose anonymous prayer, like her aunt? Did she continue to weave goats' hair, allowing her to refuse alms like her mother, or did she take up her aunt's begging basket and bowl? We know from the story that at the very end, with her mother dying, Maria could not stay where she was; the authorities were threatening to seize her hosts' property simply because they were housing women labeled as religious dissidents. Or perhaps, despite John's irenic conclusion, Maria simply despaired and, unwilling to make her own choices, joined a women's community. Or might she have even abandoned all she had learned from her mother and aunt and married a rich man? We simply do not know. Nor do we know whether she lived to face the bubonic plague that the Roman empire suffered in 542. Was she still alive, a very old woman and "holy fool," when Amida went mad in 560, a cumulative result of decades of disasters?[37] All we know from the limited Syriac texts that survive to tell this story is that she knew what it meant to give, to share, and how to define the limits of ascetic hospitality.

And we know what she wanted. John's statement is too startling, too far outside a neat unified ending, to be simply imaginary idealization. Despite the lifetime model of her energetic mother, and her commitment to remain with her mother until Euphemia died, Maria's "whole mind" was fixed on the model that she discovered when she finally emerged from her seclusion, one that differed radically from her own past and from the model of a mother whose temperament she clearly did not share. Maria is not torn. She is "single minded," whole. She knows what she wants. Yet with her aunt's death, what Maria wants becomes in that instant of possibility impossible. She must now make new choices. She must now decide whether she will take up an unplanned emulation of her aunt's very public solitude if she takes to the road.

Their biographer may not have known what Maria chose in the end. Relating the story more than thirty years later, in the late 560s, he says simply that she "remained," that she outlived the other two and that she began to emulate their examples in some form that in his view represented the religious practices of both models.

It is not surprising that John cannot be more specific. Like Maria, he was in constant motion during those years. The city John knew as Amida has never been kind to those viewed as threats to its governing political powers. Home in the nineteenth century to the largest Armenian community in Anatolia, its last Armenian church is today a roofless ruin. In 1994 William Dalrymple found some Kurdish refugees huddled in the church's west porch, and the town's last surviving Armenian was an old woman, silent and as seemingly mindless as the wandering Mary might have appeared.[38] By 2005, when several of my colleagues visited the tiny Syriac Christian community in Diyarbakır, the Kurdish refugees had taken over the whole Armenian church ruin. Yet the Syriac Church of St. Mary, at the actual site where Euphemia and Maria might have worshiped in better days, still houses the tomb of Jacob of Sarug. Its priest today is as familiar as Euphemia with the experience of imprisonment for speaking unpopular truths. And the women in the Syriac community still keep busy with yarn and food, with quilting and gardening, drying fruits and vegetables, and welcoming guests with a sacrificial generosity. The city walls, too, are still "formidable."[39]

Maria of Amida's world was very different in many ways from our own. But the lifestyle, ideals, distributive choices, and acute tensions that this enigmatic young woman faced in her turbulent world have much in common with the challenge to practice Christian sharing in any age. Maria's story and its persistent mysteries may inspire a creative praxis for those today who seek to encounter and address, in material terms, the challenges of human need and moral choice.

7

LIVING CRUNCHY AND
DOING RIGHT(S)

> Crunchiness brings wealth. Wealth leads to sog-
> giness. Sogginess brings poverty. Poverty creates
> crunchiness. From this immutable cycle we know
> that to hang on to wealth, you must keep things
> crunchy.

Thus begins the now-classic 1988 editorial "Colchester's crunchiness,"
by Nico Colchester, then deputy editor of the *Economist*.[1] In Colchester's
cycle, "sogginess" is that comfortable economic uncertainty, its vague
reassurances much in demand. "Crunchiness," on the other hand, is a no-
doubt-about-it state of affairs. "Crunchy systems are those in which small
changes have big effects," wrote Colchester. "A crunchy policy is not necessarily right, only more certain than a soggy one to deliver the results that
it deserves." In applying economic practices, he concludes, "Whatever you
decide, keep things crunchy."

Sharing the world, the second paradigm whose modern applications
are the subject of this chapter, is about living crunchy. While the first paradigm, "sensing need," focuses on inner perceptions and awareness, sharing
the world is about action. But not all actions are crunchy. Some can have
little or no effect; soggy, polite gestures at best, they float in a moral haze
that keeps the actors content and comfortable. "Soggy" organizations boast
of philanthropy but change little or nothing; they are characterized by systems that make us feel good about investments (although details seem a
bit vague) and charismatic personalities who smile but never quite take a
stand. Lives such as those of Mary and Euphemia, John Chrysostom, and
Basil of Caesarea, on the other hand, are about as crunchy as it gets.

Applying crunchy examples of radical lives and policies to how we
personally choose to "do good" and practice "human rights" in relation to all people in need (including ourselves) is no easy task. Even

when we can instinctively distinguish "soggy" from "crunchy" (or that delightful middle ground "munchy," which Colchester defines as "crunchy with a sentimentally soft centre"), there are a dizzying array of options for using economic resources to "share" material goods and resources with the rest of the world. Not all of the methods and practices of these options will work easily together. The history of economics, politics, and court justice is based on endless conflicts over systems, ideals, and implementation challenges. Christian tradition is similarly famous for its bickering over how to address poverty and do what is right to build and support culture, society, and relationships. How to do what is "right" will depend in part on what we believe about human "rights." It will also depend on how much power we have over material resources, including the motivation and will to direct them to outward causes rather than to the exclusive service of personal debts, tastes, and cravings. Crunchy action depends on embracing particular views of "enough" and on clearly perceiving genuine needs in other people. Sharing the world builds on sensing need, is ineffective without sensitive perception, but is essentially about economic and social action. Yet individual choices of practical activities and time costs will depend on personality and the limits of circumstance. To act in society is as much about receiving as it is about giving, as much about hearing, seeing, and sensing as it is about speaking and doing.

The variety of ways for sharing resources and material goods with the rest of the world, which has led to so much conflict, also offers a hopeful breadth of options to consider. Every Christian story about relieving destitution in the ancient and modern world opens new doors for the creative imagination. Every story raises questions about its constructive applications, pitfalls, and limits. Crunchy social action depends on choosing specific activities, and the more we know about the past, the better we can choose and draw our own lines. History is littered with fallout from, and inspiring models of, efforts to apply the biblical applications about generosity, ownership, and divestment. It dares us to take similar risks: to give wildly, perhaps, to play the fool, to defy injustices, to invest in the eschatological future, and to keep enough for the present to hold together body and soul.

Helpful as these generalities may be, personal action can only begin with concrete, measurable behaviors. We must inevitably face challenge and opportunity at a personal level, asking, "What are some of the very specific moral choices that I might make about my own possessions?"

For example, how might I, living in a nation glutted by goods produced with the unequal sweat of the world's poor who are paid pittance wages, follow the model of Zaccheus, the repentant tax collector in Luke 19, who promised Jesus he would "restore fourfold" any resources gained by his complicity in fraud? Zaccheus's story compels me to take a look around at all that I have purchased in life, certainly with honest wages but much of it at cut-rate discounts that were possible precisely because of international sweatshop labor. Whenever I open my closets or unpack the month's groceries, for example, the abundance reminds me of two biblical texts I first stumbled onto during college. One is Isaiah 3:14: "The plunder of the poor is in your house." The other, more wryly, is Job 20:22: "In the fullness of [her] plenty [s]he will be cramped."[2] But how do I "de-cramp"? How do I restore justice at all, let alone "fourfold"? What actions will both cleanse my conscience and return the "plunder" of a wealthy civilization's profits to its rightful owners? Ought I pack up for the Salvation Army (or better, a women-empowering shelter that also nurtures children) any clothes and possessions I find that were not made by workers I might assume were guaranteed fair trade or at least minimum wage? And if so, what do I pack up? I must, after all, be realistic and practical. Some essentials (such as books) will stay put no matter where they were made, no matter who suffered. Others are so worn that it would be rude to give them away. And how would I sell off things that remain marketable? In India the streets are clean because even rags and scraps have retail value. But in the West today, selling one's possessions to give money to the poor takes a yard sale, barter-power, perhaps an auctioneer's or real estate agent's stiff commission, and that most costly of all American commodities: time. Is it worth it? Even assuming quantitative tallies were possible, such divestment seems frankly more symbolic than effective as restorative justice. Thus we have the dilemma of capitalist consumerism, the challenge of the crunchy-seeking Christian.

"Doing right(s)" demands choices and actions that are more expansive than navel-gazing into your own closet and cupboards. It demands a gaze that looks not at marketable *things* but rather at human *people*. For early Christian authors, practicing what was "right" toward those in need meant treating the poor *as* Christ, enacting legal fairness, and providing physical services mercifully, such as food, clothing, healthcare, and hospitality, all directly contributing to building an image of the eternal "kingdom of God" or "kingdom of heaven."

The word "kingdom" (discussed further in Chapter 8) is a useful word but one that can also be problematic, whether it is about God or about heaven, and even if we believe in both. "Kingdom" implies imperial male domination, rarely good news for women. And empires, whether run by kings or queens, do not have much of a positive record for treating poor citizens (male or female) fairly. They tend to take crunchy bites out of other people's property, through colonialism, taxation, and outright conquest. It's no wonder that the phrase "kingdom of heaven" is suspect despite its best meaning: as the ultimate, eternal, and omnipresent safehouse, the transcendent and yet eternally concrete location of love, grace, truth, and justice, the site of a perfectly restored relational unity with One who loves and made us.

Perhaps in part because of this, doing "rights" today, even in the Christian tradition, tends to shift away from the traditional focus on the eschatological "kingdom." For the patristic writers, heaven (and hell) were just over the next hill. Yet Christians today, treating heaven as more of a distant ideal "other world," nonetheless share with their patristic forbears the conviction that its ideals mean nothing if they do not take shape in the present. Modern religious social action is about changing things now. We do it by applying many of the same action tools we find in the historical accounts (such as food, clothing, medical care, and legal advice) but focus more on contemporary social values: housing, jobs, education, childcare, healthcare, tolerance, and equitable behavior in our personal encounters with those whose needs seem "high risk" and whose poverty may seem to threaten our own comfort and security.

The challenge remains: to find an intersection between the historical tradition and the present that is adequately defined and discrete or adequately general in useful and realistic terms. Rather than attempt to survey—or summarize—the voluminous literature on religious practices of giving, of alms, philanthropy, and charity over the centuries in Christian tradition, I focus the following discussion much more narrowly on three common themes in contemporary relief rhetoric that might be enriched by integration with early Christian examples. These themes include justice and the "common good" in human rights language, the generosity of poverty, and hospitality. These three themes, also discussed in Maria's and Euphemia's story (Chapter 6), merely beckon the reader toward the beginning of a much wider range of possible discussions on sharing. Yet they remain fixed and useful launching points in the search for creative and crunchy choices.

HUMAN RIGHTS: JUSTICE AND
THE "COMMON GOOD"

Ancient religious ideals of social justice have been defined increasingly, at least in the West, in terms of "human rights" and, particularly in Catholic social thought, as "the common good." The appalling inhumanities of World War II and particularly the Holocaust compelled international leaders to develop global guidelines to prevent further atrocities. The development of these guidelines in the "Universal Declaration of Human Rights" (UDHR) was outlined briefly in Chapter 4. Ratified by nations as philosophically diverse as Russia, China, India, several Arab nations, and countries from Western Europe and North and South America, the UDHR developed within a common acknowledgment that (despite sharp disagreements among the various contributors) all human persons share certain innate "rights" in any culture, and that these rights deserve and compel legal protection. In the decades after the UDHR was signed on December 10, 1948, the document has served as the basis for other legal documents and affirmations about international human rights, often focusing on particular discrete groups, such as women, children, and the legal protection of various rights to reproductive and other economic and health-related choices. Throughout the development and implementation of international human rights policies, international human rights language has consistently downplayed explicit religious views in order most effectively to foster agreement among the many different religious and philosophical positions of those who are eager to work for justice and the good of their communities through a commitment to "translate" human rights language into transformative action.

Yet leaders within specific religious traditions throughout the twentieth century have also been quick to take up "rights" language in a moral push for social action. The Civil Rights Movement in America and the work of Dr. Martin Luther King, Jr., are perhaps the most obvious examples. Another area of thought in Christian tradition in which this trend is consistently evident is that of "Catholic Social Thought" (CST) and the Catholic social teachings of recent papal documents. The CST model is especially relevant to the concepts outlined in this book because of its deliberate and conscious roots in the patristic tradition. While a detailed discussion of how "rights" and "common good" language are used in CST and papal decrees belongs to a more intentionally academic study,[3] a brief summary here of several examples will illustrate how relevant these efforts are to integrating early Christian and modern religious responses to social action.

Pope Leo XIII's encyclical *Rerum Novarum* (1891), on the condition of labor, is regarded as the first major papal document on this topic. Written to address the rise of Marxism and the massive suffering that followed the factory economics of the industrial revolution in Europe, *Rerum Novarum* discussed the universal rights of all people to justice and the need to protect laborers from such things as unfair wages and child labor. Pope John XXIII's mid–Vatican II (1963) encyclical, *Pacem in Terris*, further developed Leo XIII's concerns while addressing a new generation. Subtitled "On establishing universal peace in truth, justice, charity and liberty," *Pacem in Terris* begins by affirming and defining human rights and duties. It is this encyclical that provided the lead on the specific theme of "the common good" (which Leo had earlier mentioned in passing) and its effect on the developing ideas of liberation theology in the 1970s and 1980s. *Pacem in Terris* explicitly defines the common good in political terms intended to influence "the secular administration of all civil society":

[53.] Individual citizens and intermediate groups are obliged to make their specific contributions to the common welfare. One of the chief consequences of this is that they must bring their own interests into harmony with the needs of the community, and must contribute their goods and their services as civil authorities have prescribed, in accord with the norms of justice and within the limits of their competence. Clearly then those who wield power in the state must do this by such acts which not only have been justly carried out but which also either have the common welfare primarily in view or which can lead to it.

[54.] Indeed since the whole reason for the existence of civil authorities is the realization of the common good, it is clearly necessary that, in pursuing this objective, they should respect its essential elements, and at the same time conform their laws to the circumstances of the day.[4]

Another encyclical, *Gaudiem et spes* ("Joy and Hope"),[5] issued in 1965 on the final day of Vatican II, is considered "the most authoritative and significant document of Catholic social teaching issued in the twentieth century," according to David Hollenbach, S.J., an authority on the idea of the common good in CST and a leading scholar who was to play a key role in drafting the 1986 Bishop's letter (discussed below). *Gaudiem et spes* includes an extensive discussion of the common good as it relates to solidarity, building on Thomas Aquinas and earlier moral writers to affirm social interdependence, reverence for the human person, reverence and love for enemies, the essential equality of all persons, social justice, and human solidarity in light of the Christian incarnation. It was this document, in particular, that led Latin American bishops to a new commitment to solidarity with the poor that, in a 1979 gathering in Mexico, was subsequently called the "preferential option for the poor." This movement, based on *Gaudium et spes,* gradually led other Christians around the world to place a newly emphatic stress on "how the Christian vocation is a call to solidarity with the poor in their struggle to overcome the plight of deprivation and marginalization." This logically follows from the idea of the common good in Catholic social thought, that "justice directs the activity of individual citizens and of smaller groups in society to the common good of the community as a whole."[6]

Finally, specifically addressing Americans was the document "Economic Justice for All," issued in 1986 by the U.S. Catholic bishops.[7] Summoning its readers to "conversion and action," the document includes an appeal back to the early church: "From the patristic period to the present, the Church has affirmed that misuse of the world's resources or appropriation of them by a minority of the world's population betrays the gift of creation since 'whatever belongs to God belongs to all.' "[8]

These ideas about common good and even the "preferential option for the poor" are not new. Throughout history Christians have been arguing that Gospel teachings on the poor consistently seem to argue that God considers it right and just to give preferential treatment to those who are most needy. The idea of the "common good" itself was most famously championed by Thomas Aquinas, a medieval Dominican friar, scholar, and priest who profoundly influenced Catholic moral rhetoric with his extensive interpretations of Aristotle's newly re-discovered views on political justice. For Aquinas, justice was "the premier moral virtue" that "directs a person's actions toward the good of fellow human beings."[9] In other words, common good cannot be separated from justice but rather depends on it. For Latin American liberation theologian Leonardo Boff, these ideas extend beyond human justice to encompass ecological and cosmic justice. In *Cry of the Earth, Cry of the Poor*, Boff concludes that "the common good is not that of humans alone, but is rather that of the whole cosmic community. Everything that exists and lives deserves to exist, to live, and to share life. The particular common good emerges out of harmony and synergy with the thrust of the planetary and universal common good."[10] In other words, we might say, doing rights includes doing what is environmentally right for the globe; the paradigm of sharing the world is about justice for all parts of that groaning, trembling creation that suffers the consequences of global and individual injustice and violation.

The Cappadocian poverty sermons contain similar ideas. Historically poised in the midpoint in time between the ancient Greek philosopher, Aristotle, and the medieval Latin Dominican, Aquinas, Basil and Gregory of Nazianzus, and perhaps particularly Gregory of Nyssa, shared Boff's concern that relief and empathic activities toward the needy are ultimately about cosmic balance and cosmic healing. Indeed, such Greek patristic views continue to influence Orthodox thought on cosmic and environmental balance today. The Ecumenical (Greek Orthodox) Patriarch of Constantinople, Bartholomew, has been especially active in encouraging theological discussion on environmental issues for the twenty-first century based on patristic tradition.[11]

The fourth-century sermons on poverty relief are also rich in "rights" language that is based on common-good appeals to the shared human nature of rich and poor alike, something briefly discussed in Chapter 3. "The Word orders us to share and to love one another in natural kinship," Basil wrote in his homily against usury. "After all, humankind is a civic and gregarious animal. Liberality for the purpose of restoration is a necessary part of the common life and helping one another upwards."[12] This argument has much in common with Aristotle's comments on common good, and it is likely that Aristotelian thought influenced Basil, directly or indirectly. In his homily against stockpiling, Basil explicitly refers to the "common good," writing that "riches grow useless left idle and unused in any place; but moved about, passing from one person to another, they serve the common good and bear fruit."[13] We know that Basil influenced Aquinas, who in his *Summa* quotes from this same sermon of Basil's.[14] Basil's social teachings also influenced later Greek tradition. Gennadius Scholarius II, the first ecumenical patriarch to take office in Constantinople after it was conquered by the Muslims in the fifteenth century, speaks of the common good in an extended appeal to help the needy based on Matthew 25:31–46.[15] As we saw in Chapter 3, Gregory of Nyssa and Gregory of Nazianzus appeal repeatedly to "common" race and kinship as the rationale for a justice that does not discriminate against those in need. Since "all humanity is governed by a single nature," wrote Gregory of Nyssa in his second sermon "On the love of the poor," "you belong to the common nature of all;... let all therefore be accorded common use."[16]

Their contemporary Asterius, bishop of nearby Amasea, had similar concerns. He was outraged "that we who are created with equal honor live so unequally with members of the same race."[17] Few early Christian authors wrote against slavery, but John "the Almsgiver," early seventh-century bishop of Alexandria, vigorously campaigned against treating slaves harshly, using his church funds to buy and free them from such situations when he could. His appeal for justice to slaves reveals his cultural assumption that slavery was normal in his Christian culture, but within that setting he was adamant that misuse and lack of respect for slaves as fellow human beings was not. "God has not given [slaves] to us to strike," John argued, "but to be our servants, and perhaps not even for that, but rather for them to be supported by us from the riches God has bestowed on us. What price, tell me, must a man pay to purchase one who has been honoured by creation in the likeness and similitude of God?"[18] Human rights statements thus call on all persons to determine their own individual actions based on what is in the best interest of all with whom we share the world in common across global identities and values.

THE GENEROSITY OF POVERTY

John the Almsgiver was probably a small boy on the day that a worried "Christ-loving lay person" took a walk through his village, somewhere along the Gaza strip that reaches from modern Israel down to the border with Egypt, to visit a local monk. Reaching the place at which the holy monks, Barsanuphias and John, practiced ascetic solitude while dispensing advice to visitors, he relayed the question that had been weighing on his mind: "If someone is asked to give alms but has nothing to give," he asked, "is he obliged to borrow in order to give?"[19]

This innocent question might startle a modern reader. Go into debt just so you can give your money away? Such acts are usually considered at best holy folly.[20] Yet the question shows us just how much almsgiving was viewed as a sacred duty in this villager's mind, whether he had anything of his own to give or not. Divesting to help the destitute was not just for the rich and middle class who had goods to spare. It was an ideal for everyone, including the "poor."

The monk's reply must have come as good news. "There is no need to borrow in order to give," he answered, drawing on several New Testament texts. "Indeed, someone who has nothing beyond what is needed does not have anything to give to another person. He should simply say to the person who is asking, 'Forgive me, but I only have what I need myself.'"

Those who are poor are often famous for their generosity. In praising the rural poor of his beloved Algeria during the tumultuous 1990s, novelist Yasmina Khadra described human dignity and the tragedy of over-generous giving in just such terms:

> On the sun-glazed road, I see *fellahin* breaking their backs in their fields, truck drivers hugging the steering wheel with their arms, women waiting for a forgetful bus, children jogging to school, idlers meditating on the terraces of cafés, old men rotting against fences. On their faces, despite the burden of uncertainty and the darkness of the nation's drama, I glimpse a wondrous kind of serenity—the faith of an easygoing people, generous to the point of handing over their last shirt, so humble they arouse the contempt of those who have not understood a word of the prophets...their dignity...still perceptible through the opacity of misfortune.[21]

Such sacrificial generosity is often, as here, evoked using perhaps idealistic and even romantic imagery as a way to shame the religiously smug. Such stories function like that of the widow giving her two pennies to the temple in Luke 21. Such acts often humble and inspire those who see them, and especially those who find themselves on the receiving end of such a gift from someone who has barely enough to survive. The act of giving carries power. To give is a supremely welcoming act that says "I am human too; drawing from the value of my humanness, let me honor you with this costly token of myself." But the generosity of those commonly viewed as "poor" is more than a token. Activist Jim Wallis reflects on how such generosity can, if enabled, change the world. "Poor people have resources," he writes, "Time, energy, numbers, relationships, experience, talent, faith, and even some money—when pooled together, can become very significant.... The problem is how to mobilize these assets."[22] In the majority of cases, they are most effectively mobilized in lateral actions: by working together as equals within the community, equals whose social value does not depend on their education, income, or family connections, and who work together to address and redeem the community they (and we) share.[23]

The paradigm of "sharing the world" in Christian traditions of charity is not about "us" (who "have") sharing with "them" (who need), although most philanthropy and relief rhetoric constructs it this way. Nor is it all about "us" serving ourselves. As Søren Kierkegaard remarked, "The neighbor is not the *I*; the neighbor is the *you* who is in every other human being."[24] Giving that pleases the personal tastes of the "I" may not be relevant or helpful for what *you* truly need; as one poet put it, "What good is [a gift of] cheese when I'm thirsty?"[25] Sharing the world calls for a powerful recognition of a mutual commonality of interdependence, working together as members of a body for whom the "swollen head" of pride is impossible since the head is Christ. Gregory of Nyssa pushes this theme of interdependence further in his sermon on homeless lepers by arguing that physical contact with the diseased poor—because they are the holy and beloved of God—in fact enables reciprocal healing for the so-called rich donors, who are spiritually sick from their wealth and greed. The early Christian church manual, the *Didache*, might also have encouraged this mutuality of sharing among those who are already poor with its injunction, "Do not be one who stretches out hands to receive but shuts them when it comes to giving."[26] Christianity in the first four centuries was often characterized by its reputation for material generosity, even during active persecution when possessions were anything but secure.

By the late third and early fourth century many of those who were technically "poor" had chosen to live in this way, following the example of St. Antony and others in a life of asceticism. But whether ascetic men and women were formerly rich or poor, instructions and "rules" or "canons" defining how they practiced early Christian monasticism often emphasized a careful distinction between voluntary and involuntary poverty. Voluntary poverty was admirable; involuntary poverty was recognized as inhuman and unjust suffering; and the one had a moral responsibility to the other. The "Rules" of the Syriac bishop Rabbula, for example, instruct those dedicated to an ascetic Christian life to "persevere in fasting and be diligent in prayer; they shall take care of the poor and demand justice for the oppressed."[27] A similar set of anonymous "Canons which are necessary for the monks" from the Syriac tradition says that "It is right for the monks that they shall clothe themselves with mercy and pity of atonement towards the poor and needy, and especially towards the strangers who live among them, in order that the Messiah shall confess goodness from them that 'I was a stranger and you have gathered me,' and again, 'forget not love of the strangers.' "[28]

Sharing the world is a tangible act of social equity if I, too, am willing to admit that I lack. Such sharing reminds me that my inherent dignity and my value as a human person do not depend on having a surplus of goods that I can earmark for beneficent divestment. The Gaza monk's gentle words about debt speak to me in such situations. Everything that I own is mine to share with others insofar as I, too, have a right to basic essentials necessary for survival. The real trick is deciding, in a glutted culture, how much is "enough." This decision can never be made just once; it is made anew each time we pass a store window, sort through junk mail, make decisions about broken equipment, or just get itchy for that new "something." Recognizing the dignity of others follows on recognizing my own inherent and equal dignity as a human person in relation to the poor who, too, want to share with me. If my sense of value depends on gripping at surplus goods and resources, to then use them to "prove" my superior generosity to others, perhaps something is wrong with my perceptions. My sense of personal value is very fragile indeed if it depends solely on what I have to give to others rather than (also) what they can teach me in our mutual interdependence as created beings within cosmic space.

The ideal value for social equity in Christian tradition historically affirms people whether they are "winners" or "losers." Timothy Patitsas, a Greek Orthodox ethicist who teaches and writes on Christian economic philosophy, reflects on the fact that even the needy in society are vital players in any community's economic success. Successful economic development in free capitalism depends on a creative "inefficiency" that naturally means some people fail. Arguing for the need to support this creative freedom, Patitsas encourages a return to a vision of liturgy:

> Due to our civilization's loss of an explicit dependence on liturgy, we express it [the creative "inefficiency"] heartlessly and inaccurately: Let the free market weed out the losers, we cry. But the losers have, in a sense, "died for our salvation;" one could no more have a dynamic economy without losers than a sacrificial cult without sacrificial victims. And there is no way of distinguishing ahead of time the losers from the winners. Therefore both are integral to our economic life and deserve our respect.[29]

Patitsas is not just telling readers to give a cheerful pat on the back to all the economic "losers" encountered on the streets. He is challenging us, rather, to treat them with respect as participants whose present and active role in our society—however broken and seemingly marginal—is no less important than our own.

HOSPITALITY

Both "rights" language and the reciprocal generosity of admitting one's own poverty demonstrate sharing the world as a dynamic that is characterized by divestment and lateral interrelationships, regardless of whether "we" and "they" are one of the elite, the poor, or somewhere in between. But for many Christians, the quest to translate these principles into practical activities from day to day most often evokes another "sharing" concept entirely: that of hospitality.

Hospitality can mean many different things. In the restaurant and hotel industry, where it is the operative term, food and housing are designed to be a treat, not a charity. When I was a child, hospitality meant visiting or welcoming parents' and grandparents' friends and relatives in long (and excruciatingly dull) Sunday afternoon sessions on porches and living room couches. Or else it took shape in elaborate, traditional holiday feasts that took weeks of planning and from which our mothers, who cooked and cleaned, needed days to recover. There is nothing necessarily wrong with these traditional forms of family-centered hospitality, but they are just the beginnings of many hospitable possibilities and relationships. Hospitality does not depend on poverty or need, but in religious tradition it ideally reaches beyond the family into broader society. It is a universal value, present in most if not all cultures, and is often connected with gift exchange. To welcome the stranger and "share one's bread" is an act of solidarity, an openness to divine goodness that is as ancient as the Homeric legends and as deeply rooted in Western religious tradition as the account of Abraham greeting the angelic visitors in Genesis 18. To care for and protect a guest is often regarded as a holy responsibility. When early Christian guesthouses began to be categorized into new institutions called "poorhouses" or "hospitals," these changing terms reshaped the common Christian understanding of what were ancient values for treating guests as sacred, now focusing them on the hungry, sick, and destitute, although they did not necessarily limit the broader ideals for welcoming others.

Unlike alms, whose ideal concept is centered in something *given*, the ideal of hospitality assumes receptivity in both host and guest. The dictionary pairs the word "hospitality" with "to entertain," which can include both receiving (guests) and openly considering (ideas). But competitive "hospitality"—which marked at least a few Thanksgiving, Christmas, and Easter dinners I have known—may shortchange this personal receptivity in the host's frenetic quest for a perfect performance. One of the

most powerful domestic lessons in my spiritual life was an Easter dinner that I spent most of Lent planning, most of Holy Week preparing,
and that my invited guests consumed in something under forty minutes.
Witnessing this event almost instantly converted me for life (at least in
theory) to Clement of Alexandria's philosophy of eating: "A person like
this seems to me to be all jaw and nothing else.... But let us eat that we
may live. For neither is food our business, nor is pleasure our aim; but both
are on account of our life here, which the Word is training up to immortality."[30] The problem I faced that holiday afternoon was not how quickly
my guests ate. The problem, I realized, was my own culinary competitive
nature, to say nothing of a rather misdirected Lenten and Easter focus.
I still find great pleasure in food, like to cook (sometimes) and care very
seriously about feeding the hungry, but this memory, of watching weeks
of artistry and labor disappear in a few transitory moments, keeps me
better focused on what really matters in life. Competitive hospitality was
such a sore temptation for many Victorian housewives that in her 1887
cookbook, *Miss Parloa's Kitchen Companion*, the author must remind her
readers that "housekeepers ought to feel that a cordial welcome to visitors is of more consequence than the preparation of fine dishes for their
gratification."[31]

Hospitality is not about displaying domestic power. As Esther de Waal
reflects on the Benedictine monastic model, "hospitality brings us back
to the theme of acceptance, accepting ourselves and accepting others, in a
most immediate and practical situation which we cannot evade." In fact,
she adds, "This asks of me a restraint and sensitivity, a restraint that is
comparable to chastity taken in its widest sense of meaning the refusal
to use another person as an instrument for my own pleasure or self-
gratification."[32]

When I was in college (shortly after the gourmet Easter) the Christians
who influenced me most were people who had dedicated themselves to
what were often extreme and expansive models of receptive hospitality.
They opened their homes, gave generously of their time and resources,
and were ready to listen, give rides, counsel, invite others for a spontaneous dinner, and do without luxuries to free up money and time to help
others in need. For some, these practices were a natural extension of a
small-town, middle-American heritage. For others they were new choices,
purposeful reactions against "baby boom" wealth that they had found
stifling with its hothouse social insularity and sameness. In most cases,
their hospitality went hand in hand with deliberate religious "witness,"

a verbal focus on discussing issues of faith, ideally with a heavy measure of common courtesy and sensitivity for the conversant guests. The material openness of this hospitality, combined with what was often in fact very stimulating intellectual conversation, was unlike anything I had ever experienced. Their ideals and practices profoundly shaped my own spiritual development and thinking, even while I also came to see the problems (and the burnout) that might follow such evangelistic fervor and exuberant application of biblical models for welcoming others.

Yet there's no getting around it: "sharing the world" does involve sharing oneself. Whatever boundaries we set, sharing is not a detached, impersonal activity but one fraught with all sorts of risks. Frank Schaeffer illustrates this in his memoir about growing up in L'Abri Fellowship, his parents' home-based community ministry in Switzerland. Despite the problems and personal fallout—which in his view were substantial—Schaeffer does not hesitate to honestly and uncritically praise the way his family practiced hospitality:

> My parents were not advocating compassion that someone else would carry out with tax dollars, or at arm's length, but rather they opened their home. The result was that those gathered around our table represented a cross-section of humanity and intellectual ability, from mental patients to Oxford students and all points of need in between. My mother and father marshaled arguments in favor of God, the Bible, and the saving work of Jesus Christ. But no words were as convincing as their willingness to lay material possessions, privacy, and time on the line, sometimes at personal risk and always with the understanding that if they were being taken advantage of, that was fine too.[33]

I visited the Swiss L'Abri community one summer when I was living in Geneva. Although the visit to L'Abri was very short, the intense personal encounters and subsequent friendships that developed from those few days significantly influenced me for years, not least in how they inspired a commitment to intellectual and practical openness. Even though it was clear that throwing myself into this model was not a good match for me, personally, I remain impressed with the honest integrity of anyone who takes a season (or two) to push the ideals of hospitality to their limits and see what happens. Such examples help inspire the constant quest for creative small-scale variants that might more permanently fit personal resources and gifts. As Christine Pohl writes in her exploration of contemporary hospitality models such as L'Abri, the Catholic Worker, and others against the background of John Chrysostom's sermons on sharing, "hospitality often involves small deaths and little resurrections."[34]

Intentional communities, such as monasteries and private homes that are connected by a larger and deliberately interdependent support structure, may offer the most resilient models for weathering such ups and downs. The resilience of community and the extended household is probably why such models seemed natural in the ancient world, where life depended on a person's social connection to many different people and roles in the home and in the neighborhood. Such hospitality never depended on the nuclear family alone. Coenobitic monasticism—group living—was big enough to share the work of sharing, whether in its guesthouses, hospitals, or elaborate church and community complexes. It was solitary ascetics, such as the monk at Gaza and Amma Syncletica, who realistically imposed limits, giving people permission to sometimes say no, offering a vision for sharing humanity with others without practicing material divestment.

Most modern Christian communities and nuclear households have more resources—and thus more responsibility for wise divestment—than the "Christ-loving layperson" at Gaza who had nothing beyond a willing money-lender at the door. Modern social resources for sharing the world may be structured differently from those of ancient society, but they abound nonetheless. Sharing in contemporary culture may not involve an unlimited and perpetual line of guests, but may take a different shape entirely, or may happen, as in Euphemia's chosen social activism, away from home. Yet early Christian texts demonstrate a provocative diversity in their examples and lifestyle models that might still guide contemporary choices. Euphemia, Maria, Mary, Basil's famine relief and hospital initiative, the Gregories' imaging of their homeless lepers, and Jacob of Sarug's vision of the poor as fertile soil are all empathic and practical examples of applying ideals to a very specific cultural context. These and other stories support and encourage creative variety in how we too might "keep things crunchy" in the way we use our own bit of ground.

8

EMBODYING SACRED
KINGDOM

"The very ability to scar tells the necessary story."
—Karmen MacKendrick, *Word Made Skin*[1]

For many religious Jews today, there is no more sacred place to visit and touch than the Western or "Wailing" wall, all that remains of the Second Temple in Jerusalem. Several years ago I found myself also fingering its rough stones and listening to the voices of those who wept and whispered into its battered mortar.

Coming to the Wall had not been part of my plan for that day, nor for any of the few days I was in Jerusalem. But as I emerged, disoriented, from the cellar of the Wohl Archaeological Museum, with its labyrinth of first-century Jewish ritual baths and mosaics still scorched black from the ancient Roman siege of Jerusalem, I turned a corner and abruptly found myself in a crowd of teenagers on a high lookout point. The staircase led down to the Western Wall plaza; beyond it was the Dome of the Rock and between the two was the Wall itself. After climbing down to go through the security checkpoint, I wandered around the plaza for a while, then approached the women's section of the Wall. Reaching the stones, I instinctively followed the Wall a few paces away from the crowd when, suddenly, I found myself at the foot of some steps leading up into a small enclosed room on the southernmost edge of this otherwise public space.

As I entered the room my first thought was: how small it is. This enclosure with its low ceiling and bookcase of prayer books against the opposite wall might hold a dozen women at most with these white plastic chairs pressed close together. The first sound I heard as I came into the room was a woman's weeping. The women in the room stood or sat facing the Wall itself. Here in this unexpected inner sanctum of the women's section, as I moved deeper into the room I began to listen, to watch, to open my heart to whatever I might encounter in that place, and to pray for peace.

I was praying for peace, that is; the Orthodox Jewish women around me seemed to be, far more deeply and personally, grieving the consequences of its absence.

I edged toward the side and sat down, visibly no different from them except that (like a few) my head was bare. For many minutes I sat, simply gazing at this Wall, and listened.

Inches in front of me a woman sat with her knees against the wall, swaying in prayer as if in labor with the weight of the room's collective sorrow. While a soft voice behind me continued to weep, the woman ahead murmured in Hebrew from her prayer book in a low, steady voice, like the hum of deep summer, her soft, steady drone intertwining like smoke with the softer prayers of the other women. Most of these women, I realized, were mothers in a world of sorrow and a universe of sorrows. Mothers in Jerusalem. Mothers in that very place where, as Gregory of Nyssa wrote in his fourth-century treatise criticizing pilgrimage, "Nowhere in the world are people so ready to kill each other." What had happened over the centuries, I wondered, in the very inches of space that I now inhabited? Except for this wall and a few graves, cellars, and museums, it is almost impossible in modern Jerusalem to see any first-century earth or standing stones; we are left with only the air itself and shattered traces of the quibbling, pious, warring religious and political leaders who capitalized on the ruins, the air, and the stories. I wondered who had stood here, walked through here, run, prayed, quarreled, killed, or been killed? What had they been thinking? What were their stories? Focusing on the wall itself I saw, through the charged space on that February morning, past the murmuring, chanting women, that the stone before us was smudged and scarred with the black of smoke from an ancient conflagration. What is this place, I wondered, this holy place? Where am I? I felt displaced, transferred at some level to another world. When I left the room some time later, returning down the steps to the outdoor Wall, I followed the example of others around me and backed away from it respectfully, gazing at it with each backward step, and meditating on all that it represented and all that it had witnessed. Up in a deep crevice in the rock, one of many, where the ruins of King Herod's wall ended and the lines of Arab and Crusader reconstruction began, I noticed a white bird nestled and quietly watching over these praying women: an icon of peace in a ravaged and troubled land. And when I turned away, at last, to enter again the public area of the Western Plaza that was crammed that tense week with police cars, tanks, and security checkpoints, a tiny old woman asked me for alms.

"Tzedakah charity," she whispered, her hand out. Behind her, far across the plaza under the brilliant blue sky, next to a building that advertised bar mitzvahs, a prominent sign announced the Colel Chabad, Free Soup Kitchen for the Needy. Even here, I thought. Even here the liturgy of what is most holy smudges together like a charcoal sketch of shadows of poverty and fire, here in this holy city, this embodied sacred image for the eschatological reality of both Jews and Christians around the world and across the ages.[2]

Fire, war, walls, weeping, poverty, and the archeological fragments of organizational relief in a holy place are all tokens of human need, not only in the modern world of the Middle East, but in the ancient world as well. Five or six miles west of Jerusalem, just off the desert road between Jerusalem and Jericho that is famous from the story of the Good Samaritan, traces of fire at the gate yet again cohere to a reminder of need and hospitality. This is the site of the archaeological remains of an extraordinary Judaean desert monastery, the monastery of the Christian hermit, Martyrius, founded in the fifth century. As large as a small village, this 10,000 square meter walled compound still bears witness to its once-vibrant community in its mosaics, baths, council hall, and guesthouse. The iron rings and stone mangers still mark out the stable. Outside the compound are the foundations of another stable and the guest hospice. Pilgrims and guests who stayed there as visitors, perhaps, similarly wounded or as sick as the proverbial Samaritan, might have looked down directly onto the lonely and still-dangerous road. Yet even inside a monastery where, as Derwas Chitty put it, the desert was a city, life was risky. By the time the Persians reached St. Martyrius in 616, the monks had blocked one of the two main doors to protect themselves against potential marauders. The surviving doorway could be secured by a remarkable rolling stone that still stands in its original grooves in the entrance. Nine feet in diameter, this massive circular stone could be rolled across the only available entry and wedged securely by an inside niche to effectively protect those within from the most violent of sieges. We know that it was shut on one attack because, on the threshold, just outside the doorway, the stone is torched, but inside, where the rolling wheel would have blocked all assault, the stones are untouched by flame. Who was inside and what was their fate that day? Coins found on the site suggest that even if they survived they soon abandoned the monastic complex. It remained abandoned from 616 well into the eighth century. At some point the stone was rolled back and broke in half, leaving the place exposed to all comers. Apart from modern vandalism and pillage for local stone construction, the foundations of the site remain intact, its underground cisterns ideal for whoever built the farmhouse within the compound sometime in the eighth century.

Fire scars at many levels. When I was six, my mother took me to watch a house burn down. For her it was entertainment; it left me with apocalyptic nightmares for years. Holy or terrible, fire is something that once it touches our nerves marks our memories as indelibly as its scars would mark our thresholds and our flesh. The darkened stones in Jerusalem and at the monastery of Martyrius carry their torched marks despite centuries of exposure to sun and rain. Fire can make even water burn flesh, as my brother learned at two when he grabbed a bubbling saucepan. Ancient Christian martyrs were sometimes boiled in oil. There are lots of ways to get burned.

Yet fire is also an image of what is holy, a purifier, a religious good, a symbol for justice, and a means to light and life. Moses met God in the burning bush, consumed with fire but not destroyed by it. Take off your shoes, God said; you are on holy ground. The ancients expected the end of the world to come in a final conflagration that would dissolve all material impurities. The apostle Paul points to the eschatological fire that separates gold from straw. And Salvian, the fifth-century presbyter of the church at Lérins described in Chapter 2, delighted to remind his readers of the fire in which the rich man in Luke 16 suffered because he failed to show mercy to the beggar. Instead, Salvian says, he should have given his riches away, "stopped the overflowing balls of fire with the opposed immensity of his huge wealth."[3] Scholar Cam Grey calls Salvian's treatises "blistering." Blistering indeed.

When his enemies tried to burn down the church where he was preaching in Armenia in the 370s, Basil of Caesarea preached a triumphally gloating sermon recalling how the winds turned the fire around, causing damage to the arsonists but sparing the Christian complex. He used the incident to call the congregation to a material divestment that would relieve the innocent citizens who had lost their possessions in the blaze.[4] Fire was a common image of moral evil, heresy, and hellfire in the theological rhetoric of early church controversies, and bishops did not need to look very far for literal models. In many Protestant churches today the congregation wears red on Pentecost to celebrate the Holy Spirit, that personal presence of God in something "like flames of fire." When I was a child, the Sunday liturgy was not over until the candles were snuffed.

HOLY FIRE: THE LITURGY
OF THE POOR

In the three-part paradigm around which this book is shaped—sensing need, sharing the world, and embodying sacred kingdom—it is the third image, discussed here, that is best represented by the theme of liturgy in the ancient world. Yet the word "liturgy" in modern Christian usage has almost as many conflicting meanings as the word "love." In the early church, the Greek word, *leitourgia*, from which we get "liturgy," could mean either worship or service. The practical behaviors that we associate with "public service" were never very far from early Christians' understanding of worship, of altar, of rituals, and gifts. Service to beggars, offerings given to the poor and material provisions for widows, was incorporated at a very early date into the liturgical pattern of the church "service." Widows' prayers were equated with offerings on the altar, and, as the stories of the Cappadocians, John Chrysostom, and Jacob of Sarug illustrate, many early Christian authors described aid to the physical body as literal engagement with the body of Christ. Such "liturgies" to the needy were also understood on a suprahuman level, as actions that contributed to the remaking and healing of the whole cosmic order by enacting the justice and mercy of God in space and time.

I grew up understanding liturgy as a mystery, that is, as Dennis Covington defines mystery, "not the absence of meaning but the presence of more meaning than we can comprehend."[5] As our pastors and church teachers explained Lutheran liturgy, we came to view certain worship-related theological phrases and explanations as "right" and others as misleading or frankly wrong, but none of them could ever be fully adequate. The expectations for my own liturgical practices as a member of the laity on Sunday mornings were clear enough; the mystery was in the divine. It was that aspect that made it liturgy rather than theater or play-acting. Our clergy led us with liturgical clothing, words, and actions, but we, holding as Lutherans do to the "priesthood of all believers," were also equally responsible to engage with the sacred at a less visible level, with our whole hearts and minds. As I understood it, in Christianity as in many religions, liturgy was engagement in ritual that used basic material substances to give shape to a sacred dwelling space, a cosmic "reality." To participating believers, this was no artificial construction of reality, but rather engagement in a reality that went far beyond the self, yet remained independent of the self, whether we knew it or not. For us, liturgies and sacraments were neither symbols nor reminders; they were not even something that we effected. They were engagements that, effected from the beginning of time, invited us to enter. Engaging with elementary substances of service and sacraments in what was tangible, the liturgical event marked my presence in a space intangible yet "literal," beyond my imagining or any potential for petty manipulation. Liturgical space invited reception. It was a place where, against all the odds, what I did was truly heard, understood, and mattered. You are on holy ground, God told Moses at the bush. A sketch of Moses's shoes, separated from his feet, can still be seen and touched in the Byzantine synagogue mosaic at ancient Sepphoris in Galilee. To follow God was to enter a liturgy imaged by fire: through the Red Sea and on the altar in the Holy of Holies. Open your mouth, God told Isaiah; let this holy coal from the altar change the molecular configuration and performance of your lips. My brother donned the red robe and white surplice of an altar boy, lighting the altar candles, holy flames that never once gave me a nightmare.

Holy fire moves, summoning us inward, upward. In the church that my family attended in the late 1970s, the sun streamed through an enormous, clear, four-part window behind the altar down the central aisle during the Sunday liturgies. The light was divided only by two cross-shaped beams that met above and behind the altar. Along the shadowed cross-beam the sun drew us each week with its rising, moving the boundaries of light ever forward and upward across the polished floor to the altar. The brilliance of that sun warmed the raw edges of my soul. To engage with this white-flamed immanence touched me in ways that changed me forever. I still believe that liturgy is an engagement in mystery.

Like fire, the Christian liturgy of public service to those in need is a similar inversion of destructive elements that builds an eschatological kingdom. Hunger, homelessness, inequity, and need are all elements by which lives are dragged down and destroyed. Once again, Jacob of Sarug best captures the paradoxical mystery here of christological, liturgical fire in the flesh of the poor:

> He at whose fierce heat the seraphs of fire cover their faces is here going around, in the person of the poor, begging bread from you. He before whom the cherubim of fire tremble in His exalted sphere is here going around with the beggars from house to house.... His radiance burns up the heavenly beings if they gaze upon Him, yet with beggars He is clothed in rags so that you might be set in the right by Him.[6]

No matter how we worship, how we perform our ritual and ecclesial liturgies, Christianity is grounded in the affirmation of a material world into which God took gritty, bloody, wet, personal, searing, and passionate shape. God knows there's need because God took on need. Liturgy is one of those words we use to express the complex depth of the Christian's relational and community response.

SERVICE AND COMMUNITY IN CHRISTIAN LITURGY

There is a sense in which liturgy is like the moving light and shadow of that silhouetted cross on the church floor. It is not only a "vertical" engagement between me and the divine, but its arms also move horizontally, across the community, held out to draw in, to receive, to welcome, and to define the boundaries of the physical self who engages in service in the here and now. Those who are wholly alone rarely stand with arms outstretched; the position has meaning only in relation to others.

Perhaps one of the most extraordinary recent narratives about the interconnection between the mystery of Christian liturgy and serving the hungry poor is Sara Miles's book, *Take This Bread*. A modern radical agnostic who had never before attended church, Miles wandered into an Episcopal service one morning at age forty-six almost by accident, took communion for the first time in her life, and instantly, she writes, "something outrageous and terrifying happened. Jesus happened to me." Trying to describe it rationally, Miles admits that

> It made no sense.... The disconnect between what I thought was happening—I was eating a piece of bread; what I heard someone else say was happening—the piece of bread was the "body" of "Christ," a patently untrue or at best metaphorical statement; and what I *knew* was happening—God, named "Christ" or "Jesus" was real, and in my mouth—utterly short-circuited my ability to do anything but cry.... Did the actual wine symbolically represent the imagined blood? No, because when I opened my mouth and swallowed, everything changed. It was real.[7]

Miles's conversion changed more than her life; it changed her community. Realizing that "at that Table, sharing food, we were brought into the ongoing work of making creation whole," she went on to establish a food pantry at the church that distributed food not from an adjoining hall, office, or pantry, but from the central liturgical space and the altar itself. The pantry continues to nourish more than 450 families each week who collect their groceries straight from the sanctuary. Not content with this level of outreach, Miles went on to start nearly a dozen more food pantries in the poorest parts of town. Still struggling at the end of the book to explain the mystery of this "Heavenly Feast," she reflects on the persistent power of the liturgy and her own continuing inadequacy, writing, "There was no way I could reduce that meal to a religious ritual.... I was going to have to take real communion whenever it happened, wherever it found me, in my least prepared and most unfinished moments."[8]

As Miles learned dramatically, liturgical service is ultimately inseparable from community, even for those who might choose a greater ascetic solitude than that possible in Miles's example of radical social action. In the ancient world it was often the solitary "holy" men and women, those who lived as hermits on the edge of town, who became local authorities, villagers flocking to ask their wisdom and to appeal for their power to obtain social justice, food in famine, and order the material redistribution of goods,[9] but unless they were priests they could not also offer the eucharist to their disciples. By the fifth century these monastic holy men became so respected for their social wisdom that it became routine to choose bishops from ascetic monks, rather than from its married priests or even (as with Ambrose and Gregory the Great in the west) its "secular" political leaders.[10]

Being a natural introvert, it took me years to appreciate the close relationship between the public social action that made it so painful for me to serve poor families hour after hour, day after day, in a public clinic, and the similarly difficult challenge I faced when given the chance to enter into more explicitly public liturgical practices. This became most obvious when I decided that as someone who studies the early church in the Greek-speaking Byzantine world I really ought to know more about contemporary eastern Orthodox worship. Although many of my friends were Orthodox, my initial visits to Orthodox parishes were a profound physical shock, not just at first but for many months, quite apart from the usual tensions of visiting a community of strangers. The parish I visited most often has a sanctuary in the round, with no pews and just a few chairs against the walls. Orthodox worship in such a setting is very kinetic indeed, and without the synchronized and uniform actions I knew from

Protestant and Roman Catholic experiences. Here, instead, everyone did things a little differently. This gave me some liberty, but there were certain things everyone did that I had never done before. These included public veneration of icons, liturgical kissing of various objects, and (in Lent) full-body prostrations, a ritual in which you kneel down in order to lie wholly, face down, on the ground, and then rise up again, repetitively, either during the Sunday liturgy or once a year in a direct personal encounter with each of your fellow parishioners as part of a ritual request for mutual forgiveness. In the first few weeks of my Orthodox visits, I could sit in the shadows and watch, but my physical stillness made me painfully obvious. Besides, I was convinced that I could understand this tradition only if I worked at understanding it with my whole body. Yet I felt almost catatonically reticent in such public space. This reticence had nothing to do with theology. I had done my homework and knew that, intellectually anyway, I was willing to bow, kneel, kiss icons, and even perform occasional full prostrations, if required. I was not prepared, however, to do these things in the presence of other people. It did not matter that they were, more or less, doing the same thing. I longed for everyone—just for those moments—to disappear so that, as C. S. Lewis put it in his defense of liturgical prostration, "the body should do its homage."[11] I began to come to church early to try this physical worship with as few people present as possible. I persisted only because, to my surprise, I found it deeply moving. But the excruciating "stage fright" of my introverted reticence remained for several years.

Deciding next to reach out to be more physically engaging in my own tradition, I found that more familiar liturgical practices were almost equally difficult. I encountered exactly the same discomfort during a year as a liturgical cupbearer in a small Episcopal chapel, as I faced weekly internal agonies at being in front and full view of the surprisingly large number of parishioners who turned out at eight o'clock every Sunday morning. As was also true in my Orthodox ventures, the only part that was easy was saying the words, conditioned as I was by decades of verbal liturgy and church music. But as I physically forced my body to engage in the intimacy of serving communion in full view of the crowds, with one of several priests whom I deeply respected, my hands and voice following theirs as I offered holy cup and holy words, a privilege and a service, I wanted nothing more than to disappear completely. Others tell me they experience the same fraught tension in the mere act of moving up to the front of the church to receive communion.

The public reticence of my own experience may be extreme, but it has taught me that affirming the Christian doctrine of the incarnation requires more than an intellectual exercise within our usual comfortable physical routines. It requires more than adjusting our external resources, to "live more simply," "give more generously," or "be more intentionally hospitable." Affirming incarnation mindful of the embodied nature of those in need and suffering from violence and injustice begins at the level of our own body cells, our own nerve endings, and our own volitional, nonverbal behavior, not just in relation to other people but also in relation to ourselves and how we worship, how we listen to our body, and how we pray. Our awareness on these many levels may have profound implications for how we address global issues of need and injustice.

"HOW SILENT AND QUIET IS JUSTICE"

There are many different nuances in the historically Christian relationship between the acts of caring for the needy bodies of those who were poor and the acts of church "liturgy" as we understand it today—what believers do with their bodies and physical objects during a church "service." Orthodox Christianity today includes a variety of social attitudes toward the liturgical language of serving the poor, but social service is in fact a deeply integral (if often overlooked) and vital piece of the tradition. Recent Orthodox authors who model and encourage a liturgy characterized by social justice include Jim Forest, Paul Evdokimov, Mother Maria Skobtsova, and the Ecumenical Patriarch of Constantinople.[12]

Mother Maria Skobtsova, who dedicated her life to housing and feeding the dispossessed poor in the streets of Paris, for which she died in a concentration camp in 1945, discusses the Orthodox ideal and response to social issues in her essay on "The Mysticism of Human Communion."[13] Emphasizing the importance of adequate concern for "a spiritual and mystical basis" on which to construct social action, she defines this in terms of a communing engagement with the divine:

> Who…can differentiate the worldly from the heavenly in the human soul, who can tell where the image of God ends and the heaviness of human flesh begins! In communing with the world in the person of each individual human being, we know that we are communing

with the image of God, and, contemplating that image, we touch the Archetype—we commune with God.[14]

Concluding with an explicit appeal to liturgy *as* social gospel, she writes that

> The liturgy outside the church is our sacrificial ministry in the church of the world, adorned with living icons of God, our common ministry, an all-human sacrificial offering of love, the great act of our God-manly union, the united prayerful breath of our God-manly spirit…and it seems to me that this mysticism of human communion is the only authentic basis for any external Christian activity.[15]

This grand vision for liturgy as part of everyday Christian life did not blind Mother Maria to certain obvious difficulties. The "icons" she encountered in the Paris slums indeed included disturbing neighbors, drunks, irritating students, "obnoxious ladies, or seedy old codgers."[16] But her view of a life that is defined within a liturgical framework on a broad scale—she was an energetic, optimistic, and educated woman who lived in her own home in the community, made her own decisions, and was closely connected with parish administration—is perhaps reminiscent of models like that of Euphemia described in Chapter 6. Independence did not free either Maria Skobtsova or Euphemia from necessary interdependence with the needs of those they served in the community—or from the action of the community authorities who eventually persecuted them to their death for their work.

Stories of early Christian martyrdom often contain similar liturgical identification, in which the martyr represents both Christ and a liturgy defined in terms of justice. Tarbo, for example, was a Syriac-speaking "daughter of the covenant" whose brother, Simeon, a bishop in Persia, was martyred in 341 because the Persians suspected that his Christianity meant he was a political traitor, loyal to Rome. Suspecting his extended family as well, the officials charged Tarbo, another sister, and the sister's slave with witchcraft against the Persian queen, killing the three women in a gruesome public butchery. The texts suggest that the social power of these young women lay in their quiet model of righteousness and their identity with Christ. In direct contrast to the bold and noisy injustice of their murderers, Tarbo's hagiographer praised the women by exclaiming, "How silent and quiet is justice."[17] Yet such women rarely described their vocation (when they had the opportunity to describe it at all) in these terms. When Martha, another daughter of the covenant, faced slaughter from the Persians by immolation in a fire pit, she identified herself with the young Isaac at Mount Moriah with the exception that her choice was one that expressed power: "But I *do* have wood and fire, for the wood is the cross of Jesus my Lord, and I *do* have fire too—the fire that Christ left on earth."[18]

LITURGY: TRANSFIGURING PAIN

My friend Father Michael Phillips, now an Orthodox monk, experienced the intricate elision of liturgy and service to the needy poor during three years in which he served as a residential Episcopal monk-chaplain in a halfway house for men with human immunodeficiency virus/acquired immunodeficiency syndrome (HIV/AIDS), while working simultaneously as a deacon-in-training at a "high church" parish. He recalls his various roles meeting and overlapping in a madly kinetic space that was both a challenge and a blessing.

In those days he was a member of the Brotherhood of St. Gregory (BSG), an Episcopal religious order whose members, like those in early Christian Syria, live and work in intentional households within secular society, dedicating themselves to particular social services. His bishop had assigned him the chaplaincy position and he also held another, full-time paid position in church administration in addition to a third role, on the clergy staff for St. Mary the Virgin, a staunchly "high" Anglo-Catholic parish in Manhattan.

"I'd always read a lot about the Anglo-Catholic movement and its close link both to the liturgical movement but also with social awareness," Father Michael told me one day when we met to discuss his experiences.[19] "So I knew it in a historical and theoretical sense. But at St. Mary's I experienced from the ground up—or the heart out—the intense link that can grow between those two roles."

The halfway house was not an easy place for him to live. When one of the three resident monks decided to leave the Brotherhood, Father Michael took on yet more tasks. After each long day's work in the diocesan office, he would take the train home to Yonkers, cook, and then spend his evening working with the residents on their issues and problems.

The image of blood was not just a liturgical concept for Father Michael as part of each Sunday's eucharist; it was something he sometimes had to wash off the walls at the house, when former addicts reverted to using drugs, against the rules. Expelling residents was often necessary to keep the house safe, but because he cared so much for the men he served, it was "always hard," he said, "always very, very hard."

And yet it was during this time, he says, when "my work at St. Mary's became a place that helped to transfigure the pain and grief of the house in a way that daily prayer didn't. We were only two brothers maintaining the house. We chanted the offices, which was a joy, but daily prayer was not eucharist. It wasn't that liturgy in which you bring everything and offer it in order to receive it back transformed. I found that at St. Mary's."

Although being on the clergy staff at St. Mary's might have been just one more thing to do, another exhausting commitment, in fact Father Michael found his role there restorative, in part because, in serving the altar there, he did not need to make any decisions. Like many high Anglo-Catholic liturgies, St. Mary's was "directed" by a Master of Ceremonies (M.C.). Trained in liturgical minutiae, the M.C. choreographed every move. "So I had to learn to let go of a lot of control," Father Michael sighed happily, "which was exactly what I was trying to exercise constantly at the house. I had to let go and not just let God, but let the M.C., who told us when to stand, reverence, read, and so forth."

While liturgy involves both physical activity, vocal activity, and listening, listening at St. Mary's was a very active process. "I was being fed, certainly spiritually and theologically, but also aesthetically," said Father Michael. He explained this to me in a reflection that is worth quoting at length:

> I began to ponder this link in the classic Anglo-Catholic movement, of beauty in the midst of slum work. I realized that this brought a beauty to people in the slums, that they could only have in church. The experience gave me an intuitive grasp of the balance between action and contemplation. As a deacon, I was the one who proclaims the Gospel out to the world and then brings the needs of the world back into the church through the intercessions and the litany. I found myself liturgizing what I was expected to do in my daily life: to share a gospel of love—sometimes tough love—and also to bring needs to the attention of others. This liturgical process was a body experience, and for me a very integrated one. The Sunday liturgical experience helped me stay focused on why I was at the house. In both an external as well as internal sense, I was bringing all that "stuff" with me on Sunday to this

beautiful liturgy at St. Mary's. This enabled me to transform some of
the pain and grief of the place into that liturgy, and then take my experience at St. Mary's back to the house.

Although he eventually left the Brotherhood and later joined the Orthodox
Church, Father Michael continued to reflect on this liturgical experience
within his Orthodox context even as he continued the struggle to balance
community expectations for parish life and service with his underlying
and continuing monastic vocation.

EMBODYING: MEDITATION
ON AN ICON

The transformative intersection of everyday life with the sacred realm
that Father Michael encountered in liturgical service in inner-city New
York is also a key theme in the Orthodox Christian theology of the icon.
Few icons contain imagery to suggest an explicit convergence of saint with
social welfare, but one of my favorites, that does this in an unusual pairing
of images, is a late eighteenth- or early nineteenth-century Russian icon
of Saints Basil and Alexis, in which the two men are depicted face to face
beneath a figure of Christ in glory. The icon itself is deeply scarred with
the marks of time, hard use, and an unknown but likely violent history. Its
unpainted edges and back are black with smoke and centuries of handling,
its gilded and exquisitely painted surface is chipped and cracked, lined in
several places as if blunt objects have been dragged across it. Yet despite
the scars and occasionally cracked, missing, or floating chips of paint, the
icon's three figures continue to radiate a profound sense of calm, their facial
expressions still impelling and enduring. The two saints are clearly identified, each name spelled out over his head in red Slavonic letters, perfectly
circular haloes balancing the spaces below the cloud of heaven from which
Christ radiates with a book in his left hand and his right hand raised in
blessing. Christ's high forehead shines with light as his close-set dark eyes
draw the viewer into an engagement that circles down and around, into
an image of eschatological reality that cuts through the framed lines on the
wood, to encompass the world of those who are drawn into its scene.

Basil stands on the left in full episcopal garb, his right hand in blessing and his left hand holding out the holy book. The book actually leans
toward Alexis, as if offered for consideration, for veneration. Alexis gazes

Saints Basil and Alexis (the "Man of God") standing beneath a figure of Christ in glory.
Nineteenth-century Russian icon; photo by the author.

back, open-eyed and calm, his arms crossed like a supplicant for blessing,
his feet bare, his tunic the short garb of the poor, and his features (down to
his toenails) exquisitely executed. His status as a holy man who has chosen
the life of a poor beggar is suggested only by his halo. All three are bearded,

and the fine feathering lines of hair tufts in Basil's beard hint at a rever-
ently playful touch. Of the two saints Alexis is visibly the broader, stron-
ger man, although his posture may hint at the slight stoop of a laborer or
the respectful inclination of one who humbles himself before ecclesiastical
authorities. It is Basil whose drapery suggests the slight shoulders and thin
chest one expects of someone who died young and who was indeed always
complaining about his health. They both stand slightly frontal, inviting
the viewer to enter and participate.

Beyond these obvious details, one of the most extraordinary features of
this icon—at least extraordinary to me as a historian—is that this scene is
historically impossible. Basil lived between 330 and 379. After his school-
ing at Athens and a bit of traveling into Egypt, he spent most of his episcopate in either Cappadocia or the northeastern mountains of Roman
Armenia. Alexis, a more shadowy figure, was from Rome and lived in
Syria in the middle of the fifth century. It is not unknown to place figures
from different times near one another in the same icon, but rarely if ever
are such figures depicted in such obvious visual engagement and relationship with one another as these two are here.

The story of St. Alexis has many variants, but in the earliest version,
from fifth-century Edessa, he is anonymous, simply called the "man of
God." Son of wealthy and noble parents, he fled an arranged marriage in
Rome to live anonymously among the destitute beggars who were living
in the alleys and churchyard in Edessa. Eager to escape detection hundreds of miles from home, he dressed and begged like everyone else, sharing the life of the poor in every particular except that, like Maria's aunt in
Amida and Jerusalem, he shared his food with other beggars and spent
his nights secretly stretched out in prayer. One night he was accidentally
discovered in the act of prayer by the church watchman, who insisted on
learning the truth about his identity. Later, when the beggar fell sick, the
watchman moved him to the bishop's hospital for the poor. There he died.
He was buried in an unmarked grave, leaving no sign that he ever existed.
The watchman's story inspired the bishop, Rabbula, to a heightened zeal
to care for all the poor and needy strangers, saying, "For who knows
whether there are many like this saint who delight in abasement, but
are nobles to God in their souls, not recognized by the people because of
their abasement."[20] While Basil's association with philanthropy most commonly represents traditional Christian relief activities—as administrators
and patrons of the poor—Alexis (like Maria's aunt Mary) represents the
embodied essence of those who voluntarily chose to identify very literally

with the Christ-poor themselves. The stories of such holy beggars follow themes of deliberate imitation of Christ, but they, intentionally anonymous, are to all appearances nothing more than ordinary tramps living in the midst of common, stinking, homeless humanity at its most needy. Neither priests, monks, deacons, nor "sons of the covenant," they are "holy fools," embodying the sacred in hidden form. Unlike traditional monks, they do not retreat from the world but hide their religious practices within its least appealing characteristics, in full public view.

It is the bishop Rabbula who makes this man's life into a legend, sometime during his own episcopate between 411 and 435. Even if the original Edessan "man of God" was a historical person, he and Basil could not have crossed paths, since by then Basil had been dead for thirty years. Nor does the transmission of either story refer to the other. So what are they doing together in this icon?

The full answer remains another mystery in the history of liturgy. Syriac scholar Susan Ashbrook Harvey has suggested that Ephrem, a Syriac contemporary of Basil who died at Edessa in 373 after generous service feeding and providing medical care to the sick victims of famine, may be the invisible conceptual link between Basil and Alexis, at least in Russian iconography.[21] All that I know for certain about this icon is how its eschatological gaze holds me. Entering into this gaze, remembering the two very different lives of these men, under the sovereignty of the Christ image and all that it means in my own personal life and narrative history, I find myself within a liturgical participation that simultaneously engages all three of the paradigms outlined in this book. From such a position, the viewer seems to stand in relation to the image as one who is at the same moment "sensing need," sharing the world with these fellow believers in some mysterious but prayerful and empowering manner to "go and do," and participating at the edge, yet "inside the rim" of an embodied entrance into a sacred realm.

Such a meditation on an icon, evoking the history of religious social action in the context of a timeless eschaton, is not—and must never become—some kind of ethereal escapism from "real-world" problems. Reflection must never, that is, paralyze responsible social response in the here and now. Far from it. Rather, meditative and prayerful engagement may act to challenge the viewer to what Charles Mathewes has called, in a more explicitly political context, "charitable citizenship." The relational dynamics of such iconic imagery may remind us that, for example, as Mathewes puts it,

> The basic challenge of political life is...the proper ordering of our loves into harmonious polyphony—albeit a polyphonic harmony only eschatologically attained....we must insist on this complexity...and on the possibility that good can come out of our being political in this way, however difficult the path may be.[22]

The word "political" is, after all, closely related to the Greek words *polis*, for city, and *politeia*, meaning "way of life." And the history of Christian liturgical practice is often closely linked with what another writer provocatively calls "the communion of civic good...the market economy as sacramental rite."[23] Wherever the figures of Basil and Alexis might be located within the timeless space of my favorite Russian icon—itself a time-bound block of wood that is scored with historical scars, marks, and meaning—the narrative tradition of each of these figures intersects with modern social issues just as surely as their gazes meet across the battered, gilded, cosmic space. Their intersection is located in their mutual focus on responding to the needy poor as icons of God. This thematic eschatological intersection, like the intersection of the gaze here, occurs beneath the Christ figure, who is painted in the classic pose suggesting the right hand of grace and the left-handed judgment of Matthew 25:31–46. Yet icons of the last judgment (which this is not) rarely show the poor themselves. Here we find not an image of judgment, but one of grace.

The liminal mystery, occasional anonymity, and historical dissonance of religious icons, like many of the inevitable unknowns we face in reading early Christian texts, give them an aura of timelessness. Although we may date their stories to particular remembered or historical events, the individuals in such stories and images rarely fit into neat, chronologically limited boundaries. And like iconic relationships, the Christ-poor is one that often takes us by surprise. The stark anachronism of Basil's and Alexis's shared gaze illustrates a communal dynamic that compels the viewer into a holy space that is entirely—and perhaps intentionally—outside the boundaries of logical and sequential time. It is this journey of sensing and remembering such bodies, and letting them speak to the action of our own choices, that is the essence of life lived on sacred ground.

NOTES

Epigraph: Dorothy Allison, *Bastard out of Carolina* (New York: Dutton-Penguin, 1992), 298.

CHAPTER 1

1. Jez Lowe, "Bede Weeps," from his CD, *Bede Weeps*, Fellside Recordings, Workington, Cumbria, 1993, published by Lowe Life Music, quoted with permission.

2. For Wilfrid's life and wanderings I have depended on Bede; for more on the Easter controversy and the Whitby "synod," see Benedicta Ward, *A True Easter: The Synod of Whitby 664 AD* (Oxford: SLG Press, 2007).

3. Edith Wyschogrod, "Empathy and Sympathy as Tactile Encounter," in *Crossover Queries: Dwelling with Negatives, Embodying Philosophy's Others*, ed. Edith Wyschogrod (New York: Fordham University Press, 2006), 171.

4. Quoted from the back cover of *The PIH Guide to the Community-Based Treatment of HIV in Resource-Poor Settings*, 2nd ed. [Online] 2006. Available at http://model.pih.org/files/Manuals/HIV/2006_AIDS_Manual.pdf. See also Paul E. Farmer, "Health, Human Rights, and the Corporal Works of Mercy: Reflections on New Orleans and Haiti. Address given at the House of Bishops, New Orleans, Louisiana, 21 September 2007" (publication forthcoming).

5. Joint Learning Initiative on Children and HIV/AIDS (JLICA), *Home Truths: Evidence for Action on Children Affected by HIV and AIDS: Final Report* (JLICA, 2009, and Geoff Foster, Madhu Deshmukh, and Alayne Adams (compilers), *Inside Out? Strengthening Community Responses to Children Affected by HIV/AIDS: JLICA Learning Group 2 Synthesis Report* (JLICA, 2008, in press), both available at www.jlica.org/resources/publications.php; see also Geoff Foster, *Study of the Response by Faith-Based Organizations to Orphans and Vulnerable Children: Preliminary Summary Report* (New York: World Conference of Religions for Peace and UNICEF, 2004, available at http://www.uniteforchildren.org/knowmore/files/FBO_OVC_study_summary.pdf; and Deryke Belshaw, "Enhancing the Development Capabilities of Civil Society Organizations, with Particular Reference to Christian Faith-Based Organizations," paper presented at the Global Poverty Research Group (GPRG) conference on "Reclaiming Development: Assessing the Contributions of Non-Governmental Organisations to Development

Alternatives," Institute for Development Policy and Management, University of Manchester (UK), 27–29 June 2005, GPRG-WPS-035, available at www.gprg.org/pubs/workingpapers/pdfs/gprg-wps-035.pdf.

6. See, e.g., Moshe Weinfeld, *Social Justice in Ancient Israel and in the Ancient Near East* (Minneapolis, MN: Fortress Press, 1995), esp. 25–45; Chafetz Chaim (=R. Yisrael Meir Kahan), *Ahavath Chesed: The Love of Kindness as Required by God,* trans. Leonard Oschry (New York: Feldheim Publishers, 1976); and for a modern view, R. Avroham Chaim Feuer, *The Tzedakah Treasury: An Anthology of Torah Teachings on the Mitzvah of Charity—to Instruct and Inspire* (Brooklyn, NY: Mesorah Publications, 2000). For a discussion of the similar Syriac Christian use and the relevance of this concept for other early Christian texts, see Susan R. Holman, "Healing the World with Righteousness? The Language of Social Justice in Early Christian Homilies," in *Giving in Monotheistic Religions*, ed. Miriam Frenkel and Yaacov Lev, Studien zur Geschichte und Kultur des islamischen Orients (Berlin and New York: Walter de Gruyter, forthcoming).

7. Optatus, *Against the Donatists* 3.3, trans. Mark Edwards, *Translated Texts for Historians* (Liverpool, UK: Liverpool University Press, 1997), 62.

8. Optatus 3.3, trans. Edwards, 63.

9. W. H. C. Frend, *The Donatist Church: A Movement of Protest in Roman North Africa* (Oxford: Clarendon Press, 1952), 177–87; Giovanni A. Cecconi, "Elemosina e propaganda: Un'analisi della 'Macariana persecutio' nel III libro di Ottato di Milevi," *Revue des Études Augustinennes* 36 (1990): 42–66.

10. For a recent English translation of Gregory's will, see Brian Daley, trans., *Gregory of Nazianzus* (New York: Routledge, 2006), 186–89.

11. Gregory the Great, *Ep.* 9.124. For discussion see Adam Serfass, "Slavery and Pope Gregory the Great," *Journal of Early Christian Studies* 14 (2006): 87.

12. J. van Leeuwen, *De armenwet in haar ontstaan, zin, en strekking geschiedkundig toegelicht* (Leiden: P. Engels, 1847), 6, translated in Frances Gouda, *Poverty and Political Culture: The Rhetoric of Social Welfare in the Netherlands and France, 1815–1854* (Lanham, MD: Rowman & Littlefield, 1995), 181.

13. Basil of Caesarea, *Hexaemeron* 7.5, using an example of male violence from the animal world to emphasize that marriage is a union (the Syriac translation, a loose paraphrase, says "single equality"). That Basil was opposed to domestic abuse is clear from the text that immediately follows: in 7.6, he tells the husband (again quoting from the Syriac translation) to "cast off from your person all altercation and brutality, since you are coupled for total harmony in the peace of a single life." From Robert W. Thomson, trans., *The Syriac Version of the Hexaemeron by Basil of Caesarea* (Leuven, Belgium: Peeters, 1995), 103. For a translation from the Greek, see Sister Agnes Clare Way, trans., *Saint Basil: Exegetic Homilies, The Fathers of the Church* (Washington, DC: Catholic University of America Press, 1963), 114.

14. Sister Nonna Verna Harrison, "Greek Patristic Perspectives on the Origins of Social Injustice," keynote address, The Stephen and Catherine Pappas Patristic Institute's Conference on "Evil and Suffering in the Early Church,"

Holy Cross Greek Orthodox School of Theology, Brookline, Massachusetts, October 12, 2006.

15. The challenge of vocabulary is discussed further in Chapter 4.

16. Gregory of Nazianzus, *Or.* 14.9, in Martha Vinson, trans., *St. Gregory of Nazianzus: Select Orations*, The Fathers of the Church (Washington, DC: Catholic University of America Press, 2003), 44–45, and *Or.* 14.27 (Vinson, 59–60), selections.

17. Alexander Schmemann, *For the Life of the World: Sacraments and Orthodoxy* (Crestwood, NY: St. Vladimir's Seminary Press, 2002), 123.

18. Leonardo Boff, *Cry of the Earth, Cry of the Poor*, trans. Phillip Berryman, Ecology and Justice Series (Maryknoll, NY: Orbis Books, 1997).

19. Basil of Caesarea, "Give Heed to Thyself " [*In illud: Attende tibi ipsi*], trans. Sister M. Monica Wagner, *Saint Basil: Ascetical Works* (New York: Fathers of the Church, 1950), 444.

20. Orhan Pamuk, *Istanbul: Memories of a City*, trans. Maureen Freely (London: Faber and Faber, 2005), 8.

21. Pope Paul VI, *Populorum Progressio* (1967) = On the Development of Peoples, here quoted from the U.S. Catholic Bishops' 1986 letter, "Economic Justice for All," in *Catholic Social Thought: The Documentary Heritage,* ed. David J. O'Brien and Thomas A. Shannon (Maryknoll, NY: Orbis, 1995), 606.

CHAPTER 2

1. Salvian, "The Four Books of Timothy to the Church" (*Ad Ecclesiam*) 4.4, in *The Writings of Salvian, The Presbyter*, trans. Jeremiah F. O'Sullivan (New York: CIMA, 1947), 361.

2. Idem. For a recent study of Salvian's views on the poor, see Cam Grey, "Salvian, the Ideal Christian Community and the Fate of the Poor in Fifth-Century Gaul," in *Poverty in the Roman World*, ed. Margaret Atkins and Robin Osborne (New York: Cambridge University Press), 162–82.

3. Rowan Williams, *Why Study the Past? The Quest for the Historical Church* (Grand Rapids, MI: Eerdmans, 2005), 91.

4. Webster's *Third New International Dictionary of the English Language, Unabridged,* Vol. 2 (Chicago: Encyclopedia Britannica, 1971), 1512.

5. Karmen MacKendrick, *Word Made Skin: Figuring Language at the Surface of Flesh* (New York: Fordham University Press, 2004), 14, 164.

6. Nick Flynn, *Another Bullshit Night in Suck City* (New York: Norton, 2004), 11.

7. Eve Ensler, *Insecure at Last: Losing it in Our Security-Obsessed World* (New York: Villard, 2006), 168, 200.

8. Eve Ensler, *Insecure at Last,* 9.

9. Edith Wyschogrod, "Empathy and Sympathy as Tactile Encounter," in *Crossover Queries: Dwelling with Negatives, Embodying Philosophy's Others*, ed. Edith Wyschogrod (New York: Fordham University Press, 2006), 160.

10. Salvian, *Ep.* 5, trans. O'Sullivan, *The Writings of Salvian*, 251–52.

11. Salvian, *Ep.* 4, trans. O'Sullivan, *The Writings of Salvian*, 241–50.

12. Paul L. Maier, *A Man Spoke, A World Listened: The Story of Walter A. Maier and the Lutheran Hour* (New York: McGraw-Hill, 1963), 1.

13. Phrases are taken from *The Book of Concord: The Confessions of the Evangelical Lutheran Church*, trans. and ed. Theodore G. Tappert in collaboration with Jaroslav Pelikan, Robert Fischer, and Arthur C. Piepkorn (Philadelphia: Fortress Press, 1959), 690, under the general index entry for "Monastery, monastic life."

14. Elizabeth A. Castelli, trans., "Pseudo-Athanasius, *The Life and Activity of the Holy and Blessed Teacher Syncletica*," in *Ascetic Behavior in Greco-Roman Antiquity: A Sourcebook*, ed. Vincent L. Wimbush (Minneapolis, MN: Fortress Press, 1990), 265–311.

15. Esther de Waal, *Seeking God: The Way of St Benedict*, Second Edition (Collegeville, MN: The Liturgical Press, 2001).

16. Karen Armstrong, *The Spiral Staircase: My Climb out of Darkness* (New York: Alfred A. Knopf, 2004), 297.

17. Martin Laird, *Into the Silent Land: A Guide to the Christian Practice of Contemplation* (New York: Oxford University Press, 2006), 12.

18. Daniel Rees and other members of the English Benedictine Congregation, *Consider Your Call: A Theology of Monastic Life Today* (Kalamazoo, MI: Cistercian Publications, 1978), 126.

19. Laird, *Into the Silent Land*, 12.

20. Thomas Merton, *The Asian Journal of Thomas Merton* (New York: New Directions, 1975), 157, quoting from Edward Conze, *Buddhist Thought in India* (London: Allen & Unwin, 1962), 85.

21. Alex de Waal, *Famine That Kills: Darfur, Sudan*, rev. ed., Oxford Studies in African Affairs (New York: Oxford University Press, 2005), 20–23.

22. Alexander Irwin, *Saints of the Impossible: Bataille, Weil, and the Politics of the Sacred* (Minneapolis, MN: University of Minnesota Press, 2002), 43.

23. The most comprehensive biography of Simone Weil is Simone Pétrement, *Simone Weil*, trans. Raymond Rosenthal (New York: Schocken Books, 1976). For Weil's political influence on social policy and ethical thought, see Simone Weil, *The Need for Roots: Prelude to a Declaration of Duties Towards Mankind*, trans. A. F. Wills (New York: Routledge, 1952); Simone Weil, *Waiting for God*, trans. Emma Craufurd (New York: Harper & Row, 1973); and Lawrence A. Blum and Victor J. Seidler, *A Truer Liberty: Simone Weil and Marxism* (New York: Routledge, 1989).

24. Mother Teresa, *Come Be My Light: The Private Writings of the "Saint of Calcutta"* (New York: Doubleday, 2007).

CHAPTER 3

1. Jacob of Sarug, "On the Love of the Poor"; the Syriac text is *Homiliae Selectae Mar-Jacobi Sarugensis,* Vol. 2, ed. Paul Bedjan (Paris: Lipsiae, Otto Harrassowitz, 1906), 816–36; here quoting from p. 832, lines 11 and 17. The English translation of this text used throughout this book is by Sebastian Brock (personal correspondence), used with permission.

2. Jacob of Sarug, "On the Love of the Poor;" selections from p. 828, lines 18–22, trans. Brock.

3. Gregory of Nyssa, first homily "On the Love of the Poor" (hereafter identified as *Paup.* 1), PG 46.457, my translation.

4. Jacob of Sarug, "On the Love of the Poor," selections, trans. Brock.

5. The story of Mary and Euphemia is found in John of Ephesus, *Lives of the Eastern Saints,* in *Holy Women of the Syrian Orient*, ed. and trans. Sebastian P. Brock and Susan Ashbrook Harvey (Berkeley: University of California Press, 1987), 124–33.

6. Robin Hyde, *A Home in This World* (Auckland, New Zealand: Longman Paul, 1984), 11.

7. Two authors who do address the effects of modern middle-eastern conflicts on the natural world are Adina Hoffman, in both her memoir, *House of Windows: Portraits from a Jerusalem Neighborhood* (New York: Random House, 2000), and in many of the essays she published in the *Jerusalem Post*, where she lamented the abuse of trees, including the politically induced vandalism that has destroyed groves of priceless ancient olive trees in Israel; and Jonathan Trouern-Trend, in his *Birding Babylon: A Soldier's Journal from Iraq* (San Francisco: Sierra Club Books, 2006), poignant observations on birds that live in areas disturbed by armed conflict.

8. Anna M. Silvas, "In Quest of Basil's Retreat: An Expedition to Ancient Pontus," *Antichthon* 41 (2007): 73–95.

9. Basil of Caesarea, *Hom.* 8.4. All translations of Basil's homily 8 ("In Time of Famine and Drought") and Gregory of Nyssa's two homilies "On the Love of the Poor" (*Paup.* 1 and *Paup.* 2) are from Susan R. Holman, *The Hungry Are Dying: Beggars and Bishops in Roman Cappadocia* (New York: Oxford University Press, 2001), 183–206, with occasional minor alterations.

10. *St. John Chrysostom: On Wealth and Poverty*, trans. Catharine P. Roth (Crestwood, NY: St. Vladimir's Seminary Press, 1984).

11. Severus of Antioch's "Cathedral Homilies" 9, 37, 65, 84, 102, and 116 were preached in honor of Gregory and Basil, all available in French translations published between 1912 and 1976 in *Patrologia Orientalis*.

12. Arthur Vööbus, *History of Asceticism in the Syrian Orient: A Contribution to the History of Culture in the Near East*, Corpus Scriptorum Christianorum Orientalium 197, *Subsidia* 17 (Louvain, Belgium: CSCO, 1960), 2.341; at least one sermon from such a festival survives among the cathedral homilies of Severus of Antioch, where it is homily 76; a French translation from 1919 by M. Brière is available in the *Patrologia Orientalis* series, Vol. 12.1, pp. 133–46.

13. Ambrose, *"De Tobia": A Commentary with an Introduction and Translation*, trans. Lois Miles Zucker, Patristic Studies 35 (Washington, DC: Catholic University of America, 1933).

14. Clement of Alexandria, "The Rich Man's Salvation," chapter 19, trans. G. W. Butterworth (Cambridge, MA: Harvard University Press, 1919), 311.

15. Clement of Alexandria, "The Rich Man's Salvation," 28–9, trans. Butterworth, 329–31.

16. Clement of Alexandria, "The Rich Man's Salvation," 30, trans. Butterworth, 333.

17. Clement of Alexandria, "The Rich Man's Salvation," 31, trans. Butterworth, 337, here slightly altered to better reflect the Greek's more gender-inclusive term.

18. Pontius, "The Life and Passion of Cyprian, Bishop and Martyr," trans. Ernest Wallis, ANF 5.270, 271.

19. *Vita Prima Graeca* 4, trans. and ed. Apostolos N. Athanassakis, *The Life of Pachomius (Vita Prima Graeca)* (Missoula, MT: Scholars Press, 1975), 7. See also Armand Vielleux, ed. and trans., *Pachomian Koinonia I: The Life of Saint Pachomius,* Cistercian Studies Series 45 (Kalamazoo, MI: Cistercian Publications, 1980).

20. Corruption was common. In 372 Basil admits that "ambitious men ever squander the sums collected for the poor on their own pleasures and for the distribution of gifts." [Basil, *Ep.* 92, trans. Roy J. Deferrari, *St. Basil: The Letters* (Cambridge, MA: Harvard University Press, 1926–1934), 2.137.] Thus it was that people often preferred to entrust administrative responsibilities to ascetic Christian leaders who were known to live in voluntary poverty.

21. Basil, *Ep.* 42 "To Chilo his pupil," trans. Roy J. Deferrari, *St. Basil: The Letters* (Cambridge, MA: Harvard University Press, 1926), 1.253.

22. Basil, *Ep.* 150 "To Amphilochius, as if from Heracleidas," trans. Roy J. Deferrari, *St. Basil: The Letters* (Cambridge, MA: Harvard University Press, 1928), 2.369.

23. The first imperial law attempting to control public begging, at least in Italy, dates to the emperors Gratian, Valentinian, and Theodosius in 382 (*Theodosian Code* 14:18, de mendicantibus non invalidis).

24. John Chrysostom, *Homily on Hebrews* 10.4 (PG 53.88); the translation here is from Rudolf Brändle, " 'This sweetest passage': Matthew 25:31–46 and assistance to the poor in the homilies of John Chrysostom," in *Wealth and Poverty in Early Church and Society*, ed. Susan R. Holman (Grand Rapids, MI: Baker-Academic, 2008), 130.

25. For example, John Moschus, *Spiritual Meadow* 127, in John Wortley, trans., *The Spiritual Meadow of John Moschos,* Cistercian Studies Series 139 (Kalamazoo, MI: Cistercian Publications, 1992), 104–5.

26. I explore this further in "Rich and Poor in Sophronius of Jerusalem's *Miracles of Ss. Cyrus and John*" in *Wealth and Poverty in Early Church and Society,* 103–24.

27. John Chrysostom, *In Matt. hom.* 66/67 [PG 58.630]. For English translation, see NPNF, Series 1, Vol. 10, p. 407, where it is *hom.* 66.3. For more details on Chrysostom's statistics about the poor in Antioch, see Wendy Mayer, "Poverty and Society in the World of John Chrysostom," in *Social and Political Life in Late Antiquity*, ed. William Bowden, Adam Gutteridge, and Carlos Machado, Late Antique Archaeology 3.1 (Leiden, The Netherlands: Brill, 2006), 465–84.

28. Basil of Caesarea, *Hom.* 6, "I will tear down my barns," in *The Sunday Sermons of the Great Fathers*, trans. and ed. M. F. Toal (Chicago: Henry Regnery, 1959), 3.326–27.

29. Basil, *Hom*. 8.7 (PG 31.321B), trans. Holman, *The Hungry Are Dying,* 190.

30. Basil, *Second Homily on Psalm* 14, in *Saint Basil: Exegetic Homilies*, trans. Sister Agnes Clare Way, Fathers of the Church 46 (Washington, DC: Catholic University Press, 1963), 182–83. See also Brenda Llewellyn Ihssen, "Basil and Gregory's Sermons on Usury: Credit Where Credit is Due," *Journal of Early Christian Studies* 16 (2008): 403–30.

31. Basil, *Second Homily on Psalm 14*, trans. Way, 184–87.

32. Basil, *Second Homily on Psalm 14*, trans. Way, 190.

33. Gregory of Nyssa, *Encomium of Saint Gregory Bishop of Nyssa on his Brother Saint Basil*, trans. Sr. James Aloysius Stein, Patristic Studies 17 (Washington, DC: Catholic University of America, 1928), selections from Chapter 17.

34. See, e.g., discussion in Paul W. Harkins, ed. and trans., *Saint John Chrysostom: Discourses Against Judaizing Christians* (Washington, DC: Catholic University of America Press, 1979), esp. xxi–l.

35. Gregory of Nazianzus, *Or*. 43.35, trans. C. G. Browne and J. E. Swallow, NPNF, Series 2, Vol. 7, p. 407.

36. Paris gr. 510. f. 149r. For further discussion see Leslie Brubaker, *Vision and Meaning in Ninth-Century Byzantium: Image as Exegesis in the Homilies of Gregory of Nazianzus* (New York: Cambridge University Press, 1999), 131–32 (the full-page image is Figure 20).

37. For example, Basil, *Ep*. 142. On the history of the Christian hospital prior to the Basileias, see Peregrine Horden, "The Earliest Hospitals in Byzantium, Western Europe, and Islam," *Journal of Interdisciplinary History* 35 (2005): 361–89; the entire issue of this volume of the journal is devoted to papers presented at a conference organized by Peter Brown, at Princeton in 2002, on "Poverty and Charity: Judaism, Christianity, Islam."

38. Basil, *Ep*. 94, to Elias, the provincial governor around 372, in Deferrari, *St. Basil: The Letters*, 2.149–53.

39. Gregory of Nyssa, *Paup*. 2, my translation.

40. Gregory of Nazianzus, *Or*. 43.63, trans. Browne and Swallow, NPNF, Series 2, Vol. 7, p. 416.

41. Robert Doran, *Stewards of the Poor: The Man of God, Rabbula, and Hiba in Fifth-Century Edessa*, Cistercian Studies 208 (Kalamazoo, MI: Cistercian Publications, 2006), 101.

42. "The Rules of Rabbūlā for the Clergy and the Qeiāmā," trans. Arthur Vööbus, in his *Syriac and Arabic Documents Regarding Legislation Relative to Syrian Asceticism* (Stockholm: Etse, 1960), 34–50, selections.

43. For the fifth-century narrative see "The Heroic Deeds of Mar Rabbula," trans. Robert Doran, in idem, *Stewards of the Poor*, 65–105. For further discussion see Arthur Vööbus, *History of Asceticism in the Syrian Orient: A Contribution in the History of Culture in the Near East. Vol. 2: Early Monasticism in Mesopotamia and Syria,* Corpus Scriptorum Christianorum Orientalium 197, Subsidia 17 (Louvain, Belgium: CSCO, 1960), especially Chapter 10, "Asceticism and Religion," and Chapter 11, "Asceticism and Social Concern."

44. Ps.-Amphilochius, *Tūrgāmā*, pp. 311, 317, as cited in Vööbus, *History of Asceticism in the Syrian Orient*, 341.

45. Rabbula's frequent emphasis on daughters of the covenant living secluded in their own homes and working only with women probably suggests that here he meant only when there were no "sons" of the covenant. Robert Doran demonstrates that the Syriac Acts of the Second Council at Ephesus name and quote a number of "sons of the covenant" who accompanied priests and deacons to the council.

46. John Chrysostom, *Hom.* 13 *on Ephesians*, here commenting on Eph. 4:24, trans. Gross Alexander, NPNF, Series 1, Vol. 13, pp. 115–16, slightly altered.

47. Gregory of Nyssa, *Paup.* 2 and *Paup.* 1, selections, trans. Holman, *The Hungry Are Dying*, 203, 204, 195, 205.

48. Gregory of Nazianzus, *Or.* 14.9, trans. Vinson, 44–5; and *Or.* 14.27, trans. Vinson, 59–60, selections.

49. On Macrina's domestic reforms to put household servants on the same social level and eat together with her and her mother, see Gregory of Nyssa, *The Life of Saint Macrina*, trans. Virginia Woods Callahan, Fathers of the Church (Washington, DC: Catholic University of America Press, 1967), 161–91, especially 168 and 170. For a study on Macrina's household as domestic monastery, see Philip Rousseau, "The Pious Household and the Virgin Chorus: Reflections on Gregory of Nyssa's *Life of Macrina,*" *Journal of Early Christian Studies* 13 (2005): 165–86.

50. Gregory of Nyssa, *The Life of Saint Macrina*, trans. and ed. Virginia Woods Callahan, 169.

51. Gregory of Nazianzus, epigrams *On Naucratius*, in *The Greek Anthology: Books 7–8*: "The Epigrams of St. Gregory the Theologian," trans. W. R. Paton (Cambridge, MA: Harvard University Press, 1917), 468–69.

52. Silvas, "In Quest of Basil's Retreat: An Expedition to Ancient Pontus."

53. John Chrysostom, "Fourth Sermon on Lazarus and the Rich Man," trans. Roth, 82.

54. John Chrysostom, "Sixth Sermon on Lazarus and the Rich Man," trans. Roth, 107.

55. Francine Cardman, "Poverty and Wealth as Theater: John Chrysostom's Homilies on Lazarus and the Rich Man," in *Wealth and Poverty in Early Church and Society*, 159–75.

56. John Chrysostom, "Sixth Sermon on Lazarus and the Rich Man," trans. Roth, 111–12.

57. John Chrysostom, "Seventh Sermon on Lazarus and the Rich Man," trans. Roth, 140.

CHAPTER 4

1. Richard Kearney, *On Stories* (London: Routledge, 2002), 156.

2. Kearney, *On Stories*, 83.

3. Kearney, *On Stories*, 132.

4. Edith Wyschogrod and Carl Raschke, "Heterological History: A Conversation," in *Crossover Queries: Dwelling with Negatives, Embodying Philosophy's Others*, ed. Edith Wyschogrod (New York: Fordham University Press, 2006), 327.

5. Johan Huizinga, *Erasmus and the Age of Reformation* (Princeton, NJ: Princeton University Press, 1984), 166.

6. Huizinga, *Erasmus and the Age of Reformation*, 174–75.

7. Lee Palmer Wandel, *Always Among Us: Images of the Poor in Zwingli's Zurich* (Cambridge: Cambridge University Press, 1990), 41.

8. John M. Headley, *Luther's View of Church History* (New Haven, CT: Yale University Press, 1963), 162.

9. Headley, *Luther's View of Church History*, 175.

10. See e.g., Samuel Torvend, *Luther and the Hungry Poor: Gathered Fragments* (Minneapolis, MN: Fortress Press, 2008); and Carter Lindberg, "No Greater Service to God than Christian Love: Insights from Martin Luther," in *Social Ministry in the Lutheran Tradition*, ed. Foster R. McCurley (Minneapolis, MN: Fortress Press, 2008), 50–68. I thank Carter Lindberg for these references.

11. Quoted in Wandel, *Always Among Us*, 40, n. 17.

12. Wandel (*Always Among Us*, 60) notes that this sentence is found in both Zwingli's *Commentary on True and False Religion* and in his treatise, *The Shepherd*.

13. Wandel, *Always Among Us*, 62, translating from *Commentary on True and False Religion*.

14. Heiko A. Oberman, *Luther: Man Between God and the Devil*, trans. Eileen Walliser-Schwarzbart (New York: Doubleday, 1990); a reproduction of the signatures is on p. 241.

15. J. Todd Billings, *Calvin, Participation, and the Gift: The Activity of Believers in Union with Christ* (Oxford: Oxford University Press, 2007), 39.

16. William J. Bouwsma, *John Calvin: A Sixteenth-Century Portrait* (New York: Oxford University Press, 1988), 148, here citing Calvin's *Comm*. Ps. 78.8 and *Comm*. John 4.20.

17. Elsie Anne McKee, *John Calvin on the Diaconate and Liturgical Almsgiving* (Geneva: Librairie Droz, 1984).

18. Billings, *Calvin, Participation, and the Gift*, 169, quoting Calvin, *Comm*. 2 Cor. 8.15; emphasis is in Billings.

19. Billings, *Calvin, Participation, and the Gift*, 169.

20. Quoted from Diarmaid MacCulloch, *Thomas Cranmer: A Life* (New Haven, CT: Yale University Press, 1996), 180. However, the context is Cranmer's *Vadianische Briefsammlung*, a refutation of Oecolampadius's and Zwingli's views on the eucharist; possibly Cranmer was referring only to their writings on this issue.

21. A classic source is W. K. Jordan, *Philanthropy in England 1480–1660: A Study of the Changing Pattern of English Social Aspirations* (New York: Russell Sage

Foundation, 1959). On Zurich see Wandel, *Always Among Us*, which also includes (179–95) the original text of the 1520 Alms Statute and the 1525 Poor Law.

22. Paul Welsby, *Lancelot Andrewes: 1555–1626* (London, England: SPCK, 1958), 78–80. For an essentially identical but more sensational version of Andrewes' flight and his reaction to Clapham, see Adam Nicolson, *God's Secretaries: The Making of the King James Bible* (New York: HarperCollins, 2003), 26–32.

23. Henoch Clapham, *An Epistle discoursing on the present pestilence, touching what it is, and how the people of God should carrie themselves towards God and their Neighbor therein,* 1603.

24. Paul Welsby, *Lancelot Andrewes*, 162–64.

25. For details on French social history in the nineteenth century published in English, see, e.g., Christopher Charle, *A Social History of France in the 19th Century* (Paris, France: Éditions du Seuil, 1991) and trans. Miriam Kochan (Oxford: Berg, 1994); Frances Gouda, *Poverty and Political Culture: The Rhetoric of Social Welfare in the Netherlands and France, 1815–1854* (Lanham, MD: Rowman and Littlefield, 1995), especially 173–202, "Christian Injunctions, Private Obligations, and Public Duties: The Organization and Structure of Poor Relief"; Colin Heywood, *Childhood in Nineteenth-Century France: Work, Health and Education among the 'classes populaires'* (Cambridge: Cambridge University Press, 1988); and Hanna Ballin Lewis, trans. and ed., *A Year of Revolutions: Fanny Lewald's 'Recollections of 1848'* (Providence, RI: Berghahn Books, 1997).

26. For the story of Migne's work, see R. Howard Bloch, *God's Plagiarist: Being An Account of the Fabulous Industry and Irregular Commerce of the Abbé Migne* (Chicago: University of Chicago Press, 1994).

27. For Armand de Melun (1807–1877) I have depended largely on André Gueslin, *Gens pauvres: Pauvres gens dans la France du XIXᵉ siècle* (Paris: Aubier, 1998), 158, 199–200.

28. Felix Martin-Doisy, *Histoire de la Charité pendant les quatres premiers siècles de l'ère Chrétienne.* Published in Paris by the *Annales de la Charité* on November 30, 1847, and reprinted in Liège, Belgium, in 1851.

29. Martin-Doisy, *Histoire de la Charité,* 636, my translation.

30. Stephen Colwell, *New Themes for the Protestant Clergy* (Philadelphia: Lippincott, Grambo, & Co., 1851, reprint New York: Arno Press, 1969). The 1853 edition is available as full text online at http://delta.ulib.org/ulib/data/moa/b6d/9cd/9ba/bba/dc6/7/data.txt. For a short biography of Colwell, see Bruce Morgan, "Stephen Colwell (1800–1871): Social Prophet before the Social Gospel," in *Sons of the Prophets: Leaders in Protestantism from Princeton Seminary*, ed. Hugh T. Kerr (Princeton, NJ: Princeton University Press, 1963), 123–47. Morgan notes (125) that Colwell first published the book anonymously but reissued it in 1852 under his own name. I thank Elizabeth A. Clark for her comments on an early version of this section of the chapter and await her forthcoming study on Philip Schaff.

31. Morgan, "Stephen Colwell: Social Prophet," 125.

32. Colwell, *New Themes for the Protestant Clergy*, 158.

33. John Davis, "Eastman Johnson's 'Negro Life at the South' and Urban Slavery in Washington, D.C.," *The Art Bulletin* 1998 [online] at www.findarticles .com/p/articles/mi_m0422/is_1_80/ai_54073918/print; the reference to Colwell as "proslavery" is in note 74, where Davis is referring to Colwell's 1861 pamphlet that defends American cotton brokers. Morgan identifies Colwell's views on slavery as "those of the conservatives of the northern Protestant Churches...he believed in the ultimate emancipation of the slaves but thought their lot far better than that of millions of 'free' working men in Europe and even America" (141–42).

34. Colwell, *New Themes for the Protestant Clergy*, 66.

35. Colwell, *New Themes for the Protestant Clergy*, 76.

36. Colwell, *New Themes for the Protestant Clergy*, 340–41.

37. Etienne Chastel's 1853 *Études historique sur l'influence de la charité durant les premiers siècles chrétiens et considerations sur son rôle dans les sociétés modernes* published in Paris in 1853 by Capelle. The translation by G. A. Matile was published in Philadelphia in 1857 by J. B. Lippincott. On Colwell's role in this project, see Henry C. Carey, "A Memoir of Stephen Colwell: Read Before the American Philosophical Society, Friday, November 17, 1871" (Philadelphia: Henry Carey Baird, Industrial Publisher, 1871), online at http://yamaguchy.netfirms.com/carey/ colwell.html.

38. The University of Pennsylvania Chair was a condition of Colwell's will, but his family waived it at his death. In his 1871 tribute, Carey anticipates it in good faith.

39. "The Princeton chair was inaugurated on September 27, 1871" (Morgan, "Stephen Colwell: Social Prophet," 124).

40. Colwell, *New Themes for the Protestant Clergy*, 372.

41. First published as a series of magazine articles and then in 1840 as a book, Newman's *The Church of the Fathers* was in its "fourth edition" by 1900. It is now available again after many years out of print; see John Henry Cardinal Newman, *The Church of the Fathers*, volume 5 of The Works of Cardinal Newman, Birmingham Oratory Millennium Edition (South Bend, IN: University of Notre Dame Press, 2003). For a general overview of the Oxford movement that also incidentally demonstrates its continuing place in Anglican church politics, see S. L. Ollard, *A Short History of the Oxford Movement*, originally published in 1915, in a second edition by 1932, and reissued in 1983 with a new introduction by A. M. Allchin, 150th Anniversary Oxford Movement Edition (Oxford: A. R. Mowbray).

42. Blomfield Jackson, trans., *The Treatise* de Spiritu Sancto, *the Nine Homilies of the* Hexaemeron, *and the letters of Saint Basil the Great, Archbishop of Caesarea*, NPNF, Series 2, Vol. 8. His comment on Basil is at page liv, note 12. One of the French sources he repeatedly cites is Eugène Fialon's *Étude Historique et Litteraire sur Saint Basile*, which was first published in Paris in 1861 and in its three-volume second edition by 1869. There is no ready source for Blomfield Jackson's life; interested scholarly readers may wish to inquire for archival records of King's College London. For the story of Thomas Jackson's colorful history and the schism at

St. Mary's Stoke Newington (now once again a united parish; www.stmaryn16
.org) I thank John Sabapathy (formerly of King's College London), who sent
me the short history, "Scenes of Congregational Life," that he had prepared for
the parish. Some details such as dates and family statistics have been obtained
through various internet genealogies and are thus undoubtedly imperfect. Marcus
Donovan's 1933 *After the Tractarians* (online at http://anglicanhistory.org/england/
riley/after/08.html, accessed 8/1/06) has a few details on St. Bartholemew's, Moor's
Lane (now demolished). Jackson's other published translations of patristic texts
include Theodoret's fourth-century *Ecclesiastical History* (1892), the second-
century letter from and martyrdom account of Polycarp (1898), and some extra-
canonical Gospel sayings (1900).

43. The classic work on this theme in the writings of John Chrysostom is
Rudolf Brändle, *Matt. 25:31–46 im Werk des Johannes Chrysostomus* (Tübingen,
Germany: Mohr Siebeck, 1979). For its relevance to modern theology, see Sarah
Coakley, "The Identity of the Risen Jesus: Finding Jesus Christ in the Poor,"
in *Seeking The Identity of Jesus: A Pilgrimage*, ed. Beverly Roberts Gaventa and
Richard B. Hays (Grand Rapids, MI: Eerdmans, 2008), 301–19.

44. See Elizabeth A. Clark and Diane F. Hatch, eds. and trans., *The Golden
Bough, The Oaken Cross: The Virgilian Cento of Faltonia Betitia Proba,* American
Academy of Religion Texts and Translations 5 (Chico, CA: Scholars Press, 1981),
especially the discussion on pages 118–19.

45. Pelagius, "On Riches," trans. B. R. Rees, *The Letters of Pelagius and His
Followers* (Woodridge and Rochester, NY: Boynton Press, 1991), 171–211.

46. Illustrated in Robert Etienne, *Pompeii: The Day A City Died,* trans. Caroline
Palmer, Discoveries (New York: Harry N. Abrams, 1992), 74.

47. Sinai *Cod. Gr. 339. Fol. 341v.* The image can also be found in George
Galivaris, *The Illustrations of the Liturgical Homilies of Gregory of Nazianzus*
(Princeton, NJ: Princeton University Press, 1969), Plate LXXXII, Fig. 391.

48. Jonathan M. Mann, Sofia Gruskin, Michael A. Grodin, and George J. Annas,
eds., *Health and Human Rights: A Reader* (London: Routledge, 1999), 453.

49. On how the UDHR was formed, see Johannes Morsink, *The Universal
Declaration of Human Rights: Origins, Drafting, and Intent* (Philadelphia: University of Pennsylvania Press, 1999). Morsinck discusses religious tensions on 284 ff.
Members of the drafting committee recognized that the need to be circumspect
about religious ideals was inevitable to ensure that its diverse constituency might
agree on fundamental human rights and the prevention of mutually recogniz-
able injustices without undue conflict about religion or any particular theological
position. Mary Ann Glendon's *A World Made New: Eleanor Roosevelt and the Universal Declaration of Human Rights* (New York: Random House, 2001) discusses
the debates and concerns of using religious language in the *Declaration* in further
detail.

50. Susan R. Holman, "The Entitled Poor: Human Rights Language in the
Cappadocians," *Pro Ecclesia* 9 (2000): 476–89.

51. M. F. Toal, *The Sunday Sermons of the Great Fathers* (Chicago: Henry Regnery, 1963), 55.

52. Gregory of Nazianzus, *Or.* 14.26, in *Gregory of Nazianzus*, trans. Brian Daley, S.J. (New York: Routledge, 2006), 90.

53. Gregory of Nyssa, *Paup.* 2; the Greek is at *De pauperibus amandis: Oratio duo*, ed. Arie van Heck, Gregorii Nysseni Opera 9.1 (Leiden, The Netherlands: Brill, 1967), p. 115, lines 21–23 and p. 120, lines 11–13 (also at PG 46.476 and PG 46.481).

54. The critical edition of Asterius is C. Datema, ed., *Asterius of Amaseia: Homilies I–XIV: Text, Introduction and Notes* (Leiden, The Netherlands: Brill, 1970), 6–15 (*hom.* 1 "On the Rich Man and Lazarus") and 26–37 (*hom.* 3 "Against Avarice"). Translations here are mine, but I have also consulted the now-outdated translation by G. Anderson and E. J. Goodspeed, trans., *Ancient Sermons for Modern Times by Asterius, Bishop of Amasia, circa 375–405 A.D.* (New York: The Pilgrim Press, 1904).

55. Asterius, *hom.* 1.8.1.

56. Asterius, *hom.* 3.12.3.

57. Asterius, *hom.* 3.12.1.

CHAPTER 5

1. Ephrem, *The Nisibene Hymns* 4.4, trans. J. T. Sarsfield Stopfold, in NPNF Series 2, Vol. 13, p. 172, slightly modernized. Also available online at www.piney .com/EphraimHymns.html.

2. Salmaan Keshavjee, "Bleeding Babies in Badakhshan: Symbolism, Materialism, and the Political Economy of Traditional Medicine in Post-Soviet Tajikistan," *Medical Anthropology Quarterly* 20 (2006): 72–93.

3. Tajikistan statistics here are from Keshavjee, "Bleeding Babies," 74. The infant mortality rates from the United Kingdom and Canada are from *Pocket World in Figures, 2008 Edition* (London: The Economist, 2007), 83. The rate in the United States was most recently calculated (in 2004) as 6.78 per thousand, but this number more than doubles, to 13.6, for non-Hispanic black mothers; the U.S. infant mortality rate has long been recognized as shameful compared to other developed nations (T. J. Mathews, M. S. and Marion F. MacDorman, "Infant Mortality Statistics from the 2004 Period Linked Birth/Infant Death Data Set," Centers for Disease Control *National Vital Statistics Report* 55 [14], May 2, 2007, available online at www.cdc.gov/omhd/AMH/factsheets/infant.htm).

4. Keshavjee, "Bleeding Babies," 81–84, selections.

5. Celsus, *De medicina* 2.10, trans. W. G. Spencer, *Celsus: De Medicina* (Cambridge, MA: Harvard University Press, 1935 [v. 1], 1938 [v. 2], 1938 [v. 3]), here citing 1.155.

6. Celsus, *De medicina* 2.10.6, trans. Spencer, *Celsus* 1.159.

7. Keshavjee, "Bleeding Babies," 87, n. 14.

8. Clement of Alexandria, "The Instructor," 1.6, trans. William Wilson, ANF 2.221–22.

9. *The Apocritus of Macarius Magnes* 3.8, trans. T. W. Crafer (London, England: SPCK, 1919), 80–81, slightly modernized. For further discussion of this and related early Christian texts, see Edward Engelbrecht, "God's Milk: An Orthodox Confession of the Eucharist," *Journal of Early Christian Studies* 7 (1999): 521–52.

10. Tertullian, *De corona* 3, trans. S. Thelwall, ANF 3.94.

11. Procopius, *Commentary on Isaiah*, PG 87:2552, translated in Engelbrecht, "God's Milk," 524.

12. Soranus, *Gynecology* 2.18, trans. Owsei Temkin (Baltimore: Johns Hopkins University Press, 1956), 89.

13. For an example from modern Haiti, see Paul Farmer, "Bad Blood: Spoiled Milk: Bodily Fluids as Moral Barometers in Rural Haiti," *American Ethnologist* 15 (1988): 62–83.

14. The literature on HIV/AIDS transmission to infants while *in utero* and breastfeeding is extensive. Three recent, authoritative articles on this topic include: Elaine J. Abrams, Landon Myer, Allan Rosenfield, and Wafaa M. El-Sadr, "Prevention of Mother-to-Child Transmission Services as a Gateway to Family-Based Human Immunodeficiency Virus Care and Treatment in Resource-Limited Settings: Rationale and International Experiences," *American Journal of Obstetrics and Gynecology* 197 (2007): Suppl. 3, S101–6; Anna Coutsoudis, Hoosen M. Coovadia, and Catherine M. Wilfert, "HIV, Infant Feeding and More Perils for Poor People: New WHO Guidelines Encourage Review of Formula Milk Policies," *Bulletin of the World Health Organization* 86(3) (2008): 210–14; and for a historical overview that includes a discussion of mother-to-child transmission (MTCT), see L. O. Kallings, "The First Postmodern Pandemic: 25 Years of HIV/AIDS," *Journal of Internal Medicine* 263 (2008): 218–43.

15. The ban on menstruating women receiving the eucharist was not consistent in the early church. It was standardized in Byzantine ritual only around the fourteenth century. On women serving at the altar see, for example, Kevin Madigan and Carolyn Osiek, *Ordained Women in the Early Church: A Documentary History* (Baltimore: Johns Hopkins University Press, 2005). A modern Orthodox nun observes that there is actually freedom of women's exposure to the sacred altar not only in the Holy Land today but also in some strict Greek Orthodox women's monasteries where "nuns serve in the altar." Teva Regule, "An Interview with Sister Aemiliane of the Exaltation of the Holy Cross Monastery, Thebes, Greece," *The St. Nina Quarterly* 3(4) (1999): 21.

16. Basil, *Hom.* 8.3, my translation.

17. Bernadette Brooten, especially her project on sexual ethics at Brandeis University (www.brandeis.edu/projects/fse); and Jennifer A. Glancy, *Slavery in Early Christianity* (Minneapolis, MN: Fortress Press, 2006). This is also a major theme in the memoirs of the former slave Harriet Jacobs, *Incidents in the Life of a*

Slave Girl Written by Herself, ed. L. Maria Child, originally published in 1861 and republished with an extensive introduction and supporting documents by Jean Fagan Yellin, ed. (Cambridge, MA: Harvard University Press, 2000).

18. R. A. Sanders and S. G. Sheridan, "All God's Children: Subadult Health in a Byzantine Jerusalem Monastery," *American Journal of Physical Anthropology* Suppl. 28 (1999): 239; for more information, see Blake Leyerle, "Children and Disease in a Sixth-Century Monastery," in *What Athens Has to Do with Jerusalem: Essays on Classical, Jewish, and Early Christian Art and Archaeology, in Honor of Gideon Foerster*, ed. Leonard V. Rutgers (Leuven, Belgium: Peeters, 2002), 349–72. See also Susan R. Holman, "Molded as Wax: Formation and Feeding of the Ancient Newborn," *Helios* 24 (1997): 77–95.

19. Gregory of Nazianzus, *epigrams* 24–74, in *The Greek Anthology: Books 7–8: "The Epigrams of St. Gregory the Theologian,"* trans. W. R. Paton (Cambridge, MA: Harvard University Press, 1917), 410–31. That she was physically gripping the altar as part of her prayer posture is stated in *epigrams* 46, 47, 49, and 67.

20. I thank Jennifer Glancy for a provocative discussion on the religious gendering of blood imagery in texts about Mary. Although her work is very different from that outlined here, her ideas led me to a more informed reading of these texts on Badakhshan and Nonna.

21. Statistics from *Pocket World in Figures, 2008 Edition* (London: The Economist, 2007), 31.

22. Christine Wenneras and Agnes Wold, "Nepotism and Sexism in Peer-Review," *Nature* 388 (1997): 341–43, summarized under the heading "Peer Review: Shameful," *The Economist* (May 24, 1997): 79.

23. James Westcott, "Slum Politics," [Online] www.alternet.org/story/21297.

24. Dorothy Allison, *Two or Three Things I Know for Sure* (New York: Dutton, 1995), 39.

25. See, e.g., Mariana Chilton, "Developing a Measure of Dignity for Stress-Related Health Outcomes," *Health and Human Rights* 9(2) (2006): 209–33.

26. Names have been changed in all clinic stories.

27. Adam Drewnowski and S. E. Specter, "Poverty and Obesity: The Role of Energy Density and Energy Costs," *The American Journal of Clinical Nutrition* 79 (2004): 6–16; this quote is from the abstract, p. 6.

28. Drewnowski and Specter, "Poverty and Obesity," 6, citing refs. 21 and 25.

29. Drewnowski and Specter, "Poverty and Obesity," 7, citing refs. 30 and 31.

30. Drewnowski and Specter, "Poverty and Obesity," 11, citing ref. 100.

31. Rebecca Cook, "Gender, Health, and Human Rights," in *Health and Human Rights: A Reader*, ed. Jonathan M. Mann, Sofia Gruskin, Michael A. Grodin, and George J. Annas (London: Routledge, 1999), 254.

32. Dorothy Allison, *Trash* (New York: Penguin, 1988), 156.

33. Chilton, "Developing a Measure of Dignity," 210.

34. Godfrey Fuji Noe, "'I've Been in the Storm Too Long:' Religiosity and Distress in High Poverty Neighborhoods," Ph.D. dissertation, The University

of Alabama at Birmingham, 2002), from the online abstract at wwwlib.umi.com/dissertations/fullcit/3066332.

35. Barbara Ehrenreich, *Nickel and Dimed: On (Not) Getting By in America* (New York: Henry Holt, 2001), 132.

36. On early Christian widows see Bonnie Bowman Thurston, *The Widows: A Women's Ministry in the Early Church* (Minneapolis, MN: Fortress Press, 1989).

37. *Gestae apud Zenophilum* 2, text and translation in L. Michael White, *The Social Origins of Christian Architecture* (Valley Forge, PA: Trinity Press International, 1997), 106 (Latin), 108 (English translation).

38. *P. Wisc.* II.64 = NewDocs.II.108, discussed in Adam Serfass, "Wine for Widows: Papyrological Evidence for Christian Charity in Late Antique Egypt," in *Wealth and Poverty in Early Church and Society,* ed. Susan R. Holman (Grand Rapids, MI: Baker Academic, 2008), 90, note 11.

39. Sozomen, *History of the Church* 4.25.

40. John Chrysostom, "A Sermon on Almsgiving," in *St. John Chrysostom: On Repentance and Almsgiving*, trans. Gus George Christo, Fathers of the Church (Washington, DC: Catholic University of America Press, 1998), 132.

41. T. G. Wilfong, *Women of Jeme: Lives in a Coptic Town in Late Antique Egypt* (Ann Arbor, MI: University of Michigan Press, 2002), 130.

42. Wilfong, *Women of Jeme*, 132.

43. *P. Oxy.* LXI 4131, cited in Serfass, "Wine for Widows," 99.

44. Except when they are mistaken as male monks and falsely accused of fathering children. The life of Mary/Marinos is one example of a woman disguised as a male monk who then chose to raise the child that a village woman accused her of fathering: Nicholas Constas, trans., "Life of St. Mary/Marinos," in *Holy Women of Byzantium: Ten Saints' Lives in English Translation,* ed. Alice-Mary Talbot (Washington, DC: Dumbarton Oaks, 1996), 1–12.

45. For the English translation see Athanasius, *The Life of Antony*, in *Athanasius*, trans. Robert C. Gregg (New York: Paulist Press, 1980), 29–99.

46. *O. Brit. Mus. Copt.*, Ad 23, cited in Wilfong, *Women of Jeme*, 107.

47. *Life of Saint Theodosius* in Cyril of Scythopolis, *Lives of the Monks of Palestine*, trans. R. M. Price, Cistercian Studies Series 114 (Kalamazoo, MI: Cistercian Publications, 1991), 262–63.

48. See Derwas J. Chitty, *The Desert a City* (Crestwood, NY: St. Vladimir's Seminary Press, 1995), 109.

49. Robert Doran, *Stewards of the Poor: The Man of God, Rabbula, and Hiba in Fifth-Century Edessa*, Cistercian Studies Series 208 (Kalamazoo, MI: Cistercian Publications, 2006), 100–101.

50. *Life of Maria, the Niece of Abraham* (=*Vita Sanctae Mariae, Meretricis*, PL 73.651–660) 10, in *Harlots of the Desert*, trans. Benedicta Ward, Cistercian Studies Series 106 (Kalamazoo, MI: Cistercian Publications, 1987), 99.

51. See, e.g., Scott Fitzgerald Johnson, *The Life and Miracles of Thekla: A Literary Study* (Cambridge, MA: Harvard University Press, 2006).

52. Details about Melania the Elder come from Palladius, *The Lausiac History*, trans. Robert T. Meyer, Ancient Christian Writers 34 (New York: Newman Press, 1964), chapters 9 ("female man of God"), 54.2 (on giving to churches, monasteries, guests, and prisons), and 55.3 (on reading Origen). On Origen, Palladius writes that she "was most erudite and fond of literature, and she turned night into day going through every writing of the ancient commentaries—three million lines of Origen and two and a half million lines of Gregory, Stephen, Pierius, Basil, and other worthy men. And she did not read them only once and in an offhand way, but she worked on them, dredging through each work seven or eight times" (trans. Meyer, 136–37).

53. "The Life of Melania the Younger," 26, in *The Life of Melania The Younger: Introduction, Translation, and Commentary,* trans. Elizabeth A. Clark (New York: The Edwin Mellen Press, 1984), 46. See also Palladius, *The Lausiac History* 61.

54. For Hicelia, see Cyril of Scythopolis, "Life of Theodosius," 1 in R. M. Price, trans., *Cyril of Scythopolis: The Lives of the Monks of Palestine,* Cistercian Studies Series 114 (Kalamazoo, MI: Cistercian Publications, 1991), 262. For Olympias, see the *Life of Olympias* and Sergia's *Narration Concerning St. Olympias*, trans. Elizabeth A. Clark, *Jerome, Chrysostom, and Friends: Essays and Translations* (New York: The Edwin Mellen Press, 1979), 107–57.

55. Jerome, *Ep.* 22.50, in *Jerome: Select Letters*, trans. F. A. Wright (Cambridge, MA: Harvard University Press, 1933), 133. One wonders if John the Almsgiver knew this story when he determined to give poor women a portion double that of his donation to poor men. "The Life of Our Holy Father, John the Almsgiver," Supplement by Leontius, Chapter 7, in *Three Byzantine Saints: Contemporary Biographies Translated from the Greek*, ed. and trans. Elizabeth Dawes and Norman H. Baynes (Crestwood, NY: St. Vladimir's Seminary Press, 1977), 214.

56. In John Moschus, *Spiritual Meadow* 230 = Nissen 12, trans. Wortley, *The Spiritual Meadow (Pratum Spirituale)*, Cistercian Studies Series 139 (Kalamazoo, MI: Cistercian Press, 1992), 212.

57. Renny Christopher, "'Shotgun Strategies': Working Class Literature and Violence," in *Critical Essays on the Works of American Author Dorothy Allison*, ed. Christine Blouch and Laurie Vickroy (Lewiston, NY: The Edwin Mellen Press, 2004), 126, note 5.

58. Martin L. Smith, SSJE, *Reconciliation: Preparing for Confession in the Episcopal Church* (Cambridge, MA: Cowley Press, 1985), 78.

59. Lars Eighner, *Travels with Lizbeth: Three Years on the Road and on the Streets* (New York: Ballantine Books, 1993), 198.

60. Diane White, "Beggars Can Be Choosers," *The Boston Globe*, October 1980.

61. Quoted in Tracy Kidder, *Mountains Beyond Mountains: The Quest of Dr. Paul Farmer, A Man Who Would Cure the World* (New York: Random House, 2003), 213.

CHAPTER 6

1. Patricia Hampl, *I Could Tell You Stories: Sojourns in the Land of Memory* (New York: W. W. Norton, 1999), 107.

2. John of Ephesus, *Lives of the Eastern Saints* 12, trans. Sebastian P. Brock and Susan Ashbrook Harvey, *Holy Women of the Syrian Orient* (Berkeley: University of California Press, 1987), 124–33. See further discussion in Susan Ashbrook Harvey, *Asceticism and Society in Crisis: John of Ephesus and 'The Lives of the Eastern Saints'* (Berkeley: University of California Press, 1990).

3. John of Ephesus, *Lives of the Eastern Saints* 12, trans. Brock and Harvey, 126.

4. John of Ephesus, *Lives of the Eastern Saints* 12, trans. Brock and Harvey, 128.

5. *Lives of the Eastern Saints* 12, trans. Brock and Harvey, 131.

6. *Lives of the Eastern Saints* 12, trans. Brock and Harvey, 131.

7. *Lives of the Eastern Saints* 12, trans. Brock and Harvey, 130.

8. Rabbula, "Commands and Admonitions of Mār Rabbūlā, bishop of Edessa to the Priests and the Benai Qeiāmā, Canon 24," in *Syriac and Arabic Documents Regarding Legislation Relative to Syrian Asceticism,* trans. Arthur Vööbus (Stockholm: Etse, 1960), 42.

9. Clement of Alexandria, "The Rich Man's Salvation," 12, trans. G. W. Butterworth (Cambridge, MA: Harvard University Press, 1919), 295.

10. Clement of Alexandria, "The Rich Man's Salvation," 14, trans. Butterworth, 299.

11. *Shepherd of Hermas,* Similitude 2 [= chapter 51], in *The Apostolic Fathers,* trans. Bart D. Ehrman (Cambridge, MA: Harvard University Press, 2003), 2.308–15.

12. Justin Martyr, *Apology* 1.67, in *Early Christian Fathers*, trans. Cyril C. Richardson (New York: Collier Books, 1970), 287.

13. Basil of Caesarea, *Hom.* 8.8, my translation.

14. "On Mercy and Justice" (*De misericordia et iudicio*) (PG 31.1709, lines 26–27), in *Saint Basil the Great: On Social Justice*, trans. Paul Schroeder, Popular Patristics Series (Crestwood, NY: St. Vladimir's Seminary Press, forthcoming).

15. "On Mercy and Justice," here from *Saint Basil: Ascetical Works*, trans. Sister M. Monica Wagner (New York: Fathers of the Church, 1950), 508.

16. "On Mercy and Justice," trans. Wagner, 511: "He requires a continual sharing and communicating of that which they possess that by showing mercy, sharing their goods, and conferring benefits, they may reproduce in themselves the benevolence of God."

17. *Didascalia* 18 (= 4.5–4.10), in *Didascalia Apostolorum,* trans. R. Hugh Connolly (Oxford: Clarendon Press, 1969), 156–60.

18. Commodianus, *Instructiones* 65, cited in Robert P. Maloney, "The Teachings of the Fathers on Usury: A Historical Study on the Development of Christian Thinking," *Vigiliae Christianae* 27 (1973): 245.

19. *Acts of Peter* 30, in *New Testament Apocrypha*, trans. Wilhelm Schneemelcher, revised edition, English trans. Robert McLaughlin Wilson (Louisville, KY: Westminster/John Knox Press, 1992), 2.311, 312.

20. *Lives of the Eastern Saints* 12, trans. Brock and Harvey, 129.

21. *Lives of the Eastern Saints* 12, trans. Brock and Harvey, 129.

22. Rabbula, Canon 16, in Vööbus, *Syriac and Arabic Documents*, 40.

23. *Lives of the Eastern Saints* 12, trans. Brock and Harvey, 124.

24. *Lives of the Eastern Saints* 12, trans. Brock and Harvey, 125.

25. "The Man of God: The Original Syriac Life," in Robert Doran, ed. and trans., *Stewards of the Poor: The Man of God, Rabbula, and Hiba in Fifth-Century Edessa*, Cistercian Studies Series 208 (Kalamazoo, MI: Cistercian Publications, 2006), 20, slightly altered.

26. See, e.g., Daniel Caner, *Wandering, Begging Monks: Spiritual Authority and the Promotion of Monasticism in Late Antiquity* (Berkeley: University of California Press, 2002).

27. *Lives of the Eastern Saints* 12, trans. Brock and Harvey, 125.

28. *Lives of the Eastern Saints* 12, trans. Brock and Harvey, 133.

29. Wendell Berry, *Jayber Crow* (Washington, DC: Counterpoint, 2000), 30.

30. New Revised Standard Bible.

31. Gregory of Nazianzus, *Or.* 14.29, trans. Martha Vinson, *St. Gregory of Nazianzus: Select Orations*, The Fathers of the Church (Washington, DC: Catholic University Press, 2003), 62.

32. *Didache* 1.5–6, trans. Bart D. Ehrman, *The Apostolic Fathers* (Cambridge, MA: Harvard University Press, 2003), 1.419.

33. *Lives of the Eastern Saints* 12, trans. Brock and Harvey, 124.

34. *Lives of the Eastern Saints* 12, trans. Brock and Harvey, 129.

35. *Lives of the Eastern Saints* 12, trans. Brock and Harvey, 132.

36. *Lives of the Eastern Saints* 12, trans. Brock and Harvey, 133.

37. See especially "Amida: The Measure of Madness," in Susan Ashbrook Harvey, *Asceticism and Society in Crisis*, 57–75.

38. William Dalrymple, *From the Holy Mountain: A Journey Among the Christians of the Middle East* (New York: Henry Holt, 1997), 80–82.

39. Information on the modern Syriac community of ancient Amida comes from Jean-Nicole Saint-Laurent, "Encountering the Suryoye of Turkey," *Hugoye: Journal of Syriac Studies* 9(2) (July 2006): paragraph 5, online at http://syrcom.cua .edu/Hugoye/Vol9No2/HV9N2TRSaintLaurent.html.

CHAPTER 7

1. Nico Colchester, "Colchester's Crunchiness," originally published in 1988, reprinted posthumously in *The Economist* on October 5, 1996, p. 20.

2. New American Standard Bible.

3. For more detailed discussions of this issue, see John A. Colman and William F. Ryan, eds., *Globalization and Catholic Social Thought: Present Crisis, Future Hope* (Ottawa, Canada, and Maryknoll, NY: Orbis, 2005); Kenneth R. Himes, ed., *Modern Catholic Social Teaching: Commentaries and Interpretations* (Washington, DC: Georgetown University Press, 2005); David Hollenbach,

S.J., *The Common Good and Christian Ethics* (Cambridge: Cambridge University Press, 2002); Susan R. Holman, "Out of the Fitting Room: Rethinking Patristic Social Texts on 'The Common Good,'" in Johan Leemans, Brian Matz, and Johan Verstraeten, eds., *Reading Patristic Texts on Social Ethics: Issues and Challenges for 21st Century Christian Social Thought*, Catholic University of America Studies in Early Christianity (Washington, DC: Catholic University of America Press, forthcoming); Mary M. Keys, *Aquinas, Aristotle, and the Promise of the Common Good* (Cambridge: Cambridge University Press, 2006); André Laks and Malcolm Schofield, eds., *Justice and Generosity: Studies in Hellenistic Social and Political Philosophy. Proceedings of the Sixth Symposium Hellenisticum* (Cambridge: Cambridge University Press, 1992); Brian Matz, "Patristic Sources and Catholic Social Teaching, A Forgotten Dimension: A Textual, Historical, and Rhetorical Analysis of Patristic Source Citations in the Church's Social Documents," *Annua Nuntia Lovaniensia* 59 (Leuven, Belgium: Peeters, 2008); Patrick D. Miller and Dennis P. McCann, eds., *In Search of the Common Good*, *Theology for the Twenty-First Century* (New York: T & T Clark, 2005); David J. O'Brien and Thomas A. Shannon, eds., *Catholic Social Thought: The Documentary Heritage* (Maryknoll, NY: Orbis, 1992); and Eleonore Stump, *Aquinas* (London: Routledge, 2003).

4. *Pacem in Terris* 53 and 54, from O'Brien and Shannon, *Catholic Social Thought: The Documentary Heritage*, 139–40.

5. The text is in O'Brien and Shannon, *Catholic Social Thought: The Documentary Heritage,* 166–237, especially 181–85.

6. Quotes on *Gaudium et spes* in this paragraph are from David Hollenbach, S.J., "Commentary on *Gaudium et spes (Pastoral Constitution on the Church in the Modern World)*, in Himes, ed., *Modern Catholic Social Teaching: Commentaries and Interpretations,* 266, 287, and 280, respectively.

7. O'Brien and Shannon, *Catholic Social Thought: The Documentary Heritage*, 572–680; for commentary and discussion, see Charles E. Curran, "The Reception of Catholic Social and Economic Teaching in the United States," in Himes, ed., *Modern Catholic Social Teaching: Commentaries and Interpretations*, 469–92.

8. "Economic Justice for All" 1.34, in O'Brien and Shannon, eds., *Catholic Social Thought: The Documentary Heritage*, 586, quoting from several earlier twentieth-century papal encyclicals.

9. David Hollenbach, S.J., "Commentary on *Gaudium et spes*," 279.

10. Leonardo Boff, *Cry of the Earth, Cry of the Poor* (Maryknoll, NY: Orbis, 1997), 33.

11. His All Holiness Ecumenical Patriarch Bartholomew, *Encountering the Mystery: Understanding Orthodox Christianity Today* (New York: Doubleday, 2008), especially Chapter 6, "The Wonder of Creation: Religion and Ecology," 89–119.

12. Basil, *First Homily on Psalm 14,* chapter 6 (PG 29.261), my translation.

13. Basil, *Hom.* 6.5, trans. M. F. Toal, *The Sunday Sermons of the Great Fathers* (Chicago, IL: Regnery, 1959), 3.329, slightly revised.

14. *Summa Theol.* IIaIIae.32.5 ad 2, quoting from Basil's *hom.* 6.7; Eleonore Stump (*Aquinas*, 323 and 543, n. 88) translates Aquinas as, "It is the hungry man's

bread that you withhold, the naked man's cloak that you have stored away, the shoes of the barefoot that you have left to rot, the money of the needy that you have buried underground."

15. See, e.g., *Sermones de moribus a Symeone Metaphrasta collecti*, PG 32.1168, l. 23, and Gennadius Scholarius II's *Tractatus de primo servitu Dei*, Chapter 9. Both are available online through the *Thesaurus Linguae Graeca* project at the University of California (www.tlg.uci.edu/).

16. This theme is most dominant in Gregory of Nyssa's second sermon "On the Love of the Poor."

17. Asterius, *Hom.* 1, On the rich man and Lazarus 8.1. The Greek is C. Datema, ed., *Asterius of Amasea: Homilies I–XIV; Text, Introduction and Notes* (Leiden, The Netherlands: E. J. Brill, 1970), 12, lines 6–7); English trans. by Galusha Anderson and Edgar Johnson Goodspeed, *Ancient Sermons for Modern Times by Asterius, Bishop of Amasia, circa 375–405 A.D.* (New York: The Pilgrim Press, 1904), 34.

18. "The Life of our Holy Father, John the Almsgiver," Supplement by Leontius, Chapter 33, in *Three Byzantine Saints,* trans. Elizabeth Dawes and Norman H. Baynes (Crestwood, NY: St. Vladimir's Seminary Press, 1977), 243.

19. Letter 620, in *Letters from the Desert: Barsanuphias and John,* trans. John Chryssavgis (Crestwood, NY: St. Vladimir's Seminary Press, 2003), 165.

20. But see, e.g., Kelly S. Johnson, *The Fear of Beggars: Stewardship and Poverty in Christian Ethics* (Grand Rapids, MI: Wm. B. Eerdmans, 2007), especially 217, n. 10.

21. Yasmina Khadra, *Double Blank,* trans. Aubrey Botsford (London: The Toby Press, 2005), 64.

22. Jim Wallis, *Faith Works: How to Live Your Beliefs and Ignite Positive Social Change* (New York: Random House, 2000), 104.

23. Successful inner city communities often build on such principles; see, e.g., Mark R. Gornik, *To Live in Peace: Biblical Faith and the Changing Inner City* (Grand Rapids, MI: Wm. B. Eerdmans, 2002).

24. Søren Kierkegaard, Pap. VIII^2 B 31:18, n.d., 1847, cited in *Søren Kierkegaard, Works of Love,* trans. Howard V. and Edna H. Hong (Princeton, NJ: Princeton University Press, 1995), 431.

25. Yitzhaq ibn Khalfoun, "A Gift of Cheese," trans. Peter Cole in *The Dream of the Poem: Hebrew Poetry from Muslim and Christian Spain 950–1492* (Princeton, NJ: Princeton University Press, 2007), 36.

26. *Didache* 4.5; for further discussion see Denise Buell, " 'Be not one who stretches out hands to receive but shuts them when it comes to giving:' Envisioning Christian Charity When Both Donors and Recipients Are Poor," in *Wealth and Poverty in Early Church and Society,* ed. Susan R. Holman (Grand Rapids, MI: BakerAcademic, 2008), 37–47.

27. "Rules of Rabbula," 11 in Arthur Vööbus, ed. and trans., *Syriac and Arabic Documents Regarding Legislation Relative to Syrian Asceticism* (Stockholm: Etse, 1960), 39.

28. "Canons which are Necessary for the Monks," 13, in Vööbus, *Syriac and Arabic Documents*, 73–4.

29. Timothy Patitsas, "St. Basil's Philanthropic Program and Modern Microlending Strategies for Economic Self-Actualization," in *Wealth and Poverty in Early Church and Society,* ed. Holman, 278, note 62.

30. Clement of Alexandria, "The Instructor," 2.1, trans. William Wilson, ANF 2.237, 238.

31. Maria Parloa, *Miss Parloa's Kitchen Companion: A Guide for All Who Would Be Good Housekeepers*, 21st ed. (Boston: Dana Estes and Co., 1887), 901.

32. Esther de Waal, *Seeking God: The Way of St. Benedict,* Second Edition (Collegeville, MN: Liturgical Press, 2001), 120, 122.

33. Frank Schaeffer, *Crazy for God: How I Grew Up as One of the Elect, Helped Found the Religious Right, and Lived to Take All (or Almost All) of It Back* (New York: Carroll and Graf, 2007), 134.

34. Christine D. Pohl, *Making Room: Recovering Hospitality as a Christian Tradition* (Grand Rapids, MI: Eerdmans, 1999), 186.

CHAPTER 8

1. Karmen MacKendrick, *Word Made Skin: Figuring Language at the Surface of Flesh* (New York: Fordham University Press, 2004), 154.

2. The stone that I was looking at while sitting in the room by the Western Wall is the lintel of "Barclay's Gate," originally what the Mishnah describes as the Kiphonas Gate and rediscovered in 1858 by James Turner Barclay. In the first century this gate, leading into the Herodian temple precinct, would have risen nearly twenty-nine feet above the ground. Today this lintel, a single piece of rock twenty-five feet long and seven feet high, "is above the women's area of the western wall, just over the stairway that leads into a room on its south side" [Jack P. Lewis, "James Turner Barclay: Explorer of Nineteenth-Century Jerusalem," *Biblical Archaeologist* 51 (1988): 166; on the Mishnah's description of the gate, Lewis quotes at length from B. Mazar, *The Mountain of the Lord* (Garden City, NY: Doubleday, 1975), 133–34]. In other words, the ground has risen about twenty-five feet since the first century and the scorch marks that were at my eye level are likely traces of a fire centuries before the room was built, with flames scorching the rock at thirty feet above ground. The gate itself was closed in by rock and rubble centuries ago, and cisterns were built on the other side of the closed-off wall. The room itself, part of the Maghrabi gate structure, is located below what has been the usual tourist entrance to the Dome of the Rock plaza.

3. Salvian, "The Four Books of Timothy to the Church" (*Ad Ecclesiam*) 3.12, in *The Writings of Salvian, The Presbyter*, trans. Jeremiah F. O'Sullivan (New York: CIMA, 1947), 338.

4. Basil, *Hom.* 21.9–12.

5. Dennis Covington, *Salvation on Snake Mountain* (New York: Addison Wesley, 1995), 203–4.

6. Jacob of Sarug, "On the Love of the Poor." The Syriac text is that of Paul Bedjan, ed., *Homiliae Selectae Mar-Jacobi Sarugensis* (Paris: Lipsiae, Otto Harrassowitz, 1906), Vol. 2, p. 830, lines 17–20; translation by Sebastian Brock, used with permission.

7. Sara Miles, *Take This Bread: A Radical Conversion* (New York: Ballantine Books, 2007), 58–59, 61.

8. Miles, *Take This Bread*, 77, 275; for more about the food pantry, visit www .saramiles.net/food_pantry, accessed 3/24/08.

9. Peter Brown, "The Rise and Function of the Holy Man in Late Antiquity," in his *Society and the Holy in Late Antiquity* (Berkeley: University of California Press, 1982), 103–52; and explicitly related to poverty relief dynamics in idem, *Poverty and Leadership in the Later Roman Empire* (Hanover, NH: University Press of New England, 2002).

10. Discussed recently in Claudia Rapp, *Holy Bishops in Late Antiquity: The Nature of Christian Leadership in an Age of Transition* (Berkeley: University of California Press, 2005); and in Andrea Sterk, *Renouncing the World Yet Leading the Church: The Monk-Bishop in Late Antiquity* (Cambridge, MA: Harvard University Press, 2004).

11. C. S. Lewis to Harry Blamires, quoted in Lyle W. Dorsett, *Seeking the Secret Place; The Spiritual Formation of C. S. Lewis* (Grand Rapids, MI: Brazos Press, 2004), 97.

12. See, for example, Jim Forest's website, www.incommunion.org; Paul Evdokimov, *In the World, Of the Church: A Paul Evdokimov Reader*, ed. and trans. Michael Plekon and Alexis Vinogratov (Crestwood, NY: St. Vladimir's Seminary Press, 2001); Sergei Hackel, *Pearl of Great Price: The Life of Mother Maria Skobtsova*, 1891–1945 (Crestwood, NY: St. Vladimir's Seminary Press, 1981); *Mother Maria Skobtsova: Essential Writings*, trans. Richard Pevear and Larissa Volokhonsky with an introduction by Jim Forest (Maryknoll, NY: Orbis Books, 2003); and His All Holiness Ecumenical Patriarch Bartholomew, *Encountering the Mystery: Understanding Orthodox Christianity Today* (New York: Doubleday, 2008).

13. *Mother Maria Skobtsova: Essential Writings*, 75–83.

14. *Mother Maria Skobtsova: Essential Writings*, 79.

15. *Mother Maria Skobtsova: Essential Writings*, 81–82.

16. *Mother Maria Skobtsova: Essential Writings*, 81.

17. "Persian Martyrs," in *Holy Women of the Syrian Orient*, eds. and trans. Sebastian P. Brock and Susan Ashbrook Harvey (Berkeley: University of California Press, 1987), 76.

18. "Persian Martyrs," in *Holy Women of the Syrian Orient*, 72.

19. Michael Phillips, interview with the author, May 1, 2006, used with permission.

20. "The Man of God: The Original Syriac Life," Robert Doran, ed. and trans., *Stewards of the Poor: The Man of God, Rabbula, and Hiba in Fifth-Century Edessa*, Cistercian Studies Series 208 (Kalamazoo, MI: Cistercian Publications, 2006), 24.

21. Susan Ashbrook Harvey, personal communication.

22. Charles Mathewes, *A Theology of Public Life*, Cambridge Studies in Christian Doctrine (New York: Cambridge University Press, 2007), 306–7.

23. Patricia Hampl, *The Florist's Daughter* (New York: Harcourt Inc., 2007), 79.

SUGGESTIONS FOR FURTHER READING

This brief list includes books that may be of general interest to those who wish to pursue further the theme of religious responses to poverty and social welfare in Western religious tradition. For further sources on specific topics, the reader is referred to the notes for each chapter.

Allahyari, Rebecca Anne. *Visions of Charity: Volunteer Workers and Moral Community*. Berkeley: University of California Press, 2000.

AnteNicene Fathers (ANF). Ten-volume series of English translations of select texts from the early church prior to the Nicene Council of 324; prepared in the nineteenth century, many of the translations are now outdated. The series is freely available online at www.ccel.org/fathers.html.

Atkins, Margaret, and Robin Osborne, eds. *Poverty in the Roman World*. Cambridge: Cambridge University Press, 2006.

Bartholomew, His All Holiness [the Ecumenical Patriarch of Constantinople]. *Encountering the Mystery: Understanding Orthodox Christianity Today*. New York: Doubleday, 2008.

Bartkowski, John P., and Helen A. Regis. *Charitable Choices: Religion, Race, and Poverty in the Post-Welfare Era*. New York: New York University Press, 2003.

Bonner, Michael, Mine Ener, and Amy Singer, eds. *Poverty and Charity in Middle Eastern Contexts*. Albany: State University of New York Press, 2003.

Bouma-Prediger, Steven, and Brian J. Walsh. *Beyond Homelessness: Christian Faith in a Culture of Displacement*. Grand Rapids, MI: Eerdmans, 2008.

Brown, Peter. *Poverty and Leadership in the Later Roman Empire*. The Menahem Stern Jerusalem Lectures. Hanover, NH: University Press of New England, 2002.

Claiborne, Shane. *The Irresistible Revolution: Living as an Ordinary Radical*. Grand Rapids, MI: Zondervan, 2006.

Cohen, Mark R. *Poverty and Charity in the Jewish Community of Medieval Egypt*. Princeton, NJ: Princeton University Press, 2005.

———. *The Voice of the Poor in the Middle Ages: An Anthology of Documents from the Cairo Geniza*. Princeton, NJ: Princeton University Press, 2005.

de Santa Ana, Julio. *Good News to the Poor: The Challenge of the Poor in the History of the Church*. Maryknoll, NY: Orbis, 1979.

Doran, Robert, trans. *Stewards of the Poor: The Man of God, Rabbula, and Hiba in Fifth-Century Edessa*. Cistercian Studies Series 208. Kalamazoo, MI: Cistercian Publications, 2006.

Dunn, Geoffrey D., James S. McLaren, and Lawrence Cross, eds. *Poverty and Riches*. Prayer and Spirituality in the Early Church 5. Strathfield, Australia: St. Paul's Publications, 2009.

Finn, Richard, O.P. *Almsgiving in the Later Roman Empire: Christian Promotion and Practice 313–450*. Oxford: Oxford University Press, 2006.

Frenkel, Miriam, and Yaacov Lev, eds. *Giving in Monotheistic Religions*. Studien zur Geschichte und Kultur des islamischen Orients. Berlin and New York: Walter de Gruyter, forthcoming.

Geremek, Bronislaw. *Poverty: A History*. Oxford: Blackwell, 1994.

Gornick, Mark R. *To Live in Peace: Biblical Faith and the Changing Inner City*. Foreword by Miroslav Volf. Grand Rapids, MI: Eerdmans, 2002.

Gregory of Nazianzus. *Oration* 14 ("On the love of the poor"), available in two English translations: Brian E. Daley, S.J., trans., *Gregory of Nazianzus*. New York: Routledge, 2006, 76–97; and Martha Vinson, trans., *St. Gregory of Nazianzus: Select Orations*. The Fathers of the Church. Washington, DC: Catholic University of America Press, 2003, 39–71.

Hackel, Sergei. *Pearl of Great Price: The Life of Mother Maria Skobtsova 1891–1945*, with a foreword by Metropolitan Anthony Bloom. Crestwood, NY: St. Vladimir's Seminary Press, 1982.

Hamel, Gildas. *Poverty and Charity in Roman Palestine, First Three Centuries c.e.* Berkeley and Los Angeles: University of California Press, 1990.

Hanawalt, Emily Albu, and Carter Lindberg, eds. *Through the Eye of a Needle: Judeo–Christian Roots of Social Welfare*. Kirksville, MO: Thomas Jefferson University Press, 1994.

Holman, Susan R. *The Hungry Are Dying: Beggars and Bishops in Roman Cappadocia*. New York: Oxford University Press, 2001.

———, ed. *Wealth and Poverty in Early Church and Society*. Holy Cross Studies in Patristic Theology and History. Grand Rapids, MI: BakerAcademic, 2008.

John Chrysostom. *On Wealth and Poverty*, ed. and trans. Catharine P. Roth. Crestwood, NY: St. Vladimir's Seminary Press, 1984.

Johnson, Kelly S. *The Fear of Beggars: Stewardship and Poverty in Christian Ethics*. Grand Rapids, MI: Wm. B. Eerdmans, 2007.

Kidder, Tracy. *Mountains Beyond Mountains: The Quest of Dr. Paul Farmer, A Man Who Would Cure the World*. New York: Random House, 2003.

Leemans, Johan, Brian Matz, and Johan Verstraeten, eds. *Reading Patristic Texts on Social Ethics: Issues and Challenges for 21st Century Christian Social Thought*. Catholic University of America Studies in Early Christianity. Washington, DC: Catholic University of America Press, forthcoming.

Marsh, Charles. *The Beloved Community: How Faith Shapes Social Justice, From the Civil Rights Movement to Today*. New York: Basic Books, 2005.

McCurley, Foster R., ed. *Social Ministry in the Lutheran Tradition*. Minneapolis, MN: Fortress Press, 2008.

Miles, Sara. *Take This Bread: A Radical Conversion*. New York: Ballantine Books, 2007.

Miller, Timothy S. *The Birth of the Hospital in the Byzantine Empire*. Baltimore: Johns Hopkins University Press, 1985.

Nicene and Post-Nicene Fathers (NPNF). Series 1 (8 volumes of Augustine and 6 volumes of John Chrysostom) and Series 2 (14 volumes of English translations of texts from the early church between the council of Nicaea through the eighth century); a companion to the AnteNicene Fathers (ANF), the NPNF is also freely available online at www.ccel.org/fathers.html.

Pattison, Bonnie L. *Poverty in the Theology of John Calvin*. Eugene, OR: Pickwick Publications, 2006.

Phan, Peter C. *Social Thought*. Wilmington, DE: Michael Glazier, 1984.

Pohl, Christine D. *Making Room: Recovering Hospitality as a Christian Tradition*. Grand Rapids, MI: Wm. B. Eerdmans, 1999.

Russell, Sharman Apt. *Hunger: An Unnatural History*. New York: Basic Books, 2005.

Schroeder, Paul. *St. Basil the Great: On Social Justice*. Popular Patristics Series. Crestwood, NY: St. Vladimir's Seminary Press, forthcoming.

Scott, Anthony, ed. *Good and Faithful Servant: Stewardship in the Orthodox Church*. Crestwood, NY: St. Vladimir's Seminary Press, 2003.

Skobtsova, Maria. *Mother Maria Skobtsova: Essential Writings*, with an introduction by Jim Forest. Maryknoll, NY: Orbis Books, 2003.

Torvend, Samuel. *Luther and the Hungry Poor: Gathered Fragments*. Minneapolis, MN: Fortress Press, 2008.

Wandell, Lee Palmer. *Always Among Us: Images of the Poor in Zwingli's Zurich*. New York: Cambridge University Press, 1990.

Wolf, Geralyn. *Down and Out in Providence: Memoir of a Homeless Bishop*. New York: Crossroad, 2005.

INDEX

Aachen, cathedral and palace chapel, 35
Abraham, Egyptian monk, 109–10
abuse, domestic: Basil's advice to wives, 16, 174n13
Acacius of Amida: cited by John Calvin, 76
Acts of Thomas: on alms by deception, 127
Acts of Peter: on alms from immoral sources, 127
Acts 6:1–6 (order of widows), 107
Acts 9:36–42. *See* Dorcas
Africa: ancient poverty, 13–14; modern poverty, 46
aged, homes for, 131–32; Naucratius' care for, 68, 70
alcoholism: fetal alcohol syndrome, 104; and homelessness, 29
Alexis. *See* "Man of God"
alms: Basil on distribution, 58; defined, 85; deserving recipient, 17, 57; and Donatist controversy, 13–14; giving in secret, 130; in Islam, 43; in Jewish philanthropy, 43; "making alms with alms," 129; morality of sources, 126–27; political use of, 14; redemptive, 87; rich tricked into accepting, 59; spiritual effect unrelated to donor's motives, 50. *See also* divestment
altar: identified with the poor, 23; Nonna dies while gripping, 100–101; and widows, 101
altar cloth: sale of for famine victims, 107
Ambrose of Milan, 87; Basil's influence on his sermon on usury, 55; civic authority, 154; hymn writer, 35; influence on Luther, 75; on John Calvin, 75–76
Amida, 119, 136, 138
Amphilochius, 58
Anastasis, the model for Charlemagne's chapel at Aachen, 45
Andrewes, Lancelot, 76–77
ANF. *See* AnteNicene Fathers
Anglo-Catholic movement, 166–67. *See also* Newman, John; Oxford Movement
AnteNicene Fathers, 7, 82
Antioch. *See* John Chrysostom, Severus
Antony, St., 109, 110, 149

Aquinas, Thomas: on the common good, 144–45; Basil's influence on, 146
Arian: founding of the "Great Orphanage," 6
Aristotle: on political justice, 145. *See also* common good
Armstrong, Karen: on empathy, 42; on solitude and silence, 41
Artemius, St., 111
asceticism, of rich women, 113. *See also* Hicelia; Macrina; Melania; Olympias; voluntary poverty
Asterius of Amasea, 91, 147
Augustine, 34, 87; influence on John Calvin, 76

Badakhshan: poverty and infant bleeding practices, 93–96, 115
Bagaia, bishop of, 14
Barclay's Gate, 194n2
Barsanuphias and John, ascetic advice on borrowing for alms, 147
Bartholemew, Ecumenical Patriarch, 146, 164
Basil of Caesarea, 16, 18, 53, 70, 89, 139, 146, 172; on alms, 58; on creation, 23; and Blomfield Jackson, 82–84; on greedy *vs.* needy beggars, 58; sermon against stockpiling, 60, 70; sermon on famine and drought, 54, 60, 100; homily in Armenia after a fire, 158; sermons on Psalm 14, 61; iconography, 24, 168–72; on marriage, 15, 174n13; monastic retreat, location of, 54, 68; on social action and political order, 53–55, 60–68
Basileias, 63–67; Gregory of Nazianzus and, 65, 67; ninth-century illumination, 63–65; praised by Blomfield Jackson, 84
Bede, 3–4
beggars, 54, 56, 59, 83, 108
begging: first imperial law against public begging, 178n23; prohibited in nineteenth-century France, 78–79
beguines: compared with *bnat qyama*, 66
Benedictine hospitality, 152. *See also* monasticism; de Waal, Esther